Writing
and Revising
A Portable Guide

Other *Portable* Volumes from Bedford/St. Martin's

50 Essays: A Portable Anthology
Edited by Samuel Cohen

40 Model Essays: A Portable Anthology
Jane E. Aaron

Contemporary and Classic Arguments: A Portable Anthology,
Sylvan Barnet and Hugo Bedau

From Critical Thinking to Argument: A Portable Guide,
Sylvan Barnet and Hugo Bedau

40 Short Stories: A Portable Anthology, Second Edition
Edited by Beverly Lawn

250 Poems: A Portable Anthology
Edited by Peter Schakel and Jack Ridl

12 Plays: A Portable Anthology
Edited by Janet E. Gardner

Literature: A Portable Anthology
Edited by Janet E. Gardner, Beverly Lawn, Jack Ridl,
and Peter Schakel

Writing about Literature: A Portable Guide
Janet E. Gardner

Researching and Writing: A Portable Guide
Marcia F. Muth

WRITING
and REVISING
A Portable Guide

X. J. KENNEDY

DOROTHY M. KENNEDY

MARCIA F. MUTH

Bedford/St. Martin's   BOSTON ◆ NEW YORK

For Bedford/St. Martin's

Developmental Editor: Karin Halbert
Production Editor: Kristen Merrill
Production Supervisor: Andrew Ensor
Marketing Manager: Karita dos Santos
Editorial Assistant: Christina Gerogiannis
Copyeditor: Barbara Bell
Text Design: Sandra Rigney
Cover Design: Donna Lee Dennison
Composition: TexTech
Printing and Binding: Haddon Craftsman, an R.R. Donnelley & Sons
  Company

President: Joan E. Feinberg
Editorial Director: Denise B. Wydra
Editor in Chief: Karen S. Henry
Director of Marketing: Karen Melton Soeltz
Director of Editing, Design, and Production: Marcia Cohen
Managing Editor: Elizabeth M. Schaaf

Library of Congress Control Number: 2006932269

Manufactured in the United States of America.

4   3   2   1   0
e   d   c   b

For information, write: Bedford/St. Martin's, 75 Arlington Street,
Boston, MA 02116 (617-399-4000)

ISBN-10: 0–312–67950–5
ISBN-13: 978–0–312–67950–7

Acknowledgments

*Acknowledgments and copyrights can be found at the back of the book
on pages 249–50, which constitute an extension of the copyright page.*

Preface for Instructors

This compact and flexible book offers clear guidance on every stage of the writing process, from generating ideas and planning to revising and editing. With its affordable price and process-oriented coverage, *Writing and Revising* can be used as a classroom text or as a quick reference, accommodating a variety of different teaching needs. Whether students are developing brief papers or more complicated essays drawing on multiple sources, *Writing and Revising* can help.

This book concisely advises and encourages students, bolstering their confidence as they strengthen the skills necessary for writing projects in college and beyond. The first three chapters help students begin on sound footing by explaining key processes: writing, with a spotlight feature on audience and purpose; reading, with a spotlight on literal and analytical levels; and critical thinking, with a spotlight on evidence. Chapters 4 through 7 guide students through generating ideas, planning and organizing, drafting, and developing their points. Each presents practical strategies to help students improve their papers and build their skills as college writers. For example, the planning strategies encourage a strong foundation, shaping a topic for audience and purpose as well as stating and organizing around a thesis. The rich and varied strategies for developing ideas guide students in everything from giving examples and providing details to adding visual evidence. The revision strategies in Chapter 8 encompass both macrorevising for purpose, thesis, audience, structure, and support and microrevising for emphasis, conciseness, and clarity. Chapter 9 on editing and proofreading concentrates on fixing likely problems. Its Quick Editing Guide briefly covers grammar errors, effective sentences, punctuation, mechanics, and format.

The last two chapters turn to common yet challenging expectations of college writers: arguing persuasively and integrating evidence from sources. Chapter 10, Strategies for Arguing, starts off by emphasizing the importance of choosing an arguable issue and forming a thesis. Next, this chapter presents strategies for making claims, selecting evidence, using the evidence to support appeals, reasoning logically, avoiding fallacies, and presenting three common types of arguments—taking a stand, proposing a solution, and evaluating. Chapter 11, Strategies for Integrating Sources, covers selecting and capturing supporting evidence by quoting, paraphrasing, and summarizing. It outlines methods of avoiding plagiarism and illustrates how to cite and list sources in both the MLA and APA documentation styles.

Throughout, this text offers practical help to students such as

- tables, charts, figures, and other visuals that clarify important processes and concepts and serve as quick references for review
- abundant and varied illustrations of strategies, especially ways of discovering ideas, drafting paragraphs, and developing supporting material
- frequent individual and group activities to guide students as they practice and apply the processes, skills, and strategies presented
- checklists to help students accomplish critical tasks that can improve their processes and drafts
- extensive coverage—a chapter apiece—of revising and editing, including concise explanations, examples, and checklists for fifteen common editing issues
- practical advice about making argumentative claims, selecting evidence, supporting appeals, and reasoning logically
- consistent connections between strategies for selecting and presenting information and its eventual role as supporting evidence
- discussion of plagiarism in the context of academic ethics and best practices for avoiding problems
- comprehensive illustration of conventions for citing and listing sources, innovatively organized around two key questions: Who wrote it? What type of source is it?

Additional material on writing and revising is available online at Re: Writing (bedfordstmartins.com/rewriting), Bedford/St. Martin's extensive collection of free online student and instructor resources. For students, this site provides helpful tutorials, exercises, citation guides, and model documents. For instructors, Re: Writing offers such resources as *The*

Bedford Bibliography for Teachers of Writing, The Bedford/St. Martin's Workshop on Plagiarism, and other free bibliographies, workshops, and online journals for professional development.

ACKNOWLEDGMENTS

Thanks to those who thoughtfully reviewed and helped shape the plans for this book: Laurie Buchanan, Clark State Community College; Polly Buckingham, Eastern Washington University; Craig Jacobsen, Mesa Community College; Susan K. Miller-Cochran, Mesa Community College; and Rochelle Rodrigo, Mesa Community College. Building on her earlier contributions to *The Bedford Guide for College Writers*, Tammy Sugarman, Georgia State University, supplied numerous documentation examples that have found their way into this book. Thanks also to the students whose work has enriched this book by illustrating many points of value to other college writers: Carrie Williamson, Heidi Kessler, Lillian Tsu, Lindsey Schendel, John Martin, Betsy Buffo, Alan Espenlaub, Kelly Grecian, Stephanie Hawkins, Ross Rocketto, and Donna Waite.

At Bedford/St. Martin's, many people have contributed to the evolution of this small book. Joan Feinberg, Denise Wydra, and Karen Henry initially conceived of the project and supported its development to present form. Thanks also to the many people from the marketing department and sales force who saw the need for this book, including Karita dos Santos, Jim Camp, Rory Baruth, and Elyse Courtney. Because *Writing and Revising* is adapted from *The Bedford Guide for College Writers*, many hands have contributed to the parent book and thus have strengthened this portable guide as well. Special thanks go to Beth Castrodale, who guided early steps in the development of this book, and Karin Halbert, who enriched its store of examples and patiently nurtured it to completion. Christina Gerogiannis also helped to refresh the examples and facilitated many details of manuscript preparation. Credit for a smooth production process goes to Elizabeth Schaaf and Kristen Merrill and to copyeditor Barbara Bell. Thanks also go to Sandra Rigney for the book's attractive design and to Sandy Schechter and Fred Courtright for clearing permissions.

As always, Marcia Muth is grateful to the inspirational student writers and revisers in her writing workshops, sponsored by the School of Education at the University of Colorado at Denver and Health Sciences Center, and especially to Rod Muth who continues to encourage her own writing and revising.

Contents

Writing
and Revising
A Portable Guide

1

Writing Processes

You are already a writer with long experience. In school you have taken notes, written book reports and term papers, answered exam questions, perhaps kept a journal. You've recorded minutes in community meetings and composed memos on the job. You've e-mailed friends, made shopping lists, maybe even tried your hand at writing songs or poetry. All this experience is about to pay off.

Unlike parachute jumping, writing in college is something you can go ahead and try without first learning all there is to know. In truth, nothing anyone can tell you will help as much as learning by doing. In this book our purpose is to help you write better, deeper, clearer, and more satisfying papers than you have ever written before. We encourage you to do so by diving into writing—experimenting, practicing, and building confidence as you expand your writing strategies.

WRITING, READING, AND CRITICAL THINKING

In college you will perform challenging tasks that enlarge what you already know about writing. In fact, you can view each writing task as a problem to solve, often through careful reading (see Ch. 2) and objective thinking (see Ch. 3). You will need to read—and write—actively, engaging with the ideas of others. At the same time, you will need to think critically, analyzing and judging those ideas. To help you assess your own achievement, you will use criteria—models, conventions, principles, standards. As you write and rewrite, you can evaluate what you are doing by asking specific questions:

- Have you considered your audience?
- Have you achieved your purpose?
- Have you made your point clear by stating it as a thesis or by unmistakably implying it?
- Have you supported your point with enough reliable evidence to persuade your readers?
- Have you arranged your ideas logically so that each follows from, supports, or adds to the one before it?
- Have you made the connections among ideas clear to your readers?
- Have you established an appropriate tone?

In large measure, learning to write well is learning what questions to ask as you write. Throughout this book, we include questions and suggestions to help you accomplish your writing tasks and reflect on the processes you use to write, read, and think critically.

A PROCESS OF WRITING

Writing can seem at times an overwhelming drudgery, worse than scrubbing floors; at other moments, it's a sport full of thrills—like whizzing downhill on skis, not knowing what you'll meet around a bend. Surprising and unpredictable as the process may seem, nearly all writers do similar things:

- They generate ideas.
- They plan, draft, and develop their papers.
- They revise and edit.

Although these activities form the basis of most effective writing processes, they aren't lockstep stages: you don't always proceed in a straight line. You can skip around in whatever order you like, work on several parts at a time, or circle back over what's already done. For example, while gathering material, you may feel an urge to play with a sentence until it clicks. Or while writing a draft, you may decide to look for more material. You can leap ahead, cross out, backtrack, adjust, question, test a fresh approach, tinker, polish, and, at the end, spell-check the tricky words.

Generating Ideas

The first activity in writing—finding a topic and something to say about it—is often the most challenging and least predictable. (For strategies for generating ideas, see Ch. 4.)

Finding Something to Write About. Selecting a topic is not always easy, but you may discover an idea while talking with friends, riding your bike, or even staring out the window. Sometimes a topic lies near home, in an everyday event you recall. Often your reading raises questions that call for investigation. When a particular writing assignment doesn't appeal to you, your challenge is to find a slant that does interest you. Find it, and words will flow—words that can engage readers as you accomplish your purpose. (See the graphic below.)

Discovering Material. You'll need information to shape and support your ideas—facts and figures, reports and opinions, examples and illustrations. Luckily you have numerous sources of supporting material to make your slant on a topic clear and convincing to your readers. You can recall your own experience and knowledge, you can observe things around you, you can converse with others who are knowledgeable, you can read materials that draw you to new views, and you can think critically about all the sources around you.

Planning, Drafting, and Developing

After finding a topic and beginning to gather material about it, you will plan your paper, write a draft, and then develop your ideas further. (See the graphic on p. 5.)

Planning. Having discovered a burning idea (or at least a smoldering one) to write about, and some supporting material (but maybe not enough yet), you can sort out what matters most. (For planning strategies, see

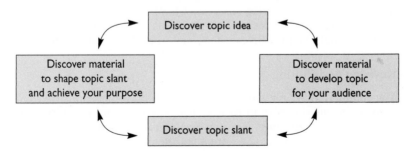

Ch. 5.) If right away you see one main point, or thesis, for your paper, test various ways of stating it, given your audience and purpose:

MAYBE   Parking in the morning before class is annoying.

OR   Parking on campus is a big problem.

Next arrange your ideas and material in a sensible order that clarifies your point. For example, you might group and label the ideas you have generated, make an outline, or analyze the main point, breaking it down into its parts:

> Parking on campus is a problem for students because of the long lines, inefficient entrances, and poorly marked spaces.

But if no clear thesis emerges quickly, don't worry. You may find one while you draft—that is, while you write an early version of your paper.

Drafting.   When your ideas first start to flow, you want to welcome them—lure them forth, not tear them apart, so they don't go back into hiding. (For drafting strategies, see Ch. 6.) Don't be afraid to take risks at this stage: you'll probably be surprised and pleased at what happens, even though your first version will be rough. Writing takes time; a paper usually needs several drafts and may need a clearer introduction, a stronger conclusion, more convincing evidence, or a revised plan. Especially when your subject is unfamiliar or complicated, you may decide to throw out your first attempt and start over as a stronger idea evolves.

Developing.   As you draft, you'll weave in explanations, examples, details, definitions, and varied evidence to make your ideas clear and persuasive. For example, you may need to define an at-risk student, illustrate the problems faced by a single parent, or supply statistics about hit-and-run accidents. If you lack specific support for your main point, you can use strategies for developing ideas (see Ch. 7), or return to strategies for generating ideas. You'll keep gaining insights and drawing conclusions while you draft. Welcome these ideas, and work them in if they fit.

Revising and Editing

You might want to relax once you have a draft, but for most writers revising begins the work in earnest. (See the visual on p. 6.) Revising means both reseeing and rewriting, making major changes so that your paper accomplishes what you want it to. After you have a well-developed

PLAN

- Identify your audience and purpose
- Decide on one main point
- State a thesis
- Organize ideas by grouping or outlining

DEVELOP

- Explain, analyze, and support
- Add examples, details, and definitions
- Supply evidence such as facts, statistics, expert testimony, and observations

DRAFT

- Start and restart
- Build paragraphs
- Open and conclude
- Create coherence

and well-organized revision, you are ready to edit: to correct errors and improve wording.

Revising.   Revision is more than just changing words. In fact, you may revise what you know and what you think while you're writing or when you pause to reread. You can then rework your thesis, reconsider your audience, shift your plans, decide what to put in or leave out, rearrange for clarity, move sentences or paragraphs around, connect points differently, or express ideas better. Perhaps you'll add costs to a paper on parking problems or switch to fathers instead of mothers as you consider teen parenthood. (For revising strategies, see Ch. 8.)

If you put aside your draft for a few hours or a day, you can reread it with fresh eyes and a clear mind. Other students can also help you—sometimes more than a textbook or an instructor can—by responding to your drafts as engaged readers.

Editing. Editing means refining details and correcting flaws that stand in the way of your readers' understanding and enjoyment. (For editing strategies, see Ch. 9.) Don't edit too early, though, because you may waste time on some part that you later revise out. In editing, you usually make these repairs:

- Get rid of unnecessary words.
- Choose livelier and more precise words.
- Replace any incorrect or inappropriate wording.
- Rearrange words in a clearer, more emphatic order.
- Combine short, choppy sentences, or break up long, confusing sentences.
- Refine transitions for continuity of thought.
- Check grammar, sentences, punctuation, and mechanics.

Proofreading. Finally you'll proofread your paper, taking a last look, checking correctness, and catching spelling or word-processing errors. (For more on proofreading, see pp. 157–59.)

Remembering What Matters Most. Like a hard game of basketball, writing a college paper is strenuous. Without getting in your way, we want to lend you all possible support and guidance throughout the writing process. So, no doubt, does your instructor, someone closer to you than any textbook writer. Still, even the best instructors and textbook writers—like the best coaches—can improve your game only so much. Advice on how to write won't make you a better writer. You'll learn more and have more fun when you take a few sentences to the hoop and make points yourself. After you sink a few baskets, you'll gain confidence in your ability and find the process of writing easier.

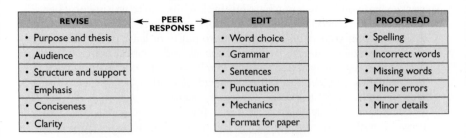

REVISE	PEER RESPONSE	EDIT	PROOFREAD
• Purpose and thesis		• Word choice	• Spelling
• Audience		• Grammar	• Incorrect words
• Structure and support		• Sentences	• Missing words
• Emphasis		• Punctuation	• Minor errors
• Conciseness		• Mechanics	• Minor details
• Clarity		• Format for paper	

■ ACTIVITY: Describing Your Writing Process

Describe your writing process. How do you get started? How do you keep writing? What process do you go through to reach a final draft? Do your steps ever vary depending on the type of writing you're doing? What step or strategy in your writing process would you most like to change?

A SPOTLIGHT ON AUDIENCE AND PURPOSE

At any moment in the writing process, two questions are worth asking:

Who is my audience?   **Why am I writing?**

Writing for Readers

Your audience, or your readers, may or may not be defined in your assignment. Consider the following examples:

ASSIGNMENT 1   Discuss the advantages and disadvantages of home schooling.

ASSIGNMENT 2   In a letter to parents of school-aged children, discuss the advantages and disadvantages of home schooling.

If your assignment defines an audience, as the second example does, you will need to think about how to approach those readers and what to assume about their relationship to your topic. For example, what points would you include in a discussion aimed at parents? How would you organize your ideas? Would you discuss advantages or disadvantages first? On the other hand, how might your approach differ if the assignment read this way?

ASSIGNMENT 3   In a short article for a professional publication for teachers, discuss the advantages and disadvantages of home schooling.

When you analyze what readers know, believe, and value, you can aim your writing toward them with a better chance of hitting your mark. Use these questions to help you write and revise for your audience.

GENERAL AUDIENCE CHECKLIST

☐ Who are your readers? What is their relationship to you?

☐ What do your readers already know about this topic? What do you want them to learn?

☐ How much detail will they want to read about this topic?

☐ What objections are they likely to raise as they read? How can you anticipate and overcome their objections?

☐ What's likely to convince them?

☐ What's likely to offend them?

■ ACTIVITY: Considering Your Audience

Write a short paragraph describing in detail a "worst" event—your worst date, worst dinner, worst car repair, or some similar catastrophe. Then revise that paragraph so that your audience is a person involved in the event—the person who went on that date with you, cooked or served the dinner, worked on your car. Now revise the paragraph again, this time writing to a person you plan to date soon, a cook at a restaurant you want to try, or a repair person working at another garage. Compare the three paragraphs. How are they similar? How do they differ?

Targeting Academic Readers

Although your future writing is likely to be aimed at a specific audience—the marketing team at work or the other members of an animal rescue group—many of your college assignments will resemble Assignment 1. Those assignments will assume that you are addressing general academic readers, represented by your instructor and possibly your classmates. General academic readers typically expect clear, logical writing that uses supporting evidence to explain, interpret, or persuade. In addition, the particular expectations of academic audiences may differ by field. For example, biologists might assume you'll supply the findings from your experiment while literature specialists might look for plenty of relevant quotations from the novel you're analyzing. Depending on the field, your readers may expect certain topics, types of evidence, and approaches. Use these questions to help you pinpoint what your college readers expect.

ACADEMIC AUDIENCE CHECKLIST

☐ How has your instructor advised you to write for readers in the field? What criteria will be used for grading your papers?

☐ What do the assigned readings in your course assume about readers and their expectations? Has your instructor recommended useful models or sample readings?

☐ What topics and issues concern readers in the field? What puzzles do they want to solve? How do they want to solve them?

☐ How is writing in the field commonly organized? For example, do writers tend to follow a persuasive pattern? That is, do they introduce the issue, state their assertion or claim, explain their reasons, acknowledge other views, and conclude? Do they use a series of conventional headings—for example, Abstract, Introduction to the Problem, Methodology, Findings, and Discussion?

☐ What evidence is typically gathered to support ideas or interpretations—facts and statistics, quotations from texts, summaries of research, references to authorities or prior studies, results from experimental research, or field notes from observations or interviews?

☐ What style, tone, and level of formality do writers in the field tend to use and readers tend to expect?

■ **ACTIVITY:** Considering an Academic Audience

Working by yourself or with a small group, use the checklist above to examine several reading or writing assignments in one of your courses. Try to identify prominent features of writing in the field. Which of these characteristics probably would be expected in student papers? How might you adjust your writing to meet those expectations? How would an academic paper differ from writing on the same topic for a general audience—for example, a letter to the editor, a newspaper article, a consumer brochure, an explanation for middle school students, or a Web page?

Writing for a Reason

Most college writing assignments ask you to write for a definite reason. For example, you might be asked to take a stand on a controversial issue and to persuade your readers to respect your position. Be careful not to confuse the sources and strategies you apply in these assignments with your ultimate purpose for writing. "To compare and contrast two things" is not a very interesting purpose; "to compare and contrast two Web sites *in order to explain their differences*" implies a real reason for writing. In most college writing, your ultimate purpose will be to explain something to your readers or to convince them of something.

To sharpen your concentration on your purpose, ask yourself from the start, What do I want to do? And, in revising, Did I do what I meant to do? You'll find that these practical questions can help you slice out irrelevant information and remove other barriers to getting your paper where you want it to go.

■ **ACTIVITY:** Considering Your Purpose

Return to the three paragraphs you wrote for the activity on page 8. Write a sentence or two summing up your purpose in writing each paragraph. Given these three purposes, how might you revise the paragraphs?

2

Reading Processes

What's so special about college reading? Don't you pick up the book, start on the first page, and keep going, just as you have ever since you met *The Cat in the Hat*? Reading from beginning to end works especially well when you are eager to find out what happens next, as in a thriller, or what to do next, as in a cookbook. On the other hand, much of what you read in college—textbooks, scholarly articles, research reports, your peers' papers—is complicated and challenging. Dense material like this often requires closer reading and deeper thinking—in short, a process for reading critically.

Reading critically is a useful skill. For assignments in this course alone, you probably will need to evaluate the strengths and weaknesses of essays by professionals and students. If you research any topic, you will need to figure out what your sources say, whether they are reliable, and how you might use their information. Critical reading is important in other courses too. For example, you might analyze a sociology report on violent children for its assumptions and implications as well as the soundness of its argument. When your writing relies on critical reading, you generally need to explain what is going on in the reading material and then go further, making your own point based on what you have read.

A PROCESS OF CRITICAL READING

Reading critically means approaching whatever you read in an active, questioning manner. This essential college-level skill changes reading from a spectator sport to a contact sport. You no longer sit in the stands, watching figure skaters glide by. Instead, you charge right into a rough-and-tumble hockey game, gripping your stick and watching out for your teeth.

Critical reading, like critical thinking (see Ch. 3), is not an isolated activity. It is a continuum of strategies that thoughtful people use every day to grapple with new information, to integrate it with existing knowledge, and to apply it to problems in daily life and in academic courses. Many readers use similar strategies:

- They get ready to do their reading.
- They respond as they read.
- They read on literal and analytical levels.

■ ACTIVITY: Describing Your Own Reading Process

How do you read a magazine, newspaper, or popular novel? What are your goals when you do this kind of reading? What's different about reading the material assigned in college? What techniques do you use for reading assignments? Which of your strategies might help your classmates, especially in classes with a lot of reading? How might you read more effectively?

Preparing to Read

College reading is active reading. Before you read, think ahead about how to approach the reading process, how to make the most of the time you spend reading.

Thinking about Your Purpose.   Naturally, your overall goal for doing most college reading is to succeed in your courses. When you begin to read, ask questions like these about your immediate purpose:

- What are you reading?
- Why are you reading?
- What do you want to do with the reading?
- What does your instructor expect you to learn from the reading?
- Do you need to memorize details, find main points, or connect ideas?
- How does this reading build on, add to, contrast with, or otherwise relate to other reading assignments in the course?

Planning Your Follow-up.   When you are assigned a specific essay, chapter, or article or are required to choose a reading about a certain topic, ask yourself what your instructor probably expects to follow the reading:

- Do you need to be ready to discuss the reading during class?
- Will you need to mention it or analyze it during an examination?
- Will you need to write about it or its topic?
- Do you need to find its main points? Sum it up? Compare it? Question it? Discuss its strengths and weaknesses? Draw useful details from it?

Skimming the Text.   Before you actively read a text, begin by skimming it, quickly reading only enough to introduce yourself to its content and organization. If the reading has a table of contents or subheadings, read those first to figure out what the material covers and how it is organized. Read the first paragraph and then the first (or first and last) sentence of each paragraph that follows. If the material has any illustrations or diagrams, read the captions.

Responding to Reading

Encourage yourself to read energetically by monitoring both what you read and how you respond to it.

Reading Deeply.   The books and articles assigned in college often require more concentration from you as a reader than simpler readings do. Use the following questions to help you understand the complexities below the surface of a reading:

- Are difficult or technical terms defined in specific ways? How might you highlight, list, or record those terms so that you can master them?
- How might you record or recall the details in the reading? How might you track or diagram interrelated ideas to grasp the connections?
- How does word choice, tone, or style alert you to the complex purpose of a reading that is layered or indirect rather than straightforward?
- How might you trace the progression of ideas in the reading? Where do you spot headings, previews of what's coming up, summaries of what's gone before, transitions, and other clues to the reading's organization?
- Does the reading include figurative or descriptive language, allusions to other works, or recurring themes? How do these elements enrich the reading?

Keeping a Reading Journal.   A reading journal helps you read actively and build a reservoir of ideas for follow-up writing. You can use a special notebook or computer file to address questions like these:

- What is the subject of the reading? What is the writer's stand?
- What does the writer take for granted? What assumptions does he or she begin with? Where are these assumptions stated or suggested?
- What evidence supports the writer's main points?
- Do you agree with what the writer is saying? Do his or her ideas clash with your ideas or call into question something you take for granted?
- Has the writer taken account of other views, opinions, or interpretations of evidence?
- What conclusions can you draw from the reading?
- Has the reading opened your eyes to new ways of viewing the subject?

Annotating the Text.   Writing notes on the page (or on a photocopy if the material is not your own) is a useful way to trace the author's points and to respond to them with questions or comments. You can underline key points, mark checks and stars by ideas when you agree or disagree, and jot questions in the margins. (For a Critical Reading Checklist, see p. 20.) When one student investigated the history of women's professional sports, she annotated a key passage from an article called "Why Men Fear Women's Teams" by Kate Rounds from the January–February 1991 issue of *Ms.*

different case from
individual sports

By contrast, women's professional (team)sports have failed   *key point*

spectacularly. Since the mid-seventies, every professional

✓   league — softball, basketball, and volleyball — has gone belly-up.

bitter tone

In 1981, after a four-year struggle, the Women's Basketball

1st example
backs up   League (WBL), backed by sports promoter Bill Byrne, folded. The
point

league was drawing fans in a number of cities, but the sponsors   *What*
women's
✓   weren't there, TV wasn't there, and nobody seemed to miss the   *teams have*
gotten these?
spectacle of a few good women fighting for a basketball.

Something   Or a (volleyball,) for that matter. Despite the success of (bikini)   *Why does she*
I know   *call it this?*
about!   volleyball, an organization called MLV (Major League Volleyball)

bit the dust in March of 1989 after nearly three years of   *2nd example* struggling for sponsorship, fan support, and television exposure.

[As with pro basketball, there was a man behind women's   *She's suspicious*

professional volleyball,] real estate investor Robert (Bat)   *of men*

Batinovich. Batinovich admits that, unlike court volleyball,

oh, great   beach volleyball has a lot of "visual T&A mixed into it." ←

      What court volleyball does have, according to former   *seeme like*

credential   MLV executive director Lindy Vivas, is strong women athletes.   *these are only*

Vivas is assistant volleyball coach at San Jose State University.   *two options*

Why do   "The United States in general," she says, "has problems

guys

always   dealing with women athletes and strong, aggressive females.   *good*

think we're   The perception is you have to be more aggressive in team sports *quote*

weak and

prissy?   than in golf and tennis, which aren't contact sports. Women

athletes are looked at as masculine and get the stigma ←

of being gay."

This student's annotations helped her deepen her reading of the article and generate ideas for her writing.

■ ACTIVITY: Annotating a Passage

Annotate the following passage from the middle of Ellen Goodman's essay "Kids, Divorce, and the Myth" from the *Boston Globe Online* (September 28, 2000).

     Not that long ago, when the divorce statistics first began to rise, many Americans comforted themselves with the belief that parents and children shared the same perspective. A child in an unhappy home would surely know it, surely suffer from it. What was right for parents—including divorce—was right for children.

     But today that seems like a soothing or perhaps self-serving myth.

     One of the myth-busters is Judith Wallerstein, who has been studying the children of divorce for over twenty-five years. Her latest book about *The Unexpected Legacy of Divorce* is written about and for the offspring of splintered families, children who carry the family rupture into their adulthood.

     This psychologist has followed 131 children of 80 California families, a small and not-so-random sample of the one million children whose parents divorce each year. Today a quarter of all adults under forty-four come from divorced homes, and

Wallerstein takes a handful of these children to show in rich detail the way divorce was and remains a life-transforming event.
Her book echoes with the laments of their tribe. These are adults who spent childhood negotiating between two parents and two homes. Some were emotionally abandoned, others were subject to the crazy postdivorce years. Some still wait for disaster, and others are stronger for the struggle.
But as the elder to their tribe, Wallerstein makes one central and challenging point: "The myth that if the parents have a poor marriage the children are going to be unhappy is not true."

A SPOTLIGHT ON READING LEVELS

Educational expert Benjamin Bloom identified six levels of cognitive activity: knowledge, comprehension, application, analysis, synthesis, and evaluation.[1] Each level acts as a foundation for the next. Each also becomes more complex and demands higher thinking skills than the previous one. (See Fig. 2.1.) Experienced readers, however, may jump among these levels, gathering information and insight as they occur.

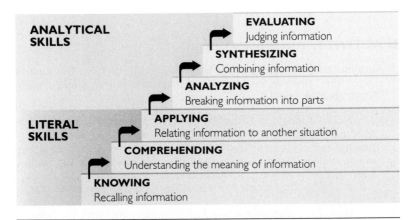

Figure 2.1   **Using Literal and Analytical Reading Skills.** The information in this figure is adapted from Benjamin S. Bloom et al., *Taxonomy of Educational Objectives, Handbook 1: Cognitive Domain* (New York: McKay, 1956).

[1]Benjamin S. Bloom et al., *Taxonomy of Educational Objectives, Handbook 1: Cognitive Domain.* Copyright © 1956 by David McKay, Inc. Reprinted with the permission of Random House, Inc.

The first three levels are literal skills. When you show that you know a fact, comprehend its meaning, and can apply it to a new situation, you demonstrate your mastery over building blocks of thought. The last three levels—analysis, synthesis, and evaluation—are critical skills. These skills take you beyond the literal level: you break apart the building blocks to see what makes them work, recombine them in new and useful ways, and judge their worth or significance. To read critically, you must engage with a piece on both literal and analytical levels.

Reading on Literal Levels

As you first tackle an unfamiliar reading, you may struggle simply to discover what—exactly—it presents to readers. When you read literally, you decode the words in the passage, figure out the meaning, and connect the information to what you already know. For example, suppose you read in your history book a passage about Franklin Delano Roosevelt (FDR), the only American president elected to four consecutive terms of office.

Becoming Aware of the Information.   Once you read the passage, even if you have little background in American history, you know and can recall the information it presents about FDR and his four terms in office.

Comprehending the Information.   To comprehend the information, you need to know that a term for a U.S. president is four years and that *consecutive* means "continuous." Thus, FDR was elected to serve for sixteen years.

Applying the Information.   To apply this knowledge, you think of other presidents—George Washington, who served two terms; Grover Cleveland, who served two terms but not consecutively; Jimmy Carter, who served one term; and Bill Clinton, who served two terms. Then you realize that being elected to four terms is unusual. In fact, the Twenty-Second Amendment to the Constitution, ratified in 1951, now limits a president to two terms.

Reading on Analytical Levels

After mastering a passage on the literal levels, you need to read on the analytical levels, probing the meaning beneath the surface. First, you analyze the information, considering its parts and implications from various angles. Then you gather related material and synthesize all of it, combining it to achieve new insights. Finally, you evaluate the significance of the information.

Analyzing the Information.   To return to FDR's four terms as president, you can ask questions to scrutinize this information from various angles, selecting a principle that suits your purpose to break the information into its components or parts. For example, you might analyze FDR's tenure in office in relation to the political longevity of other presidents. Why has FDR been the only president elected to serve four terms? What circumstances during his terms contributed to three reelections? How is FDR different from other presidents?

Synthesizing the Information.   To answer your questions, you may have to read more or review material you have read in the past. Then you begin synthesizing—combining information, pulling together the facts and opinions, identifying the evidence accepted by all or most sources, examining any controversial evidence, and drawing whatever conclusions reliable evidence seems to support. For example, it would be logical to conclude that the special circumstances of the Great Depression and World War II contributed to FDR's four terms. On the other hand, it would not be logical to conclude that Americans reelected FDR out of pity because he was a victim of polio.

Evaluating the Information.   Finally, you evaluate your new knowledge to determine its significance, both to your understanding of Depression-era politics and to your assessment of your history book's approach. For instance, you might ask yourself why the book's author has chosen to make this point. How does it affect the rest of the discussion? Does this author seem reliable? And you may also have formed your own opinion about FDR's reelections, perhaps concluding that FDR's four-term presidency is understandable in light of the events of the 1930s and 1940s, that the author has mentioned this fact to highlight the unique political atmosphere of that era, and that, in your opinion, it is evidence neither for nor against FDR's excellence as a president.

■ **ACTIVITY:** Reading Analytically

Think back to something you have read recently that helped you make a decision, perhaps a newspaper or magazine article, an electronic posting, or a college brochure. How did you analyze what you read, breaking the information into parts? How did you synthesize it, combining it with what you already knew? How did you evaluate it, judging its contribution to your decision making?

GENERATING IDEAS FROM READING

Like flints that strike each other and cause sparks, writers and readers provoke one another. For example, when your class discusses an essay, you may be surprised by the range of insights your classmates report. If you missed some of their insights during your reading, remember that they may be equally surprised by what you see.

Often you look to other writers — in books or articles — to suggest a topic, provide information about it, or help you explain it or back it up with evidence. You may read because you want to understand ideas, test them, or debate with the writer, but reading is a dynamic process. You may find that it changes your ideas instead of supporting them. Here are suggestions for unlocking the potential hidden in a good text.

Looking for Meaty Pieces.   Stimulate your thinking about current topics that intrigue you by browsing through essay collections or magazines in the library or online. Try *The Atlantic, Harper's, The New Republic, Commentary,* or a special-interest magazine like *Architectural Digest* or *Scientific American.* Check the editorials and op-ed columns in your local newspaper, the *New York Times,* or the *Wall Street Journal.* Also search the Internet on interesting subjects that challenge you to think seriously (for example, film classics or the effects of poverty on children). Look for articles that are meaty, not superficial, and that are written to inform and convince, not to entertain or amuse.

Logging Your Reading.   For several days keep a log of the articles that you find. Record the author, title, and source for each promising piece so that you can easily find it again. Briefly note the subject and point of view in order to identify a range of possibilities.

Recalling Something You Have Already Read.   What have you read lately that started you thinking? Return to a recent reading — a chapter in a humanities textbook, an article assigned in a sociology course, a research study for a biology course.

Capturing Complex Ideas.   When you find a challenging reading, do you sometimes feel too overwhelmed to develop ideas from it? If so, read it slowly and carefully. Then consider two common methods of recording and integrating ideas from sources into papers. First, try *paraphrasing,* restating the author's ideas fully but in your own words. Then try *summarizing,* reducing the author's main point to essentials. (For examples, see pp. 212–17.) Accurately restating what a reading says can help you grasp its ideas, especially on literal levels. Once you understand what it says, you are better equipped to agree with, disagree with, or question its points.

Reading Critically.   Read first literally and then analytically. Instead of just soaking up what the reading says, engage in a dialogue or conversation with the writer. Criticize. Wonder. Argue back. Demand convincing evidence. Use the following checklist to get you started as a critical reader.

CRITICAL READING CHECKLIST

☐ What problems and issues does the author raise?

☐ What is the author's purpose? Is it to explain or inform? To persuade? To amuse? In addition to this overall purpose, is the author trying to accomplish some other agenda?

☐ How does the author appeal to readers? Where do you agree, and where do you disagree? Where do you want to say "Yeah, right!" or "I don't think so!"?

☐ How does this piece relate to your own experiences or thoughts? Have you encountered anything similar? Does the topic or approach intrigue you?

☐ Are there any important words or ideas that you don't understand? If so, do you need to reread or turn to a dictionary or reference book?

☐ What is the author's point of view? What does the author assume or take for granted? Where does the author reveal these assumptions? Do they make the selection seem weak or biased?

☐ Which statements are facts that can be verified by observation, firsthand testimony, or research? Which are opinions? Does one or the other dominate the piece?

☐ Is the writer's evidence accurate, relevant, and sufficient? Do you find it persuasive?

Analyzing Writing Strategies.   Reading widely and deeply can reveal not only what others say but also how they say it and how they shape such key features as the introduction, thesis statement or main idea, major points, and supporting evidence. Ask questions like those in the Writing Strategies Checklist to help you identify writing strategies.

WRITING STRATEGIES CHECKLIST

☐ How does the author introduce the reading? In what ways does the author try to engage readers?

☐ Where does the author state or imply the main idea or thesis?

☐ How is the text organized? What are the main points used to develop the thesis? What does the selection of these points suggest about the author's approach?

☐ How does the author supply support—facts, data, statistics, expert opinions, personal experiences, observations, explanations, examples, or other information?

☐ How does the author connect or emphasize ideas for readers?

☐ How does the author conclude the reading?

☐ What is the author's tone? How do the words and examples reveal the author's attitude, biases, or assumptions?

■ **ACTIVITY:** Reading Critically

Using the advice in this chapter, critically read the following essay from the *Washington Post* Web site. First, add your own notes and comments in the margin, responding on both literal and analytical levels. Second, add notes about the writer's writing strategies. (Sample annotations are supplied to help you get started.) Finally, write out your own well-reasoned conclusions about the reading.

JAY MATHEWS

Class Struggle: Is Homework Really So Terrible?

Writer uses family example as introduction

1   My daughter recently announced, with dramatic emphasis, that she is now a second semester high school senior. This is an important milestone. The college applications have all been written, The last grades that count for much have been recorded. Time to party.

Sounds good to me!!

Writer uses humor to bond with readers

2   Except that it is not her style. She said she was going to start taking it easy, but she is still doing a lot of homework. Last week her friends told her they were going to organize

an intervention because they caught her spending several hours preparing for an exam.

Writer sets up conflict

What should I do about her? Like most American 3 parents, I am proud of my children when they meet their academic responsibilties. But I also worry when it seems too much. We want our children to have balanced lives. We often see our children's teachers as insensitive taskmasters who steal time from family life.

Writer notes TV source but digs deeper

I was fascinated by a recent report about all this on 4 *CBS Sunday Morning.* I decided to check on some of the facts and experts the program cited in hopes that would help me make up my own mind.

The CBS report said a University of Michigan study 5 showed more than a 50 percent increase in the amount of homework done by American school children twelve and under. But the actual study had some surprises.

Poor kids!

The university's Panel Study of Income Dynamics, 6 directed by economist Frank Stafford of the Institute for Social Research, has been gathering data for decades on how people use their time. They surveyed a representative sample of 3,586 children aged twelve and under in 1997, and compared the results to a similar 1981 study. As CBS reported, homework time increased 59.5 percent.

Oops—not really

But it is like raising my bowling score. A nearly 60 percent 7 improvement sounds big until you learn that my previous average was a 53. The average child in 1981 spent just one hour and twenty-four minutes a week on homework. By 1997 that had increased to two hours and fourteen minutes. That means that this allegedly overburdened American child, innocent victim of callous teachers, is averaging less than a half hour of homework each school night.

Hmm. I found books written by two experts on the 8 CBS show. One was Etta Kralovec, coauthor with John Buell of the 2000 book *The End of Homework: How Homework Disrupts Families, Overburdens Children, and Limits Learning,* and Janine Bempechat, author of the 2000 book *Getting Our Kids Back on Track: Educating Children for the Future.*

I was disappointed by the Kralovec-Buell book, 9 although that may be my fault. The authors and I seem to be on different planes of existence. Their proof that homework is an important cause of suicide among school children is a news clipping from the Harare [Zimbabwe] *Herald* referring to the case of an eleven-year-old in Hong Kong who left a note saying he jumped out of a thirty-four-story building because he didn't finish his lessons. They argue that homework is bad, in part, because it gives middle class children an unfair advantage over less financially fortunate classmates. They suggest that the problem can only be solved by a social and cultural revolution in the United States as well as the rest of the world and, I imagine, the eternal cosmos.

In other words, if you are worried because it is 1 A.M. [10] and your daughter hasn't finished her environmental studies report, Kralovec and Buell aren't much help.

Bempechat has a more practical approach. She gets [11] quickly to what research says about homework: It has no effect on achievement in early elementary grades and not much effect in the higher elementary grades, but does raise achievement in middle school and high school. Middle schoolers do better if they study at home five to ten hours a week, but more than that doesn't add anything. The greatest benefits from homework occur for high schoolers who study five to ten hours a week, and students who do more than that experience additional gains.

So should we forget about homework in the first and [12] second grades? Bempechat says no, for an intriguing reason. Children need to develop habits of work, she says, and it is likely to be easier if they start early with appropriately small obligations.

"The fifteen-minute assignment of first grade gradually [13] stretches into the three-week assignment of fifth grade," she says. "The years in between will be the training ground for our children's development into (relatively) organized and mature learners. Early experiences with homework may not contribute to children's academic development, but they certainly promote their motivational development. . . . As school gets increasingly difficult and courses become more complex, your children need to be persistent when the going gets tough. Homework, as much as you and they may hate it, will foster these strengths of character."

Kralovec and Buell will argue, perhaps, that Bempechat [14] has given in to the capitalist worship of productivity and ignores the importance of spiritual growth. That may make sense on their planet, but the need to develop habits of consistency and persistence appeals to me. The research I have done about college admissions over the past three years convinces me that success in life, as opposed to success in the application game, is the direct result of those character traits Bempechat is talking about, and they develop long before anyone ever takes an SAT.

Once we establish that homework is necessary, we can 15 discuss possible changes in the nature of the beast. My colleague Karin Chenoweth, who does the Homeroom column on this Web site and in the *Washington Post*, suggests that elementary and middle school homework be no more than an hour a day of reading and fifteen minutes of writing about that reading, with maybe twenty extra minutes of math and vocabulary work. That would certainly reduce parental struggles with dioramas, collages, and my wife's most horrific memory, the log cabin that our daughter had to construct out of Tootsie Rolls in the first grade.

There is also a very firm approach to homework, used by 16 the KIPP schools to keep low-income children on track, that might work in more affluent schools for different reasons. San Francisco–based KIPP (Knowledge Is Power Program) has fifteen schools around the country that have significantly raised the academic achievement of fifth through eighth graders in communities where such high test scores are rare. The KIPP schools enshrine homework by giving each of their teachers a cell phone and insisting that students call their teachers at any time if they have any problem completing the assignment that night. If a child appears the next day with an assignment incomplete, the parents are called to the school to talk about it.

This builds Bempechat's motivational habits, which reg- 17 ular public schools in KIPP neighborhoods often neglect. But consider the impact such a policy might have in affluent communities where the anti-homework movement has taken root. An open invitation—indeed, a requirement— that the teacher be called about any inexplicable instructions or incomprehensible problems is likely to be accepted by middle class parents with a vengeance. After a few evenings handling such calls, the teachers are likely to think more carefully about their assignments before they hand them out, and that will be good for everybody.

Of course, even good habits can be overdone. But when 18 I think about cautioning my daughter about working too hard, I remind myself that that was the way I behaved in high school. Like most people reflecting on courses and teachers that challenged them when they were teenagers, I have no regrets about those late nights.

Unless there are clear signs of emotional illness, or a   19 daily schedule that is nothing but books and papers, students like Katie are better off making their own decisions. They have acquired the character traits that Bempechat extols. They are determined to handle the responsibilities they have been given.

They may find their homework boring or frustrating, but   20 when they start earning a living they are going to have jobs with some of that, and it is best to develop coping skills early. Schools that demand a half hour a day of academic work at home, less than a fifth of the time these same children spend watching television, do not seem to me to be overdoing it.

3

Critical Thinking Processes

Critic, from the Greek word *kritikos,* means "one who can judge and discern"—in short, someone who thinks critically. College will have given you your money's worth if it leaves you better able to judge and discern— to determine what is more and less important, to make distinctions and recognize differences, to generalize from specifics, to draw conclusions from evidence, to grasp complex concepts, to choose wisely. The effective thinking that you will need in college, on the job, and in your daily life is active and purposeful, not passive and ambling. It is critical thinking.

A PROCESS OF CRITICAL THINKING

You use critical thinking every day to solve problems and make decisions. Suppose you don't have enough money both to pay your tuition and to buy the car you need to get to campus and to work. First, you might pin down the causes of your financial problem. Next, you might examine your options to find the best solution, as shown in the graphic on page 27.

■ **ACTIVITY:** Thinking Critically to Solve a Campus Problem

With classmates, identify a common problem for students at your college—juggling a busy schedule, parking on campus, changing a class, joining a social group, or some other issue. Working together, use critical thinking to explore the problem and identify possible solutions.

Problem
You can't afford both your college tuition and the car you need.

SOLUTION

❶ IDENTIFY CAUSES

Causes in your control:
Expensive vacation?
Credit card debt?

Causes out of your control:
Medical emergency?
Job loss?
Tuition increase?
Financial aid policy change?

❷ ANALYZE, SYNTHESIZE, AND EVALUATE OPTIONS

| Do without a car | *(how?)* | • Get rides with family or friends? |
| | | • Take public transportation? |

| Decrease your tuition | *(how?)* | • Take fewer courses? |

Get more money	*(how?)*	• Get a loan from the bank?
		• Get a loan from the college?
		• Get a loan from a family member?
		• Get another job?

❸ REACH A LOGICAL CONCLUSION

Apply for a short-term loan through the college for tuition.

Building Critical Thinking Skills

Using critical thinking, you can explore many problems step by step and reach reasonable solutions. Critical thinking, like critical reading, draws on a cluster of intellectual strategies and skills (see Table 3.1).

These three activities—analysis, synthesis, and evaluation—are the core of critical thinking. They are not new to you, but applying them rigorously in college-level reading and writing may be. When you approach college reading and writing tasks, instructors will expect you (and you should expect yourself) to think, read, write, and think some more as the graphic on page 29 illustrates.

TABLE 3.1 Analyzing, Synthesizing, and Evaluating

Critical Thinking Skill	Definition	Applications for Readers	Applications for Writers
Analysis	Breaking down information into its parts and elements	Analyzing the information in articles, reports, and books to grasp facts and concepts	Analyzing events, ideas, processes, and structures to understand them and explain them to readers
Synthesis	Putting together elements and parts to form new wholes	Synthesizing information from several sources, examining implications, and drawing conclusions supported by reliable evidence	Synthesizing source materials with your own thoughts to convey the unique combination to others
Evaluation	Judging according to standards or criteria	Evaluating a reading by determining standards for judging, applying them to the reading, and arriving at a conclusion about its significance or value	Evaluating something in writing by convincing readers that your standards are reasonable and that the subject either does or does not meet those standards

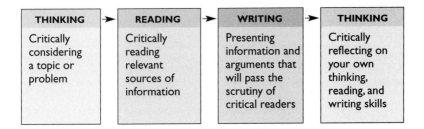

THINKING	READING	WRITING	THINKING
Critically considering a topic or problem	Critically reading relevant sources of information	Presenting information and arguments that will pass the scrutiny of critical readers	Critically reflecting on your own thinking, reading, and writing skills

■ **ACTIVITY**: Thinking Critically to Explore an Issue

You have worked hard on a group presentation that will be a major part of your grade—and each member of the group will get the same grade. Two days before the project is due, you discover that one group member has plagiarized heavily from various sources well known to your instructor. Working together with classmates, use critical thinking to explore your problem and determine what you might do.

Applying Critical Thinking to Academic Problems

Your college assignments will pose academic problems to help you gain experience grappling with them. As you do so, you'll be expected to use your critical thinking skills—analyzing, synthesizing, and evaluating—in your reading and writing. Although you could simply dive in, using each skill as needed, sometimes the very wording of an assignment or exam question will alert you to a skill that your instructor expects to assess as Table 3.2 illustrates.

TABLE 3.2   Using Critical Thinking for Academic Assignments

Critical Thinking Skill	Sample Academic Assignments
Analysis: Breaking into parts and elements based on a principle	• Describe the immediate causes of the 1929 stock market crash. • Trace the stages through which a bill becomes federal law. • Explain and illustrate the three dominant styles of parenting. • Define *romanticism*, identifying and illustrating its major characteristics.

(Continued)

TABLE 3.2 *(Continued)*

Critical Thinking Skill	Sample Academic Assignments
Synthesis: Combining parts and elements to form new wholes	• Discuss the following statement: High-minded opposition to slavery was only one cause, and not a very important one, of the animosity between North and South that in 1861 escalated into civil war.
	• Imagine that you are a trial lawyer in 1921, charged with defending Nicola Sacco and Bartolomeo Vanzetti, two anarchists accused of murder. Argue for their acquittal on whatever grounds you can justify.
Evaluation: Judging according to standards or criteria	• Present and evaluate the most widely accepted theories that explain the disappearance of the dinosaurs.
	• Defend or show weaknesses in the idea that houses and public buildings should be constructed to last no longer than twenty years.
	• Contrast the models of the solar system advanced by Copernicus and by Kepler, showing how the latter improved on the former.

■ **ACTIVITY:** Thinking Critically to Respond to an Academic Problem

Working in a small group, select one of the sample assignments in Table 3.2 or an assignment from one of your classes. Explain how you would approach the assignment in order to demonstrate your critical thinking. Have the group members share their explanations and their strategies for figuring out how to tackle their academic assignments.

A SPOTLIGHT ON EVIDENCE

As you write a college paper, you try to figure out your purpose, the position you want to take, and ways to get readers to follow your logic and accept your points. Your challenge, of course, is not just to think clearly but to demonstrate your thinking to others, to persuade them to pay attention to what you say. And sound evidence is what critical readers want to see.

Sound evidence supports your main idea or thesis, substantiating your points for readers. It also bolsters your credibility as a writer, demonstrating the merit of your position. When you write, you need to marshal enough appropriate evidence to clarify, explain, and support your ideas. You need to weave claims, evidence, and your own interpretations together into a clearly reasoned explanation or argument. And as you do so, you need to select and test your evidence so that it will convince your readers.

Using Different Types of Evidence

What is evidence? It is anything that demonstrates the soundness of a claim. Facts, statistics, expert testimony, and firsthand observations are four reliable forms of evidence (see Table 3.3 on p. 34). Other evidence might include examples, illustrations, details, and authoritative opinions. Depending on the purpose of your assignment, some kinds of evidence weigh more heavily than others. For example, readers might appreciate your memories of caring for animals on the farm in an essay recalling your childhood summers. However, they would probably discount your memories in an explanatory or argumentative paper about methods of livestock care unless you could show that your memories are representative or that you are an expert on the subject. Personal experience may strengthen an argument but generally is not sufficient as its sole support. If you are in doubt about the type of evidence an assignment requires, ask your instructor whether you should use sources or rely on personal experience and examples.

Facts.   Facts are statements that can be verified objectively, by observation or by reading a reliable account. They are usually stated dispassionately: "If you pump the air out of a five-gallon varnish can, the can will collapse." Of course, we accept many of our facts based on the testimony of others. For example, we believe that the Great Wall of China exists although we may never have seen it with our own eyes.

Sometimes people say facts are true statements, but truth and sound evidence can be confused. Consider the truth of these statements:

The tree in my yard is an oak.   *True* because it can be verified
A kilometer is 1,000 meters.   *True* using the metric system
The speed limit on the   *True* according to law
    highway is sixty-five miles
    per hour.

Fewer fatal highway accidents have occurred since the new exit ramp was built.	*True* according to research studies
My favorite food is pizza.	*True* as an opinion
More violent criminals should receive the death penalty.	*True* as a belief
Murder is wrong.	*True* as a value judgment

Some might claim that each statement is true. When you think critically, however, you should avoid treating opinions, beliefs, judgments, and personal experience as true in the same sense that verifiable facts and events are true.

Statistics.   Statistics are facts expressed in numbers. What portion of American children are poor? According to statistics from the U.S. Census Bureau, 12.9 million children (or 17.6 percent of all American children) lived in poverty in 2003 compared with 12.1 million (or 16.7 percent) in 2002. Clear as such figures seem, they can raise complex questions. For example, how significant is the increase in the poverty rate over one year? What percentage of children were poor over longer terms, ten or twenty years, for example?

Most writers, without trying to be dishonest, interpret statistics to help their causes. The statement "Fifty percent of the population have incomes above the poverty level" might substantiate the fine job done by the government of a developing nation. Putting the statement another way—"Fifty percent of the population have incomes below the poverty level"—might use the same statistic to show the inadequacy of the government's efforts.

Even though a writer is free to interpret a statistic, statistics should not be used to mislead. On the wrapper of a peanut candy bar, we read that a one-ounce serving contains only 150 calories. The claim is true, but the bar weighs 1.6 ounces. Gobble it all—more likely than eating exactly 62 percent of it—and you'll ingest 240 calories, making the candy bar a heftier snack than the innocent statistic on the wrapper suggests. Because abuses make some readers automatically distrustful, use figures fairly when you write, and make sure they are accurate. If you doubt a statistic, compare it with figures reported by several other sources. Distrust a statistical report that differs from every other report unless it is backed by further evidence.

Expert Testimony.   By *experts,* we mean people with knowledge gained from study and experience of a particular field. The test of an expert is whether his or her expertise stands up to the scrutiny of others who are knowledgeable in that field. The opinion of Michael Jordan on how to play offense in basketball or of economist and former Federal Reserve chairman Alan Greenspan on what causes inflation carries authority, but Jordan's take on the economy or Greenspan's thoughts on basketball would not be credible. Also consider whether the expert's reliability might be affected by any bias or special interest. Statistics on cases of lung cancer attributed to smoking might be better taken from government sources than from the tobacco industry.

Firsthand Observation.   Firsthand observation is persuasive. It can add concrete reality to abstract or complex points. You might support the claim "The Meadowfield waste recycling plant fails to meet state guidelines" by recalling your own observations: "When I visited the plant last January, I was struck by the number of open waste canisters and by the lack of protective gear for the workers who handle these toxic materials daily."

As readers, most of us tend to trust a writer who declares, "I was there. This is what I saw." Sometimes that trust is misplaced, however, so always be wary of a writer's claim to have seen something that no other evidence supports. Ask yourself, Is this writer biased? Might the writer have (intentionally or unintentionally) misinterpreted what he or she saw? Of course, your readers will scrutinize your firsthand observations too. Take care to reassure them that your observations are unbiased and accurate.

■ **ACTIVITY:** Looking for Evidence

Using the issue you explored with classmates for the activity on page 26, what would you need to support your identification, explanation, or solution of the problem? Working with classmates, identify the kinds of evidence that would be most useful. Where or how might you find such evidence?

Testing Evidence

As both a reader and a writer, you should always critically test and question evidence to see whether it is strong enough to carry the weight of an author's claims. Use the Evidence Checklist on page 35 to determine whether evidence is useful and trustworthy.

TABLE 3.3 Drawing on Varied Evidence

Type of Evidence	Definition	Example	Source
Facts	Information that can be confirmed or substantiated by an objective person	When employment drops, college enrollment tends to go up because people are motivated to increase their skills.	Colorado Commission on Higher Education, "Governor's Take Force to Strengthen and Improve the Community College system. Final Report, April 5, 2004," p. 16, at \<www.state.co.us/cche\>
Statistics	Factual information presented in numerical form	According to the U.S. Census Bureau, 85% of Aurora residents over age 25 have graduated from high school, 4.6% more than the national average. However, only 24.6% of this group have graduated from college, just 0.2% more than the 24.4% national average.	"Profile of Selected Social Characteristics 2000" for Aurora, Colorado, and for United States, *U.S. Census Bureau Fact* at \<http://factfinder.census.gov/home/saff/man.html?_lang=en\>
Expert Testimony	Information from a knowledgeable person whose study, research, or experience is respected by others in the field	According to Daniela Higgins, director of the Center for Workforce Development, the Career Enrichment Program at Community College of Aurora wants to attract people looking for career advancement to improve their family resources.	"Program Provides Free College Education to People Who Need Improved Job Skills and Career advancement," press release from Community College of Aurora at \<www.ccaurora.edu/news/education.html\>
Firsthand Observation	Your own accurate, unbiased eyewitness account	During my visit to Community College of Aurora to interview a workforce specialist, I observed campus publicity for programs in computer skills, paramedic and firefighter training, criminal justice, law enforcement, and early childhood education.	Your notes about your campus visit or your collection of campus materials

EVIDENCE CHECKLIST

☐ Is it accurate?
  • Do the facts and figures seem accurate based on what you have found in published sources, reports by others, or reference works?
  • Are figures or quoted facts copied correctly?

☐ Is it reliable?
  • Is the source trustworthy and well regarded?
  • Does the source acknowledge any commercial, political, advocacy, or other bias that might affect the quality of its information?
  • Does the writer supplying the evidence have appropriate credentials or experience? Is the writer respected as an expert in the field?
  • Do other sources agree with the information?

☐ Is it up-to-date?
  • Are facts and statistics current?
  • Is the information from the latest sources?

☐ Is it to the point?
  • Does the evidence back the exact claim made?
  • Is the evidence all pertinent? Does any of it drift from the point to interesting but irrelevant information? Does it obscure the absence of relevant evidence?

☐ Is it representative?
  • Are examples typical of all the things included in the writer's position?
  • Are examples balanced? Do they present the topic or issue fairly?
  • Are contrary examples acknowledged?

☐ Is it appropriately complex?
  • Is the evidence sufficient to account for the claim made?
  • Does it avoid treating complex things superficially?
  • Does it avoid needlessly complicating simple things?

☐ Is it sufficient to back the claim and persuade readers?
  • Are the amount and quality of the evidence appropriate for the claim and for the readers?

- Does the evidence accommodate or acknowledge what readers already know about the issue?
- Does the evidence answer the questions readers are likely to ask?
- Is the evidence vivid and significant?

Selecting Persuasive Supporting Evidence

Although supporting evidence can come from many sources—your experience, observation, imagination, or interaction with others—college instructors often expect you to turn to the writings of others. This expectation reflects the view that academic ideas develop through exchange: each writer reads and responds to the writing of others, building on earlier discussion while expanding the conversation. In books, articles, and reports, you can find pertinent examples, illustrations, details, and expert testimony—in short, reliable information that will show that your claims and statements are sound. You'll be more likely to find and use persuasive evidence that supports your thinking if you try to define what you need as a writer, considering questions such as those in the Purpose Checklist.

PURPOSE CHECKLIST

☐ What is the thesis you want to support or the point you want to demonstrate?

☐ Does the assignment require or suggest any specific focus—certain kinds of supporting evidence, certain types of sources, or certain ways of presenting your material?

☐ Which of your own ideas or opinions do you want to support with good evidence?

☐ Which of your ideas might you want to check, clarify, or change based on the evidence you find?

☐ Which ideas or opinions of others do you want to verify or counter?

☐ Do you want to analyze material yourself (for example, by comparing articles or Web sites that take different approaches), or do you want to find someone else's analysis?

☐ What kinds of evidence do you want to use—for example, facts, statistics, or expert testimony? Do you also want to add your own firsthand observation of the situation or scene?

Although your evidence should satisfy you as a writer, it also needs to meet the criteria of your college readers—your instructors and possibly your classmates—as the following graphic illustrates.

TWO VIEWS OF SUPPORTING EVIDENCE

COLLEGE WRITER	COLLEGE READER
• Does it support my thesis?	• Is it relevant to the purpose and assignment?
• Does it seem accurate?	• Is it reliable, given academic standards?
• Have I added enough?	• Is it of sufficient quantity, variety, and strength?
• Is it recent enough?	• Is it current, given the standards of the field?
• Is it balanced?	• Is it typical, fair, and complex?
• Will it persuade my audience?	• Does the writer make a credible case?

Using the Statement-Support Pattern

Sometimes you will know exactly what supporting evidence your paper needs. In fact, as you plan or write a draft, you may tuck in notes to yourself—find this, look that up, add some numbers here. Other times, you may sense that your evidence isn't as strong as you want it to be, but you may not know exactly what to add or where to add it. One way to determine where you need to supply supporting evidence is to examine your plan or draft, sentence by sentence.

- What does each statement claim or promise to a reader?
- Where do you provide supporting evidence to demonstrate the claim or fulfill the promise?

The answers to these questions—your statements and your supporting evidence—often fall into a common alternating pattern:

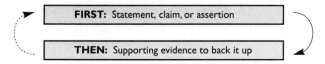

FIRST: Statement, claim, or assertion

THEN: Supporting evidence to back it up

When you spot a string of assertions without much support, you have found a place where you might need more evidence. Select your evidence carefully so that it substantiates the exact statement, claim, or assertion that precedes it. Look for relevant particulars that can strengthen and clarify your more general statement. Likewise, if you spot a string of examples, details, facts, quotations, or other evidence, introduce or conclude it with an interpretive statement that explains the point the evidence substantiates. Make sure your general statement connects and pulls together all of the particular evidence. (See also pp. 116–19 on reasoning inductively and deductively.)

When Carrie Williamson introduced the topic of her analysis, "Rainforest Destruction," she made a general statement and then supported it by quoting facts from a source. Then she repeated the statement-support pattern, backing up her next statement in turn.

The tropical rainforests are among the most biologically diverse — *Statement*
communities in the world. According to the Web site *World Rainforest Information Portal,* "more than 50 percent of all species live in tropical rainforests," and "a typical four-square-mile patch of rainforest contains up to 1,500 species of flowering plants, as many as 750 tree species, 125 mammal species, 400 bird species, 100 reptile species, 60 amphibian species, and 150 butterfly species" ("Biodiversity"). — *Supporting evidence: Statistics about species*

These amazing communities that depend on each part being intact in order to function properly and successfully are being destroyed at an — *Statement*
alarming rate. Each year the destruction claims "an area larger than Italy" (Soltani 86). — *Supporting evidence: Facts about destruction*
Many rainforest conservationists debate what the leading cause of deforestation is. — *Statement identifying cause-and-effect debate*
Regardless of which one is the major cause, the fact remains that both logging and slash-and-burn farming are destroying more and more acres of rainforests each year. — *Statement previewing points to come*

By using the statement-support pattern from the very beginning, Carrie reassured her readers that she was a trustworthy writer who would try to supply convincing evidence throughout her paper. She further strengthened this impression of reliability by following the conventions of MLA style (see Ch. 11) to credit her sources in her list of works cited:

"Biodiversity." *World Rainforest Information Portal.* Rainforest Action Network,
2001. Web. 4 Feb. 2003.

Soltani, Atossa. "Every Tree Killed Equals Another Life Lost." *Wood and Wood
Products* 100.3 (1995): 86-. *Expanded Academic ASAP.* Web. 31 Jan. 2003.

Besides checking for the statement-support pattern, consider your paper's overall purpose, organization, and line of reasoning. For example, persuasive evidence may help you define key terms, justify the significance of a problem, back up your stand on an issue, or support your solution to a problem. Table 3.4 shows some of the many ways the pattern can be used to clarify and substantiate your ideas.

TABLE 3.4   Supporting Statements with Evidence

Function of Statement	Possible Supporting Evidence
Introduce a topic	Facts or statistics to justify the importance or significance of the topic
Describe a situation	Factual examples or illustrations to convey the reality or urgency of the situation
Introduce an event	Accurate firsthand observations to describe an event that you have witnessed
Present a problem	Expert testimony or firsthand observation to establish the necessity or urgency of a solution
Explain an issue	Facts and details to clarify the significance of the issue
State your point	Facts, statistics, or examples to support your viewpoint or position
Interpret and prepare readers for evidence that follows	Facts, examples, observations, or research findings to define and develop your case
Conclude with your recommendation or evaluation	Facts, examples, or expert testimony to persuade readers to accept your conclusion

Use the Statement-Support Checklist to help you decide whether— and where—you might need evidence to support your critical thinking.

STATEMENT-SUPPORT CHECKLIST

☐ What does each statement promise that you'll deliver? What additional evidence would ensure that you have effectively kept this promise?

☐ Are your statements, claims, and assertions backed up with supporting evidence? If not, what evidence might you add?

☐ Which criteria for evidence are most important to your readers? What evidence would best meet the criteria? How much evidence would readers expect?

☐ When you read through your draft, which parts seem weak or incomplete to you?

☐ What facts or statistics would clarify your topic or substantiate your statements?

☐ What examples or illustrations would make the background or the current circumstances clearer and more compelling for readers?

☐ What comments by a reliable expert would enlighten your readers about your topic or the situation that it involves?

☐ What firsthand observation would add authenticity?

☐ Where have peer readers or your instructor suggested adding more or stronger evidence?

■ **ACTIVITY:** Supporting Critical Thinking

Working with a classmate, analyze one of your assigned readings, the essay on pages 21–25, or one of your own papers. Where does the writer use the statement-support pattern? How does the statement-support pattern affect the essay's persuasiveness? Where might the writer have stated a claim or assertion more clearly? Where might the writer have added supporting evidence?

4

Strategies for Generating Ideas

No matter how much you read or think, neither activity replaces the task of writing down the words. For most writers, the hardest part of writing comes first—confronting a blank sheet of paper or an empty screen. Fortunately, you can prepare for that moment, both for finding ideas and for getting ready to write. All of the techniques that follow have worked for some writers—both professionals and students—and some may work for you.

DISCOVERING IDEAS

When you begin to write, you need to start the ideas flowing. Sometimes ideas appear effortlessly on the paper or screen, perhaps triggered by the opportunities and resources around you—something you read, see, hear, discuss, or think about. (See the top half of the graphic on p. 42.) At other times you need an arsenal of idea generators, strategies you can use at any point in the writing process, whenever your ideas dry up or you need more examples or evidence. If one strategy doesn't work for a particular writing task, try another. (See the strategies in the lower half of the graphic, all detailed in the following pages.)

Building from Your Assignment

Learning to write is learning what questions to ask yourself. Sometimes your assignment triggers this process by raising certain questions and

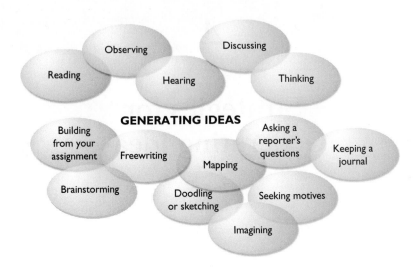

GENERATING IDEAS

Observing · Discussing · Reading · Hearing · Thinking · Building from your assignment · Freewriting · Mapping · Asking a reporter's questions · Keeping a journal · Brainstorming · Doodling or sketching · Seeking motives · Imagining

answering others. For example, Ben Martinez jotted notes on the handout as his instructor and classmates discussed the first assignment for his composition class—recalling a personal experience.

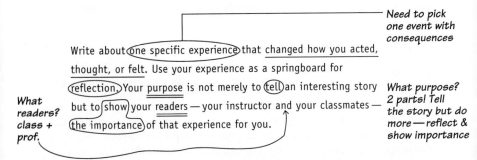

Need to pick one event with consequences

Write about one specific experience that changed how you acted, thought, or felt. Use your experience as a springboard for reflection. Your purpose is not merely to tell an interesting story but to show your readers — your instructor and your classmates — the importance of that experience for you.

What readers? class + prof.

What purpose? 2 parts! Tell the story but do more—reflect & show importance

The assignment clarified what audience to address and what purpose to try to accomplish. It also raised three big questions for Ben: Which experience should I pick? How did it change me? Why was it so important for me? His classmates asked the instructor other questions about the length, format, and due date for the essay. As class ended, Ben didn't know what he'd write about, but he had figured out which questions to tackle first, and he had several other strategies in mind for generating ideas.

Sometimes an assignment will assume that you already understand something critical—how to address a particular audience, for example, or what to include in a certain type of writing. When Amalia Blackhawk read her argument assignment, she jotted down several questions about its assumptions to ask her instructor.

Anything OK?
Or only
newspaper
type of issue?

Editor of
what?

What's my
purpose?
Persuading
readers to
respect my
view or to
agree?

My class-
mates? The
publication's
readers?

Select a campus or local issue that matters to you, and write a letter to the editor about it. Be certain to tell readers what the issue is, why it is important, and how you propose to address it. Assume that your letter will appear in a special opinion feature that allows letters longer than the usual word-count limits.

How long is
the usual letter?
How long should
mine be? Anything
else letters like this
should do?

Try these steps as you examine an assignment:

1. *Read through the assignment once* simply to discover its overall direction.
2. *Read it again,* this time highlighting or marking any information that answers questions about your situation as a writer. Does the assignment identify or suggest the readers you should address, your purpose in writing, the type of paper expected, the parts usually included in that kind of writing, or the format required? Does it specify the types of supporting evidence or the line of reasoning you should use?
3. *Jot down the questions that the assignment raises for you.* Figure out exactly what you need to decide—the type of topic to pick, the focus to develop, the issues or aspects to consider, or other guidelines to follow.
4. *List any questions that the assignment doesn't answer or ask you to answer.* Ask your instructor about these questions during or after class.

■ ACTIVITY: Building from Your Assignment

Select an assignment from this class, another course, or a textbook, and jot down some notes about it. What questions does the assignment answer for you? Which questions or decisions does it direct to you? What other questions about the assignment might you want to ask your instructor? When you finish your notes, exchange assignments with a classmate, and make notes about that assignment too. Working with your partner, compare your responses to both assignments.

Brainstorming

A *brainstorm* is a sudden insight or inspiration. As a writing strategy, brainstorming uses free association to stimulate a chain of ideas, often to personalize a topic and break it down into specifics. When you brainstorm, you start with a word or phrase and spend a specific amount of time simply scribbling a list of ideas as rapidly as possible, writing down whatever comes to mind with no editing or going back.

Brainstorming can be a group activity. In the business world, it is commonly used to fill a specific need—finding a name for a product, a corporate emblem, a slogan for an advertising campaign. In college, you can try brainstorming with a few other students or your entire class. Members of the group sit facing one another. They designate one person to record on screen, paper, or chalkboard whatever the others suggest or the best idea in the air at a busy moment. After several minutes of calling out ideas, the group can look over the recorder's list to identify useful results.

On your own, you might brainstorm to define a topic, generate an example while writing, or come up with a title for a finished paper. Martha Calbick brainstormed after her instructor assigned a paper ("Demonstrate from your own experience how the computer has significantly changed our lives"). First, she wrote the word *computer* at the top of the page and set her alarm for fifteen minutes. Then she began to scribble words and phrases. Her first thought—her kid brother's obsession with computer games—quickly led to several more.

Computer
My kid bro. thinks computers are for kids—always playing games
In 3rd grade they teach programming
Hackers—software pirates—become a programmer? big future?
Some get rich—Ed's brother wrote a program for accountants

Computers in subway stations — print tickets
Banks — shove in your plastic card
Newspaper story on man who lucked out — deposited $100 but computer credited $10,000
Class schedules and grades — all online
My report card showed a D instead of a B — big fight to correct it
Are we just numbers now?

When her alarm went off, Martha took a break. After returning to her list, she crossed out ideas that did not interest her, such as her brother's games. She circled the promising question "Are we just numbers now?" and noted how other items expressed that idea too. From her rough list, a focus began to emerge: the dehumanizing effects of computer errors.

When you want to brainstorm, try this advice:

1. *Start with a key word or phrase,* one that will launch your thoughts in a productive direction. If you need a topic, begin with a general word or phrase (for example, *computer*); if you need an example for a paragraph in progress, use a specific word or phrase (for example, *financial errors computers make*).
2. *Set a time limit.* Ten to fifteen minutes is long enough for strenuous thinking.
3. *Rapidly list brief items.* Stick to words, phrases, or short sentences that you can quickly scan later.
4. *Don't stop.* Don't worry about spelling, repetition, absurdity, or relevance. Don't judge, and don't arrange: just produce. Record whatever comes into your head as fast as your fingers can type or your pen can move. If your mind goes blank, keep going, even if you only repeat what you've just written.

When you finish, circle or check anything that suggests a provocative direction. Scratch out whatever looks useless or dull. Then try some conscious organizing: Are any thoughts related? Can you group them? If so, does the group suggest a topic?

■ **ACTIVITY:** Brainstorming

From the following list, choose a subject that interests you, that you know something about, and that you'd like to learn more about — in other words, that you might like to write on. Then brainstorm for ten minutes.

travel	fear	exercise
dieting	dreams	automobiles
family	technology	sports
advertisements	animals	education

Now look over your brainstorming list, and circle any potential topic for a paper. How well did this brainstorming exercise work for you? Can you think of any variations that would make it more useful?

■ ACTIVITY: Brainstorming with a Group

Working with a small group of your classmates — or with the entire class — choose one subject listed in the brainstorming activity that each person knows about. Brainstorm about it individually for ten minutes. Then compare and contrast the brainstorming lists of everyone in the group. Although the group began with the same subject, each writer's treatment will be unique because of differences in experience and perspective. What does this exercise tell you about group brainstorming as a strategy for generating topics for writing?

Freewriting

To tap your unconscious by *freewriting*, you simply write a series of sentences without stopping for fifteen or twenty minutes. The sentences don't have to be grammatical or coherent or stylish; just keep them flowing to unlock an idea's potential.

Generally, freewriting is most productive if it has a goal — for example, finding a topic, a purpose, or a question you want to answer. Martha Calbick wrote her topic at the top of a page and then explored her rough ideas.

> The Dehumanizing Effects of Computer Errors
>
> Computer errors — so how do they make life impersonal? You push in your plastic card and get some cash. Just a glassy screen. No human teller behind a window to look you in the face, maybe even smile. Computers make mistakes too. That man in Utica — from the newspaper — deposited $100.00 to his account and the computer misplaced a decimal point and said he had put in $10,000. Same thing when my B turned into a D. A computer knows your name and number, but it doesn't know who you are.

The result, as you can see, wasn't polished prose. It was full of false starts and little asides. Still, in twenty minutes Martha produced a paragraph to serve as a springboard for her essay.

If you want to try freewriting, here's what you do:

1. *Write a sentence or two at the top of your page or computer screen*— the idea you plan to develop by freewriting.
2. *Write steadily without stopping for at least ten minutes.* Record whatever comes to mind, even "My mind is blank," until some new thought occurs to you.
3. *Don't censor yourself.* Don't cross out false starts, misspellings, or grammar errors. Don't worry about connecting ideas or finding perfect words.
4. *Feel free to explore.* Your initial sentences may be a rough guide, but they shouldn't be a straitjacket. If you find yourself straying from your original idea, a change in direction may be valuable.
5. *Prepare yourself*—if you want to. While you wait for your pencil to start racing, you may want to ask yourself some of these questions:

   What interests you about the topic? What aspects do you care most about?

   What do you recall about this topic from your own experience? What do you know about it that the next person doesn't?

   What have you read about the topic? Observed about it? Heard about it?

   How might you feel about this topic if you were someone else—say a parent, an instructor, or a person from another country?

6. *Repeat the process, looping back to expand a good idea if you want.* Poke at the most interesting parts to see if they will further unfold:

   What does that mean? If that's true, what then? So what?

   What other examples or evidence does this statement call to mind?

   What objections might a reader raise? How might they be answered?

■ ACTIVITY: Freewriting

Choose an idea you've been thinking about or a thought from a brainstorming list. Write it at the top of a page or screen, and then freewrite about it for fifteen minutes. Share your freewriting with your classmates. If you wish, repeat this process, looping back to explore a provocative idea from your freewriting.

■ **ACTIVITY:** Invisible Writing

Invisible writing is a kind of freewriting done on a computer. After typing your topic at the beginning of a word-processing file, darken or turn off your monitor so that you can't read what's on the screen. Then freewrite. If you feel uneasy, try to relax and concentrate on the ideas. After ten minutes, turn the monitor back on, scroll to the beginning, and read what you have written.

Doodling or Sketching

If you like to fill the margins of your notebooks with doodles, harness that artistic energy to generate ideas for writing. As Elena Lopez started thinking about her collision with a teammate during a soccer tournament, she began to sketch the accident (Fig. 4.1). She added stick figures, notes, symbols, and color as she outlined a series of events and their consequences.

Try this advice as you develop ideas by doodling or sketching:

1. *Give your ideas room to grow.* Open a new file using a drawing program, doodle in pencil on a blank page, or sketch on a series of pages to capture a sequence of events.
2. *Concentrate on your topic, but welcome new ideas.* Begin with a key visual in the center or at the top of a page. Add new sketches or doodles as they occur to you; you may find that they embellish, expand, define, or redirect your initial topic.
3. *Add icons, symbols, colors, figures, labels, notes, or questions.* Freely mix visual materials and text, recording ideas without stopping to refine them.
4. *Follow up on your discoveries.* After a break, return to your pages to see how your ideas have evolved. Jot notes by your doodles, making connections, identifying sequences, noting details, or converting visual concepts into descriptive sentences.

■ **ACTIVITY:** Doodling or Sketching

Start with a doodle or sketch that illustrates your topic. Add related events, ideas, or details to develop your topic visually. Share your material with classmates, and then use their observations or questions to help you refine your direction as a writer.

Mapping

Mapping taps your visual and spatial creativity as you generate ideas. When you use mapping, you position ideas on the page or in a file to show

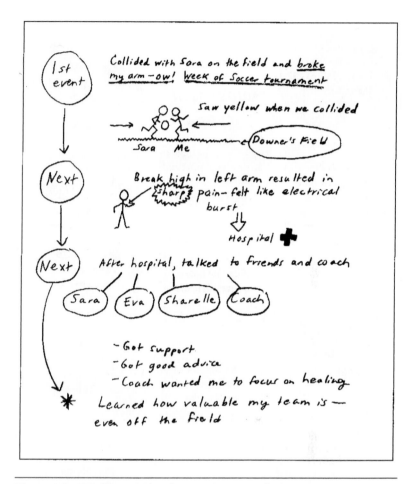

Figure 4.1   Doodling or Sketching to Generate Ideas

their relationships or relative importance—radiating outward from a key term in the center, dropping down from a key word at the top, sprouting upward from a root idea, branching out from a trunk, flowing across the page or screen in chronological or causal sequence, or following a circular, spiral, sequential, or other familiar form.

Andrew Choi used mapping to gather ideas for his proposal for revitalizing the campus radio station (Fig. 4.2). He noted ideas on differently

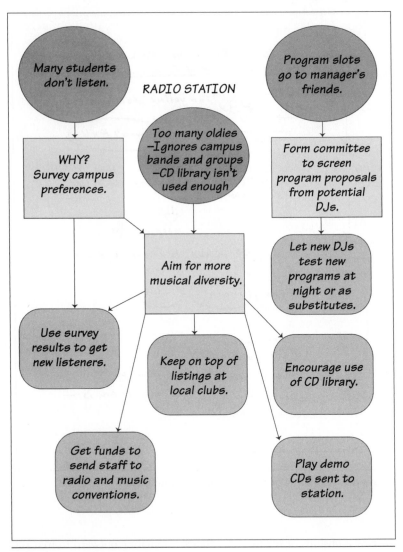

Figure 4.2   Mapping to Generate Ideas

shaped sticky notes—ovals for problems, rectangles for solutions, and rounded rectangles for implementation details. Then he moved the sticky notes around on a blank page, arranging them as he connected ideas.

Here are some suggestions for mapping:

1. *Allow space for your map to develop.* Open a new computer file, find some posterboard for arranging sticky notes or cards, or use a large page for jotting notes.
2. *Begin with your topic or a key idea.* Drawing on your imagination, memory, class notes, or reading, place a key word at the center or top of a page or screen.
3. *Add related ideas, examples, issues, or questions.* Place these points above, below, or beside your key word, adding them quickly and spontaneously.
4. *Refine the connections.* As your map evolves, use lines or arrows to connect ideas; box or circle them to focus attention; add colors to relate comparable points or to distinguish source materials from your own ideas.

After a break, continue mapping to probe one part more deeply, refine the structure, add detail, or build an alternate map from a different viewpoint. Because mapping is so versatile, you can also use it to develop graphics that present ideas in visual form.

■ ACTIVITY: Mapping

Start with a key word or idea that you know something about. Map related ideas, using visual elements to show how they connect. Share your map with classmates, and then use their questions or comments to refine your mapping.

■ ACTIVITY: Mapping with a Group

Working with a group of three to five classmates, write on a notecard the word or phrase your instructor assigns to the entire class—for example, *campus dining* or *balancing work and college.* Then spend ten or fifteen minutes writing other ideas on new note cards and arranging them around the central card. Move the cards around, and draw lines or arrows to help connect your ideas. Share each group's ideas with the entire class.

Imagining

Your imagination is a valuable resource for exploring possibilities and discovering surprising ideas, original examples, striking expressions, and unexpected relationships. Suppose your instructor asks, "What if the average North American life span were more than a century?" No doubt a longer life span would mean that more people would be old. How would that shift affect doctors and nurses, hospitals, and other medical facilities? How might city planners respond to the needs of so many more old people? What would the change mean for shopping centers? For television programming? For leisure activities? For the social security system? For taxes?

Use some of the following strategies to unleash your imagination:

1. *Speculate about changes, alternatives, and options.* What common assumption—something most people take for granted—might you question or deny? What problem or deplorable condition would you like to remedy? What changes in policy, practice, or attitude might avoid problems you foresee for the future? What different paths in life—each with challenges and opportunities—might you take?

2. *Shift your perspective.* Experiment by taking a different point of view. How would someone on the opposite side of the issue respond? How would a plant respond? An animal? A Martian? Try shifting the debate: What happens when the issue is whether people over sixty-five, not teenagers, should be allowed to drink? What happens when the time frame changes from the present to the past or future?

3. *Envision what might be.* Join the many other writers who have imagined a utopia (an ideal state) or an antiutopia. By envisioning, you can conceive of possible alternatives—a better way of treating illness, electing a president, or finding meaning in chaos.

4. *Synthesize.* Synthesizing (generating new ideas by combining previously separate ideas) is the opposite of analyzing (breaking ideas down into component parts). Synthesize to make fresh connections, fusing ideas—perhaps old or familiar—into something new.

■ **ACTIVITY:** Imagining

Begin with a problem that cries out for a solution, a condition that requires a remedy, or a situation that calls for change. Ask "What if?" or use "Suppose that . . ." to trigger your imagination. Speculate about what might be, record your ideas, and then share them with your classmates.

Asking a Reporter's Questions

Journalists assembling facts to write a news story ask themselves six simple questions—the five *W*s and an *H:*

Who?	Where?	Why?
What?	When?	How?

In the lead, or opening paragraph, of a good news story, the writer tries to condense the whole story into a sentence or two that answer all six questions.

A giant homemade fire balloon [*what*] startled residents of Costa Mesa [*where*] last night [*when*] as Ambrose Barker, 79, [*who*] zigzagged across the sky at nearly 300 miles per hour [*how*] in an attempt to set a new altitude record [*why*].

Later in the story, the reporter will add details, using the six basic questions to generate more about what happened and why.

You also can use these six helpful questions to generate specific details for your college papers. The questions can help you explore the significance of a childhood experience, analyze what happened at some moment in history, or investigate a campus problem. Their purpose is to help you gather ideas. Don't worry if some of them go nowhere or lead to repetitious answers. Later you'll weed out irrelevant points, keeping only those that look promising for your topic.

For a topic that is not based on your personal experience, you may need to read or conduct interviews to answer some of the questions. For example, take the topic of the assassination of President John F. Kennedy. Notice how each question can lead to further questions.

- *Who* was John F. Kennedy? What was his background? What kind of person was he? What kind of president? Who was with him when he was killed? Who was nearby? Who do most people believe shot him?
- *What* happened to Kennedy—exactly? What events led up to the assassination? What happened during the assassination? What did the people around the president do? What did the media representatives do? What did everyone across the country do? Ask someone who remembers the event what he or she did on hearing about it.
- *Where* was Kennedy assassinated? In what city? On what street? Where was he going? What was he riding in? Where was he sitting? Where did the shots likely come from? Where did the shots hit him? Where did he die?
- *When* was he assassinated—what day, month, year, time? When did Kennedy decide to go to this city? When—precisely—were the shots fired? When did he die? When was a suspect arrested?
- *Why* was Kennedy assassinated? What are some of the theories of the assassination? What solid evidence is available to explain it? Why has this event caused so much controversy?
- *How* was Kennedy assassinated? What kind of weapon was used? How many shots were fired? What specifically caused his death? How can we get at the truth of this event?

■ ACTIVITY: Asking a Reporter's Questions

Choose one of the following topics, or use one of your own:

A memorable event in history or in your life
A concert or other performance you have attended
An accomplishment on campus
An occurrence in your city
An important speech
A proposal for change
A questionable stand someone has taken

Answer the six reporter's questions about the topic. Then write a sentence or two synthesizing the answers to the six questions. Incorporate that sentence into an introductory paragraph for an essay you might write later.

Seeking Motives

In a surprisingly large part of your college writing, you will try to explain the motives behind human behavior. In a history paper, you might consider how George Washington's conduct shaped the U.S. presidency. In a psychology report, you might try to explain the behavior of participants in an experiment. In a literature essay, you might analyze the motives of Hester Prynne in *The Scarlet Letter*. Because people, including characters in fiction, are so complex, identifying their motives is challenging.

According to philosopher-critic Kenneth Burke, if you want to understand any human act, you can break it down into a set of five basic components, a *pentad,* and ask questions about each one. While covering much the same ground as the reporter's questions, Burke's pentad differs in that it can show how the components of a human act affect one another. This line of thought can take you deeper into the motives for human behavior than most reporters' investigations ever go.

Suppose that you are preparing to write a political science paper on President Lyndon Baines Johnson (LBJ). Right after John Kennedy's assassination in 1963, Vice President Johnson was sworn in as president. A year later he was elected to the office by a landslide. By 1968, however, Johnson had decided not to run for a second term as president. You decide to use Burke's pentad to investigate why he made that decision.

1. *The act:* What was done?
   Announcing the decision to leave office without standing for reelection.

2. *The actor:* Who did it?
   President Johnson.
3. *The agency:* What means did the person use to make it happen?
   A televised address to the nation.
4. *The scene:* Where, when, and in what circumstances did the act happen?
   Washington, D.C., March 31, 1968. Protesters against the Vietnam war were gaining numbers and influence. The press was increasingly critical of the escalating war. Senator Eugene McCarthy, an antiwar candidate for president, had made a strong showing against LBJ in the New Hampshire primary election.
5. *The purpose or motive for acting:* What could have made the person do it?
   LBJ's motives might have included wanting to avoid a probable defeat, escape further personal attacks, spare his family, make it easier for his successor to pull the country out of the war, and ease bitter dissension among Americans.

To carry Burke's method further, you can pair each component with another—act to actor, agency, scene, and purpose, for example—and begin fruitful lines of inquiry by asking questions about the pairs:

PAIR   actor to agency
QUESTION   What did LBJ [actor] have to do with his televised address [agency]?
ANSWER   Commanding the attention of a vast audience, LBJ must have felt he was in control, even though he was unable to control the situation in Vietnam.

Not all the paired questions will prove fruitful; some may not even apply. But one or two might reveal valuable connections and start you writing.

■ ACTIVITY: Seeking Motives

Choose an action that puzzles you—perhaps something you, a family member, or a friend has done; a decision of a historical or current political figure; or something in a movie, television program, or literary selection. Then apply Burke's pentad to this action to try to determine the motive for the action. If you want, you can also pair up the components to perceive deeper relationships. When you believe you understand the motivation behind the action, write a paragraph explaining the action, and share it with your classmates.

Keeping a Journal

Journal writing richly rewards anyone who faithfully engages in it every day or several times a week. You can write anywhere or anytime; all you need is a notebook, a writing implement, and a few minutes to record an entry. To keep a valuable journal, you need only the honesty and willingness to set down what you genuinely think and feel.

Your journal will become a mine studded with priceless nuggets—thoughts and observations, reactions and revelations that are yours for the taking.

Reflective Journal Writing.   What do you write in your journal? When you make an entry, put less emphasis on recording what happened, as you would in a diary, than on reflecting about what you do or see, hear or read, learn or believe. An entry can be a list or an outline, a paragraph or an essay, a poem or a letter you don't intend to send, even a page of doodling. Describe a person or a place, set down a conversation, or record insights into your actions or those of others. Consider your pet peeves, your fears, your dreams, your convictions or moral dilemmas, or the fate of the world if you were in charge. Use your experience as a writer to nourish and inspire your writing, recording what worked, what didn't, and how you reacted in each instance.

Responsive Journal Writing.   Sometimes you respond to something in particular—to your reading for an assignment, to classroom discussions, to a movie, to a conversation or observation. This type of journal entry is more focused than the reflective entry. Faced with a long paper to write, you might assign *yourself* a response journal. Then, when the time comes to draft your paper, you will have plenty of material to quarry. (For more on responding to reading, see Ch. 2.)

Warm-up Journal Writing.   To prepare for an assignment, you can group ideas, scribble outlines, sketch beginnings, capture stray thoughts, record relevant material. Of course, what starts as a quick warm-up comment on an essay you've read (or a responsive journal entry) may turn into the draft of a paper. In other words, don't let the categories here constrain you. A journal can be just about anything you want it to be, and the best journal is the one that's most useful to *you*.

■ **ACTIVITY:** Keeping a Journal

Keep a journal for at least a week. Each day record your thoughts, feelings, observations, and reactions. Reflect on what happens, and respond to what you read. At the end of the week, bring your journal to class, and read aloud to your classmates the entry you like best.

■ ACTIVITY: Keeping an E-journal

Keeping an e-journal is as simple as creating a file and making entries by date or subject. Record ideas, feelings, impressions, images, memories, quotations, or any writing you like. You will quickly notice how easy it is to copy and paste inspiring parts of e-mail, interesting quotations from Web pages, or even digitized images and sounds into your e-journal. Just be sure that you identify the source of material that you copy so that you won't later confuse it with your original writing. As your e-journal grows, you will develop a ready source of support for your writing assignments.

GETTING READY TO WRITE

Once you have generated a suitable topic and some ideas related to that topic, you are ready to get down to the job of actually writing.

Setting Up Circumstances

If you can write only with your shoes off or with a can of soda nearby, set yourself up that way. Some writers need a radio blaring rap music; others need quiet. Create an environment that puts you in the mood for writing.

Devoting a Special Place to Writing.   Your place should have good lighting and space to spread out. It may be a desk in your bedroom, the dining room table, or a quiet cubicle in the library—someplace where no one will bother you and where your mind and body will be ready to settle in for work. Try to make it a place where you can leave your projects and keep handy your pens, paper, computer, dictionary, and other reference materials.

Establishing a Ritual.   Some writers find that a ritual relaxes them and helps them get started. You might open a soda, straighten your desk, turn the radio on (or off), and create a new file on the computer.

Reducing Distractions.   Most of us can't prevent interruptions, but we can reduce them. If you are expecting your boyfriend to call, call him before you start writing. If you have small children, write when they are asleep or at school. Use your voice mail to record calls. Let people around you know you are serious about writing, and then give your full attention to it. Learn to block out the noises around you and concentrate on your writing.

Exhausting Your Excuses.   If you, like most writers, are an expert procrastinator, help yourself run out of reasons not to write. Is your room annoyingly jumbled? Straighten it. Sharpen those pencils, throw out that trash, and make that phone call. Then, with your room, your desk, and your mind in order, sit down and write.

Relocating.   If you're not getting anywhere with your writing, look for a new place to write. Move from the college library to home or from the kitchen to your bedroom. Or try an unfamiliar place — a bowling alley, a restaurant, an airport.

Choosing the Best Time to Write.   Some people think best early in the morning; others favor the small hours, when the world — and their stern self-critic — is still. Writing at dawn or in the wee hours also reduces the distraction of other people.

Writing on a Schedule.   Many writers find that it helps to write at a regular time each day. This method worked marvels for English novelist Anthony Trollope, who would start at 5:30 A.M., write 2,500 words before 8:30 A.M., and then go to his job at the post office. (He wrote more than sixty books.) Even if you can't set aside the same time every day, it may help to decide that you're going to sit down at four this afternoon and write for an hour. Or if you get stuck, vary your schedule.

Preparing Your Mind

Sometimes you'll be struck by an idea, an image, or a powerful urge to write. When that kind of miracle happens, even if you're taking a shower or getting ready to go to a movie, yield to impulse and write. You can also encourage your ideas and words to flow by talking and thinking about your writing.

Talking about Your Writing.   Discuss your ideas with a classmate, friend, or roommate, encouraging questions, comments, and suggestions. Talk in person, by phone, or through e-mail. Or talk to yourself, using a voice-activated tape recorder, while you sit in a traffic jam, walk your dog, or ride your bike.

Keeping a Notebook or Journal Handy.   Always have some paper in your pocket or backpack or on the night table to write down good ideas that pop into your mind. Imagination can strike in the supermarket checkout line, in the doctor's waiting room, or during a lull on the job.

Reading.   The step from reading to writing is a short one. Even when you're just reading for fun, you start to involve yourself with words. Who knows? You might also hit on something useful for your paper. Or read purposefully: Set out to read and take notes.

Use the questions in the Discovery Checklist to help you get ready to write.

DISCOVERY CHECKLIST

☐ Is your environment organized for writing? What changes might help you reduce distractions and procrastination?

☐ Have you scheduled enough time to get ready to write? How might you adjust your schedule or your expectations to encourage productivity?

☐ Is your assignment clear? What additional questions might you want to ask about what you are expected to do?

☐ Have you generated enough ideas that interest you? What other strategies for generating ideas might help you expand, focus, or deepen your ideas?

5

Strategies for Planning

Starting to write often seems a chaotic activity, but you can use the strategies in this chapter to help create order. For most papers, you first want to consider your audience and purpose and then focus on a central point or thesis. To help you arrange your material sensibly, the chapter also includes advice on grouping ideas and on outlining. Although no strategy appeals to every writer or fits every situation, you can use the ideas here to expand your options as a writer.

SHAPING YOUR TOPIC FOR YOUR PURPOSE AND YOUR AUDIENCE

As you work on your college papers, you may feel as if you're juggling—selecting weighty points and lively details, tossing them into the air, catching each one as it falls, deftly keeping them all moving in sequence. Busy as you are simply keeping points and details in the air, your performance almost always draws a crowd. Your instructor, your classmates, or other readers expect you to attend to their concerns as you try to achieve your purpose—generally informing, explaining, or persuading.

Thinking carefully about your audience and purpose can help you plan a paper more effectively. If you want to show your classmates and instructor the importance of an event, you'll have to decide how much detail about the event your readers need. Those who have gotten speeding tickets, for instance, will need less information about the experience than those who haven't. However, to achieve your purpose, you'll need to

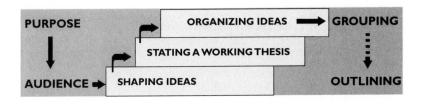

go beyond what happened to why the event mattered to you. No matter how many tickets your readers have gotten, they won't know exactly how that experience changed you unless you share that information with them. They might assume that you were worried about being late to class or paying higher insurance rates when, in fact, you had suddenly realized how narrowly you escaped having an accident like your cousin's and how that recognition motivated you to change your driving habits.

Similarly, if you want to persuade county officials to adopt your proposal for changing the way absentee ballots are distributed to college students, you'll need to support your idea with reasons and evidence— drawing on state election laws and legal precedents familiar to those readers as well as on the experiences of student voters. In fact, you may need to show not only how your proposal would solve existing problems but also why it would improve the situation more effectively than other proposals.

Although your assignment may help you begin to define your purpose and audience, you can refine your understanding using the Planning Checklist.

PLANNING CHECKLIST

☐ What is your purpose? What would you like to accomplish in your paper? How would you like your readers to react to your paper? Do you want them to smile, think, or agree? To understand, learn, accept, respect, care, change, or reply? How might you plan your writing to accomplish your aims?

☐ Who are your readers? If they are not clearly identified in your assignment or by your situation, who are they? What do you assume these readers know or want to know? What opinions do they hold? What do they find informative or persuasive? How might you plan your writing to appeal to them?

☐ How might you narrow and focus your ideas about the topic, given what you know or assume about your audience and

purpose? Which slant would best accomplish your purpose?
What points about the topic would appeal most strongly to
your readers? What details would engage or persuade them?

☐ What qualities of good writing have been discussed in your
class, explained in your syllabus, or identified in assigned
readings? What criteria for college writing have emerged
from exchanges of drafts with classmates or comments from
your instructor? How might you shape your writing to
demonstrate desirable qualities to your readers?

■ **ACTIVITY:** Considering Purpose and Audience

Think back to a recent writing task—a college essay, a job application,
a report or memo at work, a message to a relative, a letter to a campus
office, or some other text. Write a brief description of your situation as
a writer at that time. What was your purpose? Who—exactly—were
your readers? How did you account for both as you planned your writing? How might you have made your writing more effective?

STATING AND USING A THESIS

Most pieces of effective writing are unified around one main point. That
is, all the subpoints and details are relevant to that point. Generally, after
you have read an essay, you can sum up the writer's main point in a sentence, even if the author has not stated it explicitly. We call this summary
statement a *thesis.*

Often a thesis is *explicit,* plainly stated in the writing itself. In "The
Myth of the Latin Woman: I Just Met a Girl Named María," an essay from
The Latin Deli (Athens: University of Georgia Press, 1993), Judith Ortiz
Cofer states her thesis in the last sentence of the first paragraph: "You can
leave the Island, master the English language, and travel as far as you
can, but if you are a Latina, especially one like me who so obviously
belongs to Rita Moreno's gene pool, the Island travels with you." This
clear statement, strategically placed, helps readers see her main point.

Sometimes a thesis is *implicit,* clearly indicated rather than directly
stated. In "The Niceness Solution," a selection from Bruce Bawer's
Beyond Queer (New York: Free Press, 1996), Paul Varnell describes an
ordinance "banning rude behavior, including rude speech," passed in
Raritan, New Jersey. After discussing a 1580 code of conduct, he identifies four objections to such attempts to limit free speech. He concludes

with this sentence: "Sensibly, Raritan Police Chief Joseph Sferro said he would not enforce the new ordinance." Although Varnell does not state his main point in one concise sentence, readers know that he opposes the New Jersey law and any other attempts to legislate "niceness."

The purpose of most academic and workplace writing is to inform, to explain, or to convince. To achieve any of these purposes, you must make your main point crystal clear. A thesis sentence helps you clarify that idea in your own mind and stay on track as you write. It also helps your readers readily see your point and follow your discussion. Sometimes you may want to imply your thesis, but if you state it explicitly, you ensure that readers cannot miss it.

■ **ACTIVITY:** Identifying Theses with a Group

Working in a small group, select and carefully read several essays assigned in your class. Then, individually, write out the thesis for each essay. Of course, some thesis sentences are stated outright (explicit), while others are indicated (implicit). Compare and contrast the thesis statements that you identified with those your classmates found, and discuss the similarities and differences. How can you account for the differences? Try to agree on a thesis statement for each essay.

Discovering Your Working Thesis

It's rare for a writer to develop a perfect thesis statement early in the writing process and then to write an effective essay that fits the thesis exactly. What you should aim for is a *working thesis* — a statement that can guide you but that you will ultimately refine. Ideas for a working thesis are probably all around you.

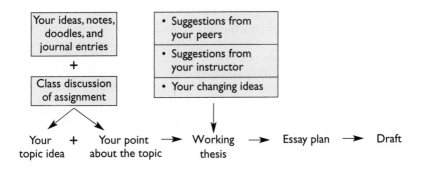

A useful thesis contains not only the key words that identify your topic but also the point you want to make or the attitude you intend to express. Your topic identifies the area you want to explore. To convert a topic to a thesis, you need to add your own slant, attitude, or point.

Topic   +   Slant or attitude or point   =   Working thesis

Suppose your instructor has asked you to identify and write about a specific societal change. After listening to discussion in class and thinking about the topic, you decide to focus on changes in formal courtesy.

TOPIC IDEA   Old-fashioned formal courtesy

Now you experiment, auditioning ideas that will make the topic your own.

AUDITION   Old-fashioned formal courtesy is a thing of the past.

Although your audition sentence emphasizes change, it's still a circular statement, repeating rather than advancing a workable point. It doesn't say anything new about old-fashioned formal courtesy; it simply offers a definition of *old-fashioned*. You still need to find and state your own slant—maybe examining why things have changed.

TOPIC IDEA + SLANT	Old-fashioned formal courtesy + its decline as gender roles have changed
WORKING THESIS	As the roles of men and women have changed in our society, old-fashioned formal courtesy has declined.

Beginning with this working thesis, you could focus on how changing attitudes toward gender roles have caused changes in courtesy. Later, when you revise, you may refine your thesis further, perhaps restricting it to courtesy toward the elderly, toward women, or, despite stereotypes, toward men. Figure 5.1 suggests ways of developing a thesis. (For advice about revising a thesis, see pp. 138–40.)

Once you have a working thesis, be sure its point accomplishes the purpose of your assignment. For example, suppose your assignment asks you to compare and contrast two local newspapers' coverage of a Senate election. Ask yourself what the point of that comparison and contrast is. Simply noting a difference won't be enough to satisfy most readers.

NO SPECIFIC POINT	The *Herald*'s coverage of the Senate elections was different from the *Courier*'s.
WORKING THESIS	The *Herald*'s coverage of the Senate elections was more thorough than the *Courier*'s.

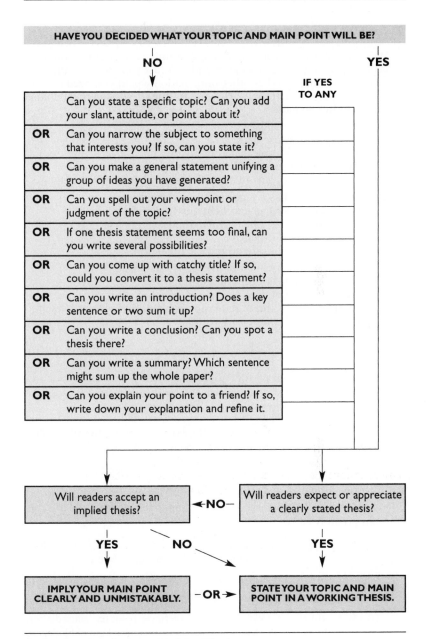

HAVE YOU DECIDED WHAT YOUR TOPIC AND MAIN POINT WILL BE?

NO   **YES**

IF YES TO ANY

Can you state a specific topic? Can you add your slant, attitude, or point about it?

OR Can you narrow the subject to something that interests you? If so, can you state it?

OR Can you make a general statement unifying a group of ideas you have generated?

OR Can you spell out your viewpoint or judgment of the topic?

OR If one thesis statement seems too final, can you write several possibilities?

OR Can you come up with catchy title? If so, could you convert it to a thesis statement?

OR Can you write an introduction? Does a key sentence or two sum it up?

OR Can you write a conclusion? Can you spot a thesis there?

OR Can you write a summary? Which sentence might sum up the whole paper?

OR Can you explain your point to a friend? If so, write down your explanation and refine it.

| Will readers accept an implied thesis? | ◄–NO– | Will readers expect or appreciate a clearly stated thesis? |

YES   **NO**   **YES**

| **IMPLY YOUR MAIN POINT CLEARLY AND UNMISTAKABLY.** | –OR► | **STATE YOUR TOPIC AND MAIN POINT IN A WORKING THESIS.** |

Figure 5.1   Developing a Working Thesis

■ ACTIVITY: Discovering a Thesis

Write a sentence, a working thesis, that unifies each of the following groups of details. Then compare and contrast your theses with those of your classmates. What other information would you need to write a good paper on each topic? How might the thesis statement change as you write the paper?

1. Cigarettes are expensive.
   Cigarettes can cause fires.
   Cigarettes cause unpleasant odors.
   Cigarettes can cause health problems for smokers.
   Secondhand smoke from cigarettes can cause health problems.

2. Clinger College has a highly qualified faculty.
   Clinger College has an excellent curriculum in my field.
   Clinger College has a beautiful campus.
   Clinger College is expensive.
   Clinger College has offered me a scholarship.

3. Crisis centers report that date rape is increasing.
   Most date rape is not reported to the police.
   Often the victim of date rape is not believed.
   Sometimes the victim of date rape is blamed or blames herself.
   The effects of date rape stay with a woman for years.

Stating a Thesis

Once you have a notion of your topic and main point, these four suggestions may help you state or improve a workable thesis that can guide your planning and drafting.

1. *State the thesis sentence exactly.* Replace vague or general wording with concise, detailed, and down-to-earth language.

   TOO GENERAL   There are a lot of troubles with chemical wastes.

   Are you going to deal with all chemical wastes, all over the world, throughout all of history? Are you going to list all the problems they can possibly cause?

   MORE SPECIFIC   Careless dumping of leftover paint is to blame for a recent outbreak of skin rashes in Atlanta.

2. *State just one central idea in the thesis sentence.* If your paper is going to focus on one point, your thesis should state only one main idea.

   TOO MANY IDEAS   Careless dumping of leftover paint has caused a serious problem in Atlanta, and a new kind of biodegradable paint offers a promising solution to one chemical waste dilemma.

ONE CENTRAL IDEA   Careless dumping of leftover paint has caused a serious problem in Atlanta.

OR   A new kind of biodegradable paint offers a promising solution to one chemical waste dilemma.

3. *State your thesis positively.* You can usually find evidence to support a positive statement, but you'd have to rule out every possible exception to prove a negative one. Negative statements also may sound halfhearted and seem to lead nowhere.

NEGATIVE   Medical scientists do not know what causes breast cancer.

POSITIVE   The causes of breast cancer remain a challenge for medical scientists.

Presenting the topic positively as a "challenge" could lead to a paper about an exciting quest. Besides, showing that medical scientists are working on the problem would be relatively easy with just an hour of online or library research.

4. *Limit your thesis to a statement that you can demonstrate.* A workable thesis is limited so that you can support it with sufficient convincing evidence. It should stake out just the territory that you can cover thoroughly within the length assigned and the time available, and no more.

DIFFICULT TO SHOW   For centuries, popular music has announced vital trends in Western society.

DIFFICULT TO SHOW   My favorite piece of music is Handel's *Messiah*.

The first thesis above could inform a whole encyclopedia of music; the second would require you to explain why that symphony is your favorite, contrasting it with all the other musical compositions you know. The following thesis sounds far more workable for a brief essay.

POSSIBLE TO SHOW   In the past two years, an increase in the number of preteenagers has resulted in a comeback for heavy metal on the local concert scene.

Unlike vague or broad claims, a limited thesis statement narrows and refines your topic, thus restricting your essay to a reasonable scope.

TOO VAGUE   Native American blankets are very beautiful.

TOO BROAD   Native Americans have adapted to many cultural shifts.

POSSIBLE TO SHOW   Members of the Apache tribe are skilled workers in high-rise construction.

■ ACTIVITY: Examining Thesis Statements

Discuss each of the following thesis sentences with your classmates. Answer these questions for each:

Is the thesis stated exactly?
Does the thesis state just one idea?
Is the thesis stated positively?
Is the thesis sufficiently limited for a short essay?
How might the thesis be improved?

1. Teenagers should not get married.
2. Cutting classes is like a disease.
3. Students have developed a variety of techniques to conceal inadequate study from their instructors.
4. Older people often imitate teenagers.
5. Violence on television can be harmful to children.
6. I don't know how to change the oil in my car.

Using a Thesis to Organize

Often a good, clear thesis suggests an organization for your ideas.

WORKING THESIS	Despite the disadvantages of living in a downtown business district, I wouldn't live anywhere else.
FIRST ¶S	Disadvantages of living in the business district
NEXT ¶S	Advantages of living there
LAST ¶	Affirmation of your fondness for downtown city life

A clear thesis also helps to organize you, keeping you on track as you write. Just putting your working thesis into words can stake out your territory. Your thesis can then direct you as you select details and connect sections of the essay. Its purpose is to guide you on a quest, not to limit your ideas.

As you write, however, you don't have to cling to a thesis for dear life. If further investigation changes your thinking, you can change your thesis.

WORKING THESIS	Because wolves are a menace to people and farm animals, they ought to be exterminated.
REVISED THESIS	The wolf, a relatively peaceful animal useful in nature's scheme of things, ought to be protected.

You can restate your thesis at any time—as you write, as you revise, and as you revise again.

ORGANIZING YOUR IDEAS

When you organize an essay, you choose a sensible order for the parts, an order that shows your readers how the ideas are connected. Often your organization will not only help readers follow your points but also reinforce your emphases by moving from beginning to end or from least to most significant, as Table 5.1 illustrates.

Grouping Your Ideas

While exploring a topic, you will usually find a few ideas that seem to belong together. In a paper about driving in Manhattan, for example, you might have two facts on city traffic jams, four actions of city drivers, and three problems with city streets. But similar ideas seldom appear together in your notes because you did not discover them all at the same time. To identify an effective order for your ideas, you'll need to sort them into groups and arrange them in sequences. Here are five common ways to work:

1. *Rainbow connections.* List all the main points you're going to express. Don't recopy the rest of your material. Use highlighting or colored pencils to mark points that go together with the same color. When you write, follow the color code, dealing with related ideas at the same time.
2. *Linking.* Make a list of major points, and then draw lines (in color if you like) to link related ideas. Number each linked group to identify a sequence for discussing the ideas. Figure 5.2 illustrates a linked list for an essay on Manhattan driving. The writer has connected related points and supplied each linked group with a heading that will probably inspire a topic sentence to introduce each major division of the essay. Because one point, "chauffeured luxury cars," failed to relate to any other, the writer will leave it out.
3. *Solitaire.* Collect notes and ideas on roomy (5-by-8-inch) note cards. To organize, spread out the cards, and then arrange and rearrange them, as you would the cards in a game of solitaire. When each idea seems to lead to the next, gather all the cards into a deck in that order. As you write, deal yourself a card at a time and translate its contents into sentences. This technique is particularly helpful when you are writing about literature or from research.
4. *Slide show.* If you are familiar with Microsoft PowerPoint or other presentation software, write your notes and ideas on "slides" (the software equivalent of blank sheets). When you're done, the program gives you the option of viewing your slides one by one or viewing the

TABLE 5.1 Using Spatial, Chronological, and Logical Organization

Organization	Movement	Typical Use	Example
Spatial	Left to right, right to left, bottom to top, top to bottom, front to back, outside to inside	• Describing a place or a scene • Describing a person's physical appearance	You might describe an ocean vista, moving from the rocky beach with its tidepools to the plastic buoys floating offshore and then to the sparkling water meeting the glowing sky.
Chronological	What happens first, second, and next, continuing until the end	• Narrating an event • Explaining steps in a procedure	You might narrate the events that led up to an accident leaving home late, stopping to do an errand, speeding along the highway, racing up to the intersection.
Logical	General to specific, specific to general, least important to most important, cause to effect, problem to solution	• Explaining an idea • Persuading readers to accept a stand, a proposal, or an evaluation	You might analyze the effects of the 1997 El Niño by selecting four major consequences, placing the most important one last for emphasis.

cab drivers

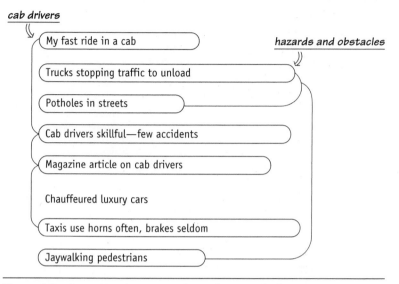

My fast ride in a cab

hazards and obstacles

Trucks stopping traffic to unload

Potholes in streets

Cab drivers skillful—few accidents

Magazine article on cab drivers

Chauffeured luxury cars

Taxis use horns often, brakes seldom

Jaywalking pedestrians

Figure 5.2   Grouping Ideas Using the Linking Method

entire collection. In PowerPoint, choose View and then Slide Sorter to shuffle and reshuffle your slides into a logical order.

5. *Clustering.* Like mapping (see pp. 48–51), clustering is a visual method useful for generating as well as grouping ideas. In the middle of a piece of paper, write your topic in a word or a phrase. Then think of the major divisions into which this topic might be organized. For an essay called "Manhattan Drivers," the major divisions might be the *types* of Manhattan drivers: (1) taxi drivers, (2) bus drivers, (3) truck drivers, (4) New York drivers of private cars, and (5) out-of-town drivers of private cars. Arrange these divisions around your topic, and circle them too. Draw lines out from the major topic to the subdivisions (Fig. 5.3). You now have a rough plan for an essay.

Around each division, make another cluster of details you might include — examples, illustrations, facts, statistics, bits of evidence, opinions. Circle each specific item, and connect it to the appropriate type of driver. When you write your paper, you can expand the details into one paragraph for each type of driver.

This technique lets you know where you have enough specific information to make your paper clear and interesting and where you don't. If one subtopic has no small circles around it — like "bus drivers" in Figure 5.3 — you should think of some specifics to expand it or drop it.

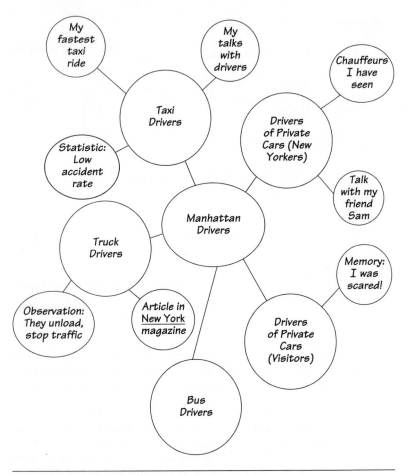

Figure 5.3   Grouping Ideas Using the Clustering Method

■ **ACTIVITY:** Clustering

Generate clusters for three of the following topics. With your classmates, discuss which one of the three would probably help you write
the best paper.

teachers	fast food	civil rights
Internet sites	leisure activities	substance abuse
my favorite restaurants	musicians	technology

■ ACTIVITY: Grouping Ideas on the Computer

Here are some of the easy computer tools you can use to highlight, categorize, and shape your thinking by distinguishing your points on a screen:

Highlighting

Boxing

Showing color

Using **bold,** *italics,* or underlining

• Adding bullets

1. Numbering

Changing fonts

Varying print sizes

To use these features, click on their icons on your toolbar, or use your menu. You can also see your experiments with organization by using an option like Track Changes or by creating a table or column of ideas in a separate window to the left of your text.

Outlining

A familiar way to organize is to outline. Whether brief or detailed, a written outline acts like a map. It shows where you are starting from, where you can stop along the way, and where you are going. If you get lost, you can consult it to get back on track.

How do you arrive at a useful outline? Some writers like to begin with a working thesis. A clear thesis can suggest how to develop an outline, allowing the plan for the paper to grow naturally from the idea behind it. Others prefer to start with a loose informal outline—perhaps just a list of points to make. Still others, especially those laying out a research paper or complicated argument, like to follow a detailed formal outline. However, some writers simply freeze up when they try to outline what they want to say. A more useful tool for them might be a *revision outline,* an outline prepared after writing to identify what actually appears in a draft and to diagnose what might need to be added or changed (see pp. 141–42).

An outline discussed during a peer exchange or submitted with your essay can also act as a map or skeletal summary for your readers. Sometimes it can even help a writer respond to readers' suggestions. For example, if readers find your writing mechanical, a loose informal outline may free up your ideas. On the other hand, if readers find your writing disorganized and hard to follow, a more detailed plan might be especially useful. Experiment with the various types and uses of outlines to learn what helps you plan effectively.

Making a Thesis-guided Outline.   Your working thesis may identify points that you can use to organize your paper. (If it doesn't, you may want to revise your thesis and then return to your outline, or vice versa.) For example, suppose you are assigned an anthropology paper on the people of Melanesia. You decide to focus on the following idea:

> *Working thesis: Although the Melanesian pattern of family life may look strange to Westerners, it fosters a degree of independence that rivals our own.*

Laying out ideas in the same order they follow in the two parts of this thesis statement, you might make a simple outline like this:

1. *Features that appear strange to Westerners*
   - *A woman supported by her brother, not her husband*
   - *Trial marriages common*
   - *Divorce from her children possible for any mother*

2. *Admirable results of system*
   - *Wives not dependent on husbands for support*
   - *Divorce between mates uncommon*
   - *Greater freedom for parents and children*

This informal outline suggests an essay that naturally falls into two parts: (1) features that seem strange and (2) admirable results of the system. When you are creating a thesis-guided outline, look for the key element of your working thesis that can suggest a logical outline, as Table 5.2 illustrates (pp. 76–77).

Developing an Informal Outline.   For in-class writing, brief essays, and familiar topics, a short or informal outline, also called a *scratch outline,* may serve your needs. Jot down a list of points in the order you plan to make them. Use this outline, for your eyes only, to help you get organized, stick to the point, and remember good ideas under pressure. The following example outlines a short paper explaining how outdoor enthusiasts can avoid illnesses carried by unsafe drinking water. It simply lists each of the methods for treating potentially unsafe water that the writer plans to explain in the paper.

> *Working thesis: Campers and hikers need to ensure the safety of the water they drink from rivers or streams.*

Introduction: Treatments for potentially unsafe drinking water

1. *Small commercial filter*
   — *Remove bacteria and protozoa including salmonella and E. coli*
   — *Use brands convenient for campers and hikers*

2. *Chemicals*
   — *Use bleach, chlorine, or iodine*
   — *Follow general rule: 12 drops per gallon of water*

3. *Boiling*
   — *Boil for 5 minutes (Red Cross) to 15 minutes (National Safety Council)*
   — *Store in a clean, covered container*

Conclusion: Using one of three methods of treating water, campers and hikers can enjoy safe water from natural sources.

This simple outline could easily fall into a five-paragraph essay or grow to eight paragraphs: introduction, conclusion, and three paragraphs or pairs of paragraphs in between. You probably won't know until you write the paper exactly how many paragraphs you'll need.

An informal outline can be even briefer than the preceding one. To answer an exam question or prepare a very short paper, your outline might be no more than an *outer plan*—three or four phrases jotted in a list:

Isolation of region
Tradition of family businesses
Growth of electronic commuting

Making an informal outline also can help you develop your ideas. Say you plan a how-to essay analyzing the process of buying a used car, beginning with this thesis:

Working thesis: Despite traps that await the unwary, preparing yourself before you shop can help you find a good used car.

The key word in this thesis is *preparing*. When you ask yourself how the buyer should prepare before shopping for a used car, you're likely to outline several ideas:

— *Read car magazines and* <u>*Consumer Reports*</u>*.*
— *Check ads in the newspapers.*

TABLE 5.2   Organizing by Questioning the Key Element of Your Thesis

Key Element of Thesis	Examples of Key Element	Sample Thesis Statement	Question You Might Ask	Possible Organization of Outline
Plural word	Words such as *benefits, advantages, teenagers,* or *reasons*	A varied personal exercise program has four main advantages.	What are the types, kinds, or examples of this word?	List outline headings based on the categories or cases you identify.
Key word identifying an approach or vantage point	Words such as *claim, argument, position, interpretation,* or *point of view*	*Wylie's interpretation* of Van Gogh's last paintings unifies aesthetic and psychological considerations.	What are the parts, aspects, or elements of this approach?	List outline headings based on the components you identify.
Key word identifying an activity	Words such as *preparing, harming,* or *improving*	*Preparing* a pasta dinner for surprise guests can be an easy process.	How is this activity accomplished, or how does it happen?	Supply a heading for each step, stage, or element that the activity involves.

One part of the sentence subordinate to another	Sentence part beginning with a qualification such as *because*, *although*, or *despite*	*Although* the new wetland preserve will protect only some wildlife, it will bring several long-term benefits to the region.	What does the qualification include, and what does the main statement include?	Use a major heading for the qualification and another for the main statement.
General evaluation that assigns a quality or value to someone or something	Evaluative words such as *typical*, *unusual*, *valuable*, or *notable*	When other parents meet Sandie Burns on the soccer field sidelines, they may be surprised to see her wheelchair, but they soon discover that she is a *typical* soccer mom.	What examples, illustrations, or clusters of details will show this quality?	Add a heading for each extended example or each group of examples or details you want to use.
Claim or argument advocating a certain decision, action, or solution	Words such as *should*, *could*, *might*, *ought to*, or *must*	In spite of these tough economic times, the student Senate *should* strongly recommend extended hours for the library computer lab.	Which reasons and evidence will justify this opinion? Which will counter the opinions of others who disagree with it?	Provide a heading for each major justification or defensive point; add headings for countering reasons.

—Make phone calls to several dealers.
—Talk to friends who have bought used cars.
—Know what to look and listen for when you test-drive.
—Have a mechanic check it out.

After starting your paper with some horror stories about people who got taken by car sharks, you can discuss, point by point, your bits of advice. Of course, you can always change the sequence, add or drop an idea, or revise your thesis as you go along.

Preparing a Formal Outline.   A *formal outline* is an elaborate guide, built with time and care, for a long, complex paper. Because major reports, research papers, and senior theses require so much work, some professors and departments ask a writer to submit a formal outline at an early stage and to include one in the final draft. A formal outline shows how ideas relate to one another—which ones are equal and important (coordinate) and which are less important (subordinate). It clearly and logically spells out where you are going. If you outline again after writing a draft, you can use the revised outline to check your logic and to reveal where revisions are needed.

When you make a full formal outline, follow these steps:

1. Place your thesis statement at the beginning.
2. List the major points that support and develop your thesis, labeling them with roman numerals (I, II, III).
3. Break down the major points into divisions with capital letters (A, B, C), subdivide those using arabic numerals (1, 2, 3), and subdivide those using lowercase letters (a, b, c). Continue until your outline is fully developed. If a very complex project requires further subdivision, use arabic numerals and lowercase letters in parentheses.
4. Indent each level of division in turn: the deeper the indentation, the more specific the ideas. Align like-numbered or -lettered headings under one another.
5. Cast all headings in parallel grammatical form. (See pp. 173–74 on parallelism.) Use phrases or sentences but not both in the same outline.

A *formal topic outline* for a long paper about city and small-town drivers might be constructed this way:

Drivers in Cities and Small Towns

Working thesis: Different lifestyles cause city drivers to be more aggressive than small-town drivers.

I. Lifestyles of drivers
  A. Fast-paced, stress-filled lifestyle of city drivers
      1. Aggressive
      2. Impatient
      3. Tense
      4. Often frustrated
  B. Slow-paced lifestyle of small-town drivers
      1. Laid-back
      2. Patient
      3. Relaxed
      4. Not easily upset
II. Resulting behavior as drivers
  A. City drivers
      1. Little consideration for other drivers
          a. Blowing horn
          b. Shouting
          c. Not using proper signals
              (1) Turning across lanes
              (2) Stopping without warning
      2. Disregard for pedestrians
      3. Violation of speed limits
          a. Running red lights
          b. Having many accidents
  B. Small-town drivers
      1. Consideration for other drivers
          a. Driving defensively
          b. Yelling less
          c. Signaling
              (1) Turning
              (2) Stopping
      2. Regard for pedestrians
      3. Attention to speed limits
          a. Observing traffic lights
          b. Having fewer accidents

■ ACTIVITY: Evaluating an Outline

Discuss the sample formal topic outline on pages 78–79 with some of your classmates or the entire class, considering the following questions:

- Would this outline be useful in organizing an essay?
- How is the organization logical? Is it easy to follow? What are other possible arrangements for the ideas?
- Is this outline sufficiently detailed for a paper? Can you spot any gaps?
- What possible pitfalls would the writer using this outline need to avoid?

A topic outline may not be thorough enough to pinpoint what you want to say, how to say it, or how ideas are related. If so, consider *a formal sentence outline,* simply writing complete sentences for the headings or turning topic headings into sentences—specifying ideas, changing wording, or even reworking your thesis as needed. A sentence outline can clarify what you intend to say and help you draft topic sentences and paragraphs, but you cannot be sure how everything fits together until you write the draft itself.

Drivers in Cities and Small Towns

Working thesis: Because of their more stressful lives, city drivers are more aggressive than small-town drivers.

I. The lives of city drivers are more stressful than are the lives of small-town drivers.

    A. City drivers are always in a hurry.

        1. They are impatient.

        2. They are often frustrated.

    B. Small-town drivers live slower-paced lives.

        1. They are relaxed.

        2. They are seldom frustrated on the streets.

II. As a result of the tension they live with constantly, city drivers are more aggressive than small-town drivers are.

    A. City drivers are aggressive.

        1. They show little consideration for other drivers.

            a. They blow their horns often.

            b. They shout at other drivers frequently.

    2. They show little respect for pedestrians.

    3. They do not obey traffic laws.

        a. They do not use proper signals.

        b. They turn across lanes.

        c. They stop without warning.

        d. They speed.

    4. They have many accidents.

B. Small-town drivers are laid-back.

    1. They are considerate of other drivers.

        a. They drive carefully.

        b. They rarely yell or honk at other drivers.

    2. They show concern for pedestrians.

    3. They obey traffic laws.

        a. They use proper signals.

        b. They turn properly.

        c. They stop slowly.

        d. They speed less.

    4. They have fewer accidents.

CAUTION: Because an outline divides or analyzes ideas, some instructors and other readers disapprove of categories with only one subpoint, reasoning that you can't divide anything into one part. Let's say that your outline on earthquakes lists a 1 without a 2:

D. Probable results of an earthquake include structural damage.

    1. Houses are stripped of their paint.

Logically, if you are going to discuss the probable results of an earthquake, you need to include more than one result:

D. Probable results of an earthquake include structural damage.

    1. Houses are stripped of their paint.

    2. Foundations crack.

    3. Road surfaces are damaged.

    4. Water mains break.

Not only have you now come up with more points, but you have also placed the most important last for emphasis.

■ ACTIVITY: Outlining

1. Using one of your groups of ideas from the activities in Chapter 4, construct a formal topic outline that might serve as a guide for an essay.

2. Now turn that topic outline into a formal sentence outline.

3. Discuss both outlines with your classmates and your instructor, bringing up any difficulties you encountered. If you come up with a better way to organize your ideas, change the outline.

4. Write an essay based on your outline.

6

Strategies for Drafting

Learning to write well involves learning key questions to ask yourself: How can I begin this draft? What should I do if I get stuck? How can I flesh out the bones of my paper? How can I end effectively? How can I keep my readers with me? In this chapter we offer advice to get you going and keep you going, drafting the first paragraph to the last.

STARTING AND RESTARTING

A playful start may get you hard at work before you know it. Here are some suggestions.

- **Time yourself.** Set your watch, alarm, or egg timer, and vow to draft a page before the buzzer sounds. Don't stop for anything. If you're writing drivel, just push on. You can cross out later.
- **Slow to a crawl.** If speed quotas don't work, time yourself to write with exaggerated laziness, maybe a sentence every fifteen minutes.
- **Scribble on a scrap.** If you dread the blank sheet of paper, try starting on scrap paper, the back of a list, or a small notebook.
- **Begin writing the most appetizing part.** Start in the middle or at the end, wherever the thoughts come easily to mind. As novelist Bill Downey observes, "Writers are allowed to have their dessert first."
- **State your purpose.** Set forth what you want to achieve: to tell a story? to explain something? to win a reader over to your way of thinking?

- **Slip into the reader's shoes.** Put yourself in your reader's place. Start writing what you'd like to find out from the paper.
- **"Nutshell" it.** Briefly summarize the paper you want to write. Condense your ideas into one small, terse paragraph. Later you can expand each sentence until the meaning is clear and all of your points are adequately supported.
- **Shrink your immediate job.** Break the writing task into smaller parts, and do only the first one. Vow to turn out, say, just the first two paragraphs.
- **Find a provocative title.** Write down a dozen possible titles for your paper. If one sounds strikingly good, don't let it go to waste!
- **Tape-record yourself.** Talk a first draft into a tape recorder. Then play it back. Then write. Even if you find it hard to transcribe your spoken words, this technique may get you thinking.
- **Speak up.** On your feet, before an imaginary cheering crowd, state your opening paragraph. Then—quick!—get it on tape or write it down.
- **Take short breaks.** Even if you don't feel tired, take a break every half hour or so. Get up, walk around the room, stretch, or get a drink of water. Two or three minutes should be enough to refresh your mind.

When you have to write a long or demanding essay that you can't finish in one sitting, you may return to it only to find yourself stalled. You tromp your starter, and nothing happens. Your engine seems reluctant to turn over. Try the following suggestions for getting back on the road.

- **Leave hints for how to continue.** If you're ready to quit, jot down any remaining ideas. Tell yourself what you think might come next, or write the first sentence of the next section. When you come back to work, you will face not a blank wall but rich and suggestive graffiti.
- **Pause in midstream.** End a writing session by breaking off in midsentence or midparagraph. Just leave a sentence trailing off into space, even if you know how you want it to end. When you return to your task, you can start writing again immediately.
- **Repeat.** If the next sentence refuses to appear, simply recopy the last one until that shy creature emerges on the page.
- **Reread.** When you return to work, spend a few minutes rereading what you have already written or what you have planned.
- **Switch instruments.** Do you write at the computer? Try writing in longhand. Or drop your pen to type. Try writing on note cards or colored paper.

- **Change activities.** When words won't come, do something else. Run, walk your dog, cook your favorite meal, or nap. Or reward yourself— after you arrive at a certain point in your labors—with a trip to the vending machine, a text message to a friend, or a TV show. All the while, your unconscious mind will be working on your writing task.

■ ACTIVITY: Organizing Your Drafts

Using your word processor menu options, set the margin widths, line spacing, print size, and other aspects of your paper's format and page layout. If your instructor has not specified formatting, customize your files to produce pages with 1-inch margins and double-spacing, using 12-point type.

Next, whether you store your work on disks or on the hard drive of your own computer, figure out a simple file-naming convention and folder system to make it easy for you to keep track of your work. Some students prefer file names that identify the course, term, assignment, and draft number, while others note the paper topic or activity with the draft number—Eng101F2006-1-1 or Argument-1. When you revise a draft, be sure to duplicate and rename the file— Eng101F2006-1-2 or Argument-2—instead of simply reworking the original file. Then all the versions of your paper will be available in case you want to retrieve writing from an early draft or your instructor wants to review the stages of your writing process. Use the menu or the help screen to create a folder for each course, and store all your drafts for the class there.

PARAGRAPHING

An essay is written not in large, indigestible lumps but in *paragraphs*— small units, each more or less self-contained, each contributing some new idea in support of the thesis or main point of the essay. Writers focus on one idea at a time, stating it, developing it, illustrating it with examples or a few facts—showing readers, with plenty of detailed evidence, exactly what they mean. (For more on developing ideas within paragraphs, see Ch. 7.)

Paragraphs can be as short as one sentence or as long as a page. Sometimes the length is governed by the audience, the purpose of the writing, or the medium in which it appears. Journalists expect newspaper readers to gobble up facts like popcorn, quickly skimming articles with short one- or two-sentence paragraphs. College writers, in contrast, should assume their readers' willingness to read through well-developed paragraphs.

When readers see a paragraph indentation, they interpret it as a pause, a chance for a deep breath. After that signpost, they expect you to concentrate on a new aspect of your thesis for the rest of that paragraph. In this way, your sequence of paragraphs guides readers through your writing: your opening paragraph draws them in, your body paragraphs focus their attention, and your concluding paragraph wraps up the discussion.

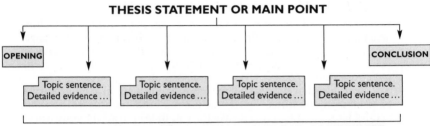

Using Topic Sentences

A *topic sentence* spells out the main idea of a paragraph in the body of an essay. It guides you as you write, and it hooks your readers as they discover what to expect and how to interpret the rest of the paragraph. As the topic sentence establishes the focus of the paragraph, it also relates the paragraph to the thesis of the essay, supporting the topic and main point of the essay as a whole. (For this reason, much of the advice on writing topic sentences for paragraphs also extends to writing thesis statements for essays.) To convert an idea to a topic sentence, you need to add your own slant, attitude, or point.

Main idea   +   Slant or attitude or point   =   Topic sentence

How do you write a good topic sentence? Make it interesting, accurate, and limited. The more pointed and lively your topic sentence, the more it will interest your readers. Even a dull and vague start can be enlivened once you zero in on a specific point:

MAIN IDEA + SLANT	Television + Everything that's wrong with it
DULL START	There are many things wrong with television.
POINTED TOPIC SENTENCE	Of all the shoddy television programming, what I dislike most is melodramatic news.
¶ PLAN	Illustrate the point with two or three melodramatic news stories.

A topic sentence also should be an accurate guide to the rest of the paragraph so that readers expect just what the paragraph delivers:

INACCURATE GUIDE	An emergency may not be a common event, but emergency preparedness should be. [The paragraph explains several types of household emergencies, not preparedness.]
ACCURATE TOPIC SENTENCE	Although an emergency may not be a common event, emergency preparedness should be routine in every home.
¶ PLAN	Explain how a household can prepare for an emergency with a medical kit, a well-stocked pantry, and a communication plan.

Finally, a topic sentence should be limited so you don't mislead or frustrate readers about what the paragraph covers.

MISLEADING SENTENCE	Seven factors have contributed to the increasing obesity of the average American. [The paragraph discusses only one.]
LIMITED TOPIC SENTENCE	Portion size is a major factor that contributes to the increasing obesity of average Americans.
¶ PLAN	Define healthy portion sizes, contrasting them with the large portions common in restaurants and packaged foods.

Opening with a Topic Sentence

Usually the topic sentence appears first in the paragraph, followed by sentences that clarify, illustrate, and support what it says. It is typically a statement but can be a question, alerting the reader to the topic without giving away the punchline. The following example comes from "The Virtues of the Quiet Hero," Senator John McCain's essay about "honor, faith, and service," presented on October 17, 2005, as part of the "This I Believe" series on National Public Radio's *All Things Considered*. Here and in all the following examples, we have put the topic sentence in *italics*.

Years later, I saw an example of honor in the most surprising of places. As a scared American prisoner of war in Vietnam, I was tied in torture ropes by my tormentors and left alone in an empty room to suffer through the night. Later in the evening, a guard I had never spoken to entered the room and silently loosened the ropes to relieve my suffering. Just before morning, that same guard came back and re-tightened the ropes before his less humanitarian comrades returned. He never said a word to me. Some months later on a Christmas morning, as I stood alone in the prison courtyard, that same guard walked up to me and stood next to me for a few moments. Then with his sandal, the guard drew a cross in the dirt. We stood wordlessly there for a minute or two, venerating the cross, until the guard rubbed it out and walked away.

This paragraph moves from a general statement to specific examples. The topic sentence clearly states at the outset what the paragraph is about. The second sentence introduces the situation that McCain is recalling. Then the next half dozen sentences supply two concrete, yet concise, illustrations of his central point.

Placing a Topic Sentence Near the Beginning

Sometimes the first sentence of a paragraph acts as a transition, linking what has gone before with what is to come. In this case, the second sentence might be the topic sentence. This pattern is illustrated in the following paragraph from "You Wanna Take This Online?" by Jeff Chu (*Time*, August 8, 2005). The paragraph before this one recounts thirteen-year-old Taylor Hern's discovery of her name on an online "List of Hos" and ends with her question: "'Who would actually make time in their schedule to do something like that?'"

Turns out, many of her peers would. *Technology has transformed the lives of teens, including the ways they pick on one another.* If parents and teachers think it's hard to control mean girls and bullying boys in school, they haven't reckoned with cyberspace. Cyberbullying can mean anything from posting pejorative items like the List of Hos to spreading rumors by e-mail to harassing by instant message. It was experienced in the preceding two months by 18 percent of 3,700 middle schoolers surveyed by researchers at Clemson University. Their study is scheduled to be presented at this month's American Psychological Association meeting. The phenomenon peaks at about age 13; 21 percent of eighth-graders surveyed reported being cyberbullied recently. And incidents of online bullying are like roaches: for every one that's reported, many more go unrecorded. "Our statistics are conservative," says Clemson psychologist Robin Kowalski. "Part of the problem is kids not recognizing that what's happening is a form of bullying."

Ending with a Topic Sentence

Occasionally a writer, especially one trying to persuade the reader to agree with an argument, piles detail on detail. Then, with a dramatic flourish, the writer concludes with the topic sentence, as student Heidi Kessler does in this paragraph:

> A fourteen-year-old writes to an advice columnist in my hometown newspaper that she has "done it" lots of times and sex is "no big deal." At the neighborhood clinic where my aunt works, a hardened sixteen-year-old requests her third abortion. A girl-child I know has two children of her own, but no husband. A college student in my dorm now finds herself sterile from a "social disease" picked up during casual sexual encounters. Multiply these examples by thousands. *It seems clear to me that women, who fought so hard for sexual freedom equal to that of men, have emerged from the battle not as joyous free spirits but as the sexual revolution's walking wounded.*

This paragraph moves from the particular to the general—from four examples about individuals to one large statement about American women at the end. By the time you come to the end of the paragraph, you might be ready to accept the conclusion in the topic sentence.

Implying a Topic Sentence

It is also possible to find a perfectly unified, well-organized paragraph that has no topic sentence at all, like the following from "New York" by Gay Talese (*Esquire,* July 1960):

> Each afternoon in New York a rather seedy saxophone player, his cheeks blown out like a spinnaker, stands on the sidewalk playing "Danny Boy" in such a sad, sensitive way that he soon has half the neighborhood peeking out of windows tossing nickels, dimes, and quarters at his feet. Some of the coins roll under parked cars, but most of them are caught in his outstretched hand. The saxophone player is a street musician named Joe Gabler; for the past thirty years he has serenaded every block in New York and has sometimes been tossed as much as $100 a day in coins. He is also hit with buckets of water, empty beer cans and eggs, and chased by wild dogs. He is believed to be the last of New York's ancient street musicians.

No one sentence neatly sums up the writer's idea. Like most effective paragraphs that do not state a topic sentence, this one contains something just as good—a *topic idea*. The author doesn't allow his paragraph to wander aimlessly. He knows exactly what he wants to achieve—a description of how Joe Gabler, a famous New York street musician, plies his trade. Because Talese keeps this purpose firmly in mind, the main point—that Gabler meets both reward and abuse—is clear to the reader as well.

■ ACTIVITY: Shaping Topic Sentences

Discuss each of the following topic sentences with your peer group, answering these questions:

Will it catch readers' attention?
Is it accurate?
Is it limited?
How might you develop the idea in the rest of the paragraph?
Can you improve it?

1. Television commercials stereotype people.
2. Living away from home for the first time is hard.
3. It's good for a child to have a pet.
4. A flea market is a good place to buy jewelry.
5. Pollution should be controlled.
6. Everybody should recycle waste.

WRITING AN OPENING

Even writers with something to say may find it hard to begin. Often they are so intent on writing a brilliant opening that they freeze, unable to write at all. They forget even the essentials—setting up the topic, sticking to what's relevant, and establishing a thesis. If you feel like a deer paralyzed by headlights when you face your first page, try these ways of tackling the opening.

- Start with your thesis statement, with or without a full opening paragraph. You can fill in the rest later.
- Write your thesis statement—the one you planned or one you'd now like to develop—in the middle of the page. Then go back to the top of the page, and concisely add the background a reader needs to appreciate where you're going.
- Write a long beginning for your first draft; then cut it down to the most dramatic, exciting, or interesting essentials.
- Simply set down words—any words—on paper, without trying to write an arresting opening. Then rewrite later.
- Write the first paragraph last, after you know exactly where your essay goes.
- Move your conclusion to the beginning, and write a new ending.
- Write a summary for yourself and your readers.

Your opening paragraph should intrigue readers—engaging their minds and hearts, exciting their curiosity, drawing them away from their preoccupations into the world you create in your writing. Use the Opener Checklist as you hunt for an effective opening that fits your paper. Then read the sample opening paragraphs that follow.

OPENER CHECKLIST

- ☐ What vital background might readers need?
- ☐ What general situation might help you narrow down to your point?
- ☐ What facts or statistics might make your issue compelling?
- ☐ What powerful anecdote or incident might introduce your point?
- ☐ What striking example or comparison would engage a reader?
- ☐ What question will your thesis—and your essay—answer?
- ☐ What lively quotation would set the scene for your essay?
- ☐ What assertion or claim might be the necessary prelude for your essay?
- ☐ What points should you preview to prepare a reader for what will come?
- ☐ What would compel someone to keep on reading?

Beginning with a Story

Often a simple anecdote can capture your readers' interest and make a good beginning. Here is how Nicholas Kulish opens his essay "Guy Walks into a Bar" (*New York Times,* February 5, 2006):

> Recently my friend Brandon and I walked along Atlantic Avenue in Brooklyn looking for a place to watch a football game and to quench our thirst for a cold brew. I pushed open the door and we were headed for a pair of empty stools when we both stopped cold. The bar was packed with under-age patrons.

Most of us, after an anecdote, want to read on. What will the writer say next? What does the anecdote have to do with the essay as a whole?

Commenting on a Topic

Sometimes a writer expands on a topic, bringing in vital details, as David Morris does as he opens his article "Rootlessness" (*Utne,* May/June 1990):

> Americans are a rootless people. Each year one in six of us changes residences; one in four changes jobs. We see nothing troubling in these statistics. For most of us, they merely reflect the restless energy that made America great. A nation of immigrants, unsurprisingly, celebrates those willing to pick up stakes and move on: the frontiersman, the cowboy, the entrepreneur, the corporate raider.

After baldly stating his point, Morris supplies statistics to support his contention and briefly explains the phenomenon. This same strategy can be used to present a controversial opinion: open with the opinion, and then back it up with examples.

Asking a Question

An essay can begin with a question and answer, as James H. Austin begins "Four Kinds of Chance," in *Chase, Chance, and Creativity: The Lucky Art of Novelty* (New York: Columbia UP, 1978):

> What is chance? Dictionaries define it as something fortuitous that happens unpredictably without discernible human intention. Chance is unintentional and capricious, but we needn't conclude that chance is immune from human intervention. Indeed, chance plays several distinct roles when humans react creatively with one another and with their environment.

That Austin begins to answer the question in the first paragraph leads readers to expect the answer to continue in the rest of the essay.

Ending with the Thesis Statement

Opening paragraphs often end by stating the essay's main point. After capturing readers' attention with an anecdote, gripping details, or pertinent examples, you lead readers in exactly the direction you want your essay to go. In his response to the question "Should Washington stem the tide of both legal and illegal immigration?" ("Symposium," *Insight on the News,* March 11, 2002), Daniel T. Griswold uses this strategy to begin his answer:

> Immigration always has been controversial in the United States. More than two centuries ago, Benjamin Franklin worried that too many German immigrants would swamp America's predominantly British culture. In the mid-1800s, Irish immigrants were scorned as lazy drunks, not to mention Roman Catholics. At the turn of the century a wave of "new immigrants"—Poles, Italians, Russian Jews—were believed to be too different ever to assimilate into American life. *Today the same fears are raised about immigrants from Latin America and Asia, but current critics of immigration are as wrong as their counterparts were in previous eras.*

WRITING A CONCLUSION

The final paragraphs of an essay linger longest in readers' minds. Consider E. B. White's conclusion to "Once More to the Lake" in *One Man's Meat* (Gardiner, ME: Tilbury House, 1941). In the essay, White describes returning with his young son to a vacation spot White had loved as a child. At the end of the essay, in an unforgettable image, he recalls how old he really is and realizes the inevitable passing of generations:

> When the others went swimming my son said he was going in, too. He pulled his dripping trunks from the line where they had hung all through the shower and wrung them out. Languidly, and with no thought of going in, I watched him, his hard little body, skinny and bare, saw him wince slightly as he pulled up around his vitals the small, soggy, icy garment. As he buckled the swollen belt, suddenly my groin felt the chill of death.

White's classic ending opens with a sentence that points back to the previous paragraph but also looks ahead. Then White leads us quickly to his final chilling insight. And then he stops.

It's easy to suggest what not to do at the end of an essay. Don't leave your readers half expecting you to go on. Don't restate everything you've already said. Don't introduce a brand-new topic that leads away from your point. And don't signal that the end is near with an obvious phrase like "As I have said . . ."

How do you write an ending, then? Use the Conclusion Checklist as you tackle your ending. Then read the sample concluding paragraphs that follow.

CONCLUSION CHECKLIST

☐ What restatement of your thesis would give readers a
satisfying sense of closure?

☐ What provocative implications of your thesis might answer
"What now?" or "What's the significance of what I've said?"

☐ What snappy quotation or statement would wrap up your
point?

☐ What closing facts or statistics might confirm the merit of
your point?

☐ What final anecdote, incident, or example might round out
your ideas?

☐ What question has your essay answered?

☐ What assertion or claim might you want to restate?

☐ What summary might help a reader pull together what you've
said?

☐ What would make a reader sorry to finish such a satisfying
essay?

Ending with a Quotation

An apt quotation can neatly round out an essay, as literary critic Malcolm
Cowley shows in *The View from Eighty* (New York: Viking, 1980), his discussion of the pitfalls and compensations of old age:

> "Eighty years old!" the great Catholic poet Paul Claudel wrote in his
> journal. "No eyes left, no ears, no teeth, no legs, no wind! And when all
> is said and done, how astonishingly well one does without them!"

Stating or Restating Your Thesis

In a sharp criticism of American schools, humorist Russell Baker in
"School vs. Education" ends by stating his main point, that schools do
not educate:

> Afterward, the former student's destiny fulfilled, his life rich with
> Oriental carpets, rare porcelain, and full bank accounts, he may one day
> find himself with the leisure and the inclination to open a book with a
> curious mind, and start to become educated.

Ending with a Brief Emphatic Sentence

For an essay that traces causes or effects, evaluates, or argues, a deft concluding thought can reinforce the main idea. In "Don't Mess with Mother"
(*Newsweek*, September 19, 2005), Anna Quindlen ends her essay about the
environmental challenges posed by post-Katrina New Orleans this way:

> New Orleans will be rebuilt, but rebuilt how? In the heedless, grasping
> fashion in which so much of this country has been built over the past fifty
> years, which has led to a continuous loop of floods, fires and filth in the air
> and water? Or could the new New Orleans be the first city of a new era, in
> which the demands of development and commerce are carefully balanced
> against the good of the land and, in the long run, the good of its people?
> We have been crummy stewards of the Earth, with a sense of knee-jerk
> entitlement that tells us there is always more where this came from.
>   There isn't.

Stopping When the Story Is Over

Even a quiet ending can be effective, as long as it signals clearly that the
essay is finished. Journalist Martin Gansberg simply stops when the
story is over in his account of the fatal stabbing of a young woman, Kitty
Genovese, in full view of residents of a Queens, New York, apartment
house. The residents, unwilling to become involved, did nothing to inter-
fere. Here is the last paragraph of his article "Thirty-eight Who Saw
Murder Didn't Call Police" (*New York Times*, March 17, 1964):

> It was 4:25 A.M. when the ambulance arrived to take the body of
> Miss Genovese. It drove off. "Then," a solemn police detective said, "the
> people came out."

■ ACTIVITY: Opening and Concluding

Openings and conclusions frame an essay, contributing to the unity
of the whole. The opening sets up the topic and main idea; the conclusion reaffirms the thesis and rounds off the ideas. Discuss the following with your classmates.

1. Here are two possible opening paragraphs for a student essay on
   the importance of teaching children how to swim.

   A. Humans inhabit a world made up of over 70 percent water. In
      addition to these great bodies of water, we have built millions
      of swimming pools for sports and leisure activities. At one time
      or another most people will be faced with either the danger of

drowning or the challenge of aquatic recreation. For these reasons, it is essential that we learn to swim. Being a competitive swimmer and a swimming instructor, I fully realize the importance of knowing how to swim.

B. Four-year-old Carl, curious like most children, last spring ventured out onto his pool patio. He fell into the pool and, not knowing how to swim, helplessly sank to the bottom. Minutes later his uncle found the child and brought him to the surface. Because Carl had no pulse, his uncle administered CPR until the paramedics arrived. Eventually the child was revived. During his stay in the hospital, his mother signed him up for beginning swimming classes. Carl was a lucky one. Unlike thousands of other children and adults, he got a second chance.

   a. Which introduction is more effective? Why?
   b. What would the body of this essay consist of? What kinds of evidence would be included?
   c. Write a suitable conclusion for this essay.

2. Here are the introductory and concluding paragraphs from two student essays. How effective are they? Could they be improved? If so, how? If they are satisfactory, explain why. What would be a catchy yet informative title for each essay?

A. Recently a friend down from New York astonished me with stories of several people infected—some with AIDS—by stepping on needles washed up on the New Jersey beaches. This is just one incident of pollution, a devastating problem in our society today. Pollution is increasing in our world because of greed, apathy, and Congress's inability to control this problem. . . .

    Wouldn't it be nice to have a pollution-free world without medical wastes floating in the water and washing up on our beaches? Without garbage scattered on the streets? With every corporation abiding by the laws set by Congress? In the future we can have a pollution-free world, but it is going to take the cooperation of everyone, including Congress, to ensure our survival on this Planet Earth.

B. The divorce rate has risen 700 percent in this century and continues to rise. More than one out of every two couples who are married end up in divorce. Over one million children a year are affected by divorce in the family. From these statistics it is clear that one of the greatest problems concerning the family today is divorce and the adverse effects it has on our society. . . .

    Divorce causes problems that change people for life. The number of divorces will continue to exceed the 700 percent figure unless married couples learn to communicate, to accept their mates unconditionally, and to sacrificially give of themselves.

ACHIEVING COHERENCE

Effective writing proceeds in some sensible order, each sentence following naturally from the one before it. Yet even well-organized prose can be hard to read unless it is *coherent* and effectively integrates its elements. To make your writing coherent, you can use various devices that tie together words in a sentence, sentences in a paragraph, paragraphs in an essay.

Adding Transitional Words and Sentences

You use transitions every day to help the people around you follow your train of thought. For example, you might say to a friend, "Well, *on the one hand*, a second job would help me save money for tuition. *On the other hand*, I'd have less time to study." But some writers rush through, omitting links between thoughts or mistakenly assuming that connections they see will automatically be clear to readers. Often just a transitional word, phrase, or sentence inserted in the right place can transform a disconnected passage into a coherent one.

Many words and phrases signal connections between or within sentences. In Table 6.1, these *transitional markers* are grouped by purpose or the kind of relationship or connection they establish.

Occasionally a whole sentence serves as a transition. In this excerpt from an essay by Marsha Traugot about adopting older and handicapped children, the opening of a paragraph harks back to the one before while simultaneously suggesting a new direction. We have italicized the transitional sentence.

> . . . Some exchanges hold monthly meetings where placement workers looking for a match can discuss waiting children or families, and they also sponsor parties where children, workers, and prospective parents meet informally.
>
> *And if a match still cannot be made?* Exchanges and other child welfare organizations now employ media blitzes as aggressive as those of commercial advertising. . . .

By repeating the key word *match* in her transitional sentence and by inserting the word *still*, Traugot makes clear that what follows will build on what has gone before. At the same time, by making the transitional sentence a rhetorical question, Traugot promises that the new paragraph will introduce new material, in this case answering the question.

TABLE 6.1   Using Transitional Markers

	Common Transitions
To Mark Time	then, soon, first, second, next, recently, the following day, in a little while, meanwhile, after, later, in the past, still
To Mark Place or Direction	in the distance, close by, near, far away, above, below, to the right, on the other side, opposite, to the west, next door
To Summarize or Restate	in other words, to put it another way, in brief, in simpler terms, on the whole, in fact, in a word, to sum up, in short, in conclusion, to conclude, finally, therefore
To Relate Cause and Effect or Result	therefore, accordingly, hence, thus, for, so, consequently, as a result, because of
To Add, Amplify, or List	and, also, too, besides, as well, moreover, in addition, furthermore, in effect, second, in the second place, again, next
To Compare	similarly, likewise, in like manner
To Concede	whereas, on the other hand, with that in mind, still, and yet, even so, in spite of, despite, at least
To Contrast	on the other hand, but, or, however, unlike, nevertheless, on the contrary, conversely, in contrast, instead
To Indicate Purpose	to this end, for this purpose, with this aim
To Express Condition	although, though
To Give Examples or Specify	for example, for instance, in this case, in particular, to illustrate
To Qualify	for the most part, by and large, with few exceptions, mainly, in most cases, generally, some, sometimes, typically
To Emphasize	it is true, truly, indeed, of course, to be sure, obviously, without doubt, evidently, clearly, understandably

Supplying Transitional Paragraphs

Transitions can be even longer than sentences. In a long, complicated essay, moving clearly from one idea to the next sometimes requires a short transition paragraph.

> So far, we have been dwelling on the physical and psychological effects of driving nonstop for more than two hundred miles. Now let's reflect on causes. Why do people become addicted to their steering wheels?

Use a transition paragraph only when you sense that your readers might get lost if you don't—lead them by the hand, for example, as you change direction or return from one branch of argument to your main trunk.

Using Repetition

Another way to clarify the relationship between two sentences, paragraphs, or ideas is to repeat a key word or phrase. Such purposeful repetition almost guarantees that readers will understand how all the parts of a passage fit together. Notice the repetition of the word *anger* in the following paragraph (the italics are ours) from *Of Woman Born* (New York: Norton, 1976) by poet Adrienne Rich. In this complex paragraph, the writer explores her relationship with her mother. The repetition holds all the parts together, making the paragraph's ideas coherent.

> And I know there must be deep reservoirs of *anger* in her; every mother has known overwhelming, unacceptable *anger* at her children. When I think of the conditions under which my mother became a mother, the impossible expectations, my father's distaste for pregnant women, his hatred of all that he could not control, my *anger* at her dissolves into grief and *anger* for her, and then dissolves back again into *anger* at her: the ancient, unpurged *anger* of the child.

Strengthening Pronouns

Because they always refer back to nouns or other pronouns, pronouns serve as transitions by making readers refer back as well. Notice how certain pronouns (in italics) hold together the following paragraph from "Misunderstood Michelle" by columnist Ellen Goodman in *At Large* (New York: Summit Books, 1981):

> I have two friends who moved in together many years ago. *He* looked upon this step as a trial marriage. *She* looked upon it as, well, moving in together. *He* was sure that in a matter of time, after *they* had built up trust

and confidence, *she* would agree that marriage was the next logical step. *She*, on the other hand, was thrilled that here at last was a man *who* would never push *her* back to the altar.

The paragraph contains other transitions, too: time markers like *many years ago, in a matter of time,* and *after; on the other hand,* which indicates contrast; and the repetition of words related to marriage — *trial marriage, marriage,* and *the altar.* All serve the main purpose of transitions: keeping readers on track.

■ ACTIVITY: Identifying Transitions

Go over one of the papers you have already written for this or another course, and circle all the transitional devices you find. Then share your paper with a classmate. Can the classmate find additional transitions? Does the classmate think you need transitions where you don't have any?

7

Strategies for Developing

How can you spice up your general ideas with the stuff of real life? How can you tug your readers deeper and deeper into your essays until they say, "I see just what you mean"? Well-developed essays have that power because they back up general points with evidence that comes alive for readers. In this chapter we cover more than a dozen strategies for developing your writing. (Also see Ch. 10 for strategies commonly used in argumentative papers.) Although you may choose to use only one method within a single paragraph, a strong essay almost always requires a combination of developmental strategies.

Whenever you develop a piece of writing or return to it to revise, you face a challenge: How do you figure out what to do? Sometimes you may suspect that you've wandered into a writers' cafeteria, a local hangout offering a huge buffet lunch. You watch others load their plates, but you still hesitate. Which foods will taste best? Which will be healthy choices? Which will make your meal a relaxing experience? How much will fit on your plate? For you as a writer, the answers depend on your situation, the clarity of your main idea or thesis, and the state of your draft, as the Development Checklist on page 102 suggests.

GIVING EXAMPLES

An example—the word comes from the Latin *exemplum,* "one thing chosen from among many"—is a typical instance that illustrates a whole type or kind. Giving examples to support a generalization is probably the

DEVELOPMENT CHECKLIST

Purpose

☐ Does your assignment recommend or require specific methods of development?

☐ Which developmental strategies might be most useful to explain, inform, or persuade?

☐ What type of development might best achieve your specific purpose?

Audience

☐ Which developmental strategies would best clarify your topic for your readers?

☐ Which would best demonstrate your thesis to your readers?

☐ What kinds of evidence would your specific readers prefer? Which developmental strategies might present this evidence most effectively?

Thesis

☐ What kinds of development does your thesis promise or imply you will supply?

☐ What sequence of developmental strategies would best support your thesis?

Essay Development

☐ Has a reader or peer editor pointed out ideas in your draft that need fuller or more effective development?

☐ Where might your readers have trouble following or understanding without more or better development?

Paragraph Development

☐ Should any paragraphs with one or two sentences be developed more fully?

☐ Should any long paragraphs with generalizations, repetition, and wordy phrasing be developed differently so that they are richer and deeper?

most common means of development. This example from *In Search of Excellence* (New York: Harper & Row, 1982) by Thomas J. Peters and Robert H. Waterman Jr. explains the success of America's top corporations.

> Although he's not a company, our favorite illustration of closeness to the customer is car salesman Joe Girard. He sold more new cars and trucks, each year, for eleven years running, than any other human being. In fact, in a typical year, Joe sold more than twice as many units as whoever was in second place. In explaining his secret of success, Joe said: "I sent out over thirteen thousand cards every month."
>
> Why start with Joe? Because his magic is the magic of IBM and many of the rest of the excellent companies. It is simply service, overpowering service, especially after-sales service. Joe noted, "There's one thing that I do that a lot of salesmen don't, and that's believe the sale really begins *after* the sale—not before. . . . The customer ain't out the door, and my son has made up a thank-you note." Joe would intercede personally, a year later, with the service manager on behalf of his customer. Meanwhile he would keep the communications flowing.

Notice how Peters and Waterman focus on the specific, Joe Girard. They don't write *corporation employees* or even *car salespeople*. Instead, they zero in on one particular man to make the point come alive. The specific example of Joe Girard makes closeness to the customer *concrete* to readers: he is someone readers can relate to.

Joe Girard	Level 4: Specific example
Car salespeople	Level 3: Even more specific group
Corporation employees	Level 2: More specific group
America's top corporations	Level 1: General group or category

The ladder of abstraction shown here moves up from the general—America's top corporations—to a specific person—Joe Girard. To check the level of specificity in one of your paragraphs or outlines, draw a ladder of abstraction for it. Do the same to restrict a broad subject to a topic you can manage in a short essay. If you haven't climbed up to the fourth or fifth level, you are probably being too general and need to add specifics.

An example doesn't always have to be a specific individual. Sometimes you can create a picture of something readers have never encountered or give an abstraction a recognizable personality and identity. Using this strategy, Jonathan Kozol makes real the plight of illiterate people in our health-care system in this paragraph from *Prisoners of Silence:*

Breaking the Bonds of Adult Illiteracy in the United States (New York: Continuum, 1980):

> Illiterates live, in more than literal ways, an uninsured existence. They cannot understand the written details on a health insurance form. They cannot read waivers that they sign preceding surgical procedures. Several women I have known in Boston have entered a slum hospital with the intention of obtaining a tubal ligation and have emerged a few days later after having been subjected to a hysterectomy. Unaware of their rights, incognizant of jargon, intimidated by the unfamiliar air of fear and atmosphere of ether that so many of us find oppressive in the confines even of the most attractive and expensive medical facilities, they have signed their names to documents they could not read and which nobody, in the hectic situation that prevails so often in those overcrowded hospitals that serve the urban poor, had ever bothered to explain.

Examples aren't doodads you add to a paragraph for decoration; they are what holds your readers' attention and shows them that your writing makes sense. By using examples, you make your ideas more concrete and tangible. Giving plenty of examples is one of the writer's chief tasks. When you need more, you can generate them at any point in the writing process. Begin with your own experience, even with a topic about which you know little, or try conversing with others, reading, digging in the library, or browsing on the Web. (For ways to generate ideas, see Ch. 4.)

Consider the questions in the following checklist when you use examples in your writing.

EXAMPLE CHECKLIST

☐ Are your examples relevant to your main idea or thesis?

☐ Are your examples the best ones you can think of? Will readers find them strong and appropriate?

☐ Are your examples really specific? Or do they just repeat generalities?

☐ From each paragraph, can you draw a ladder of abstraction to at least the fourth level?

■ ACTIVITY: Giving Examples

To help you get in the habit of thinking specifically, fill in a ladder of abstraction for five of the following general subjects. Then share your ladders with classmates, and compare and contrast your specifics with theirs. Here are two examples:

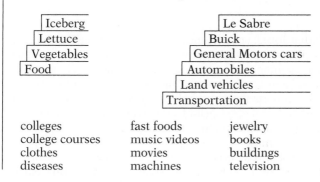

| Iceberg |
| Lettuce |
| Vegetables |
| Food |

| Le Sabre |
| Buick |
| General Motors cars |
| Automobiles |
| Land vehicles |
| Transportation |

colleges	fast foods	jewelry
college courses	music videos	books
clothes	movies	buildings
diseases	machines	television

PROVIDING DETAILS

A *detail* is any specific, concrete piece of information—a fact, a bit of the historical record, your own observation. Details make scenes and images more realistic and vivid for readers. They also back up generalizations, convincing readers that the writer can make broad assertions with authority.

Mary Harris "Mother" Jones tells the story of her life as a labor organizer in *The Autobiography of Mother Jones* (Chicago: Kerr, 1925, 1980). She lends conviction to her general statement about a coal miner's lot at the end of the nineteenth century with ample evidence from her own experience and observations.

Mining at its best is wretched work, and the life and surroundings of the miner are hard and ugly. His work is down in the black depths of the earth. He works alone in a drift. There can be little friendly companionship as there is in the factory; as there is among men who build bridges and houses, working together in groups. The work is dirty. Coal dust grinds itself into the skin, never to be removed. The miner must stoop as he works in the drift. He becomes bent like a gnome.

His work is utterly fatiguing. Muscles and bones ache. His lungs breathe coal dust and the strange, damp air of places that are never filled with sunlight. His house is a poor makeshift and there is little to encourage him to make it attractive. The company owns the ground it stands on, and the miner feels the precariousness of his hold. Around his house is mud and slush. Great mounds of culm [the refuse left after coal is screened], black and sullen, surround him. His children are perpetually grimy from playing on the culm mounds. The wife struggles with dirt, with inadequate water supply, with small wages, with overcrowded shacks.

Although Mother Jones, not a learned writer, relies on short, simple sentences, her writing is clear and powerful because of the specific details she uses. Her opening makes two general statements: (1) mining "is wretched work," and (2) the miner's "life and surroundings" are "hard and ugly." She supports these generalizations with a barrage of factual evidence and detail, including well-chosen verbs: "Coal dust *grinds* itself into the skin." The result is a moving, convincingly detailed portrait of the miner and his family.

In *Lipstick Jihad: A Memoir of Growing Up Iranian in America and American in Iran* (New York: Public Affairs, 2005), Azadeh Moaveni uses details to evoke the "drama and magic" she experienced during a childhood visit to Iran.

> To my five-year-old suburban American sensibilities, exposed to nothing more mystical than the Smurfs, Iran was suffused with drama and magic. After Friday lunch at my grandfather's, once the last plates of sliced cantaloupe were cleared away, everyone retired to the bedrooms to nap. Inevitably there was a willing aunt or cousin on hand to scratch my back as I fell asleep. Unused to the siesta ritual, I woke up after half an hour to find the bed I was sharing with my cousin swathed in a tower of creamy gauze that stretched high up to the ceiling. "Wake up," I nudged him, "we're surrounded!" "It's for the mosquitoes, *khareh*, ass, go back to sleep." To me it was like a fairy tale, and I peered through the netting to the living room, to the table heaped with plump dates and the dense, aromatic baklava we would nibble on later with tea. The day before I had helped my grandmother, Razi joon, make *ash-e gooshvareh*, "earring stew"; we made hoops out of the fresh pasta, and dropped them into the vat of simmering herbs and lamb. Here even the ordinary had charm, even the names of stews.

To guide readers through her details, Moaveni uses transitions — chronological (*After Friday lunch, after half an hour, The day before*), spatial (*through the netting to the living room*), and thematic (*To me it was like a fairy tale*). (For more on transitions, see pp. 97–100.)

Quite different from Moaveni's personal, descriptive details are Guy Garcia's objective facts in "Influencing America" (*Time*, August 13, 2005). Garcia heaps up statistical details to substantiate his claim that Hispanics are "helping to define" mainstream America even though they face "prejudice and enormous social and economic hurdles."

Nearly a quarter of all Latinos live in poverty; the high school drop out rate for Latino youths between the ages of 16 and 19 is 21%—more than triple that of non-Hispanic whites. Neo-nativists like Pat Buchanan and Samuel Huntington still argue that the "tsunami" of non–English speakers from Latin America will destroy everything that America stands for. Never mind that most Hispanics are religious, family-centric, enterprising, and patriotic. In the *Time* poll, 72% said they considered moral issues such as abortion and issues of faith important or very important. This year the government announced that undocumented workers were pouring billions into Social Security and Medicare for benefits that they would never be allowed to claim. Of the 27,000 troops serving in the U.S. armed forces who are not U.S. citizens, a large percentage are from Mexico and the rest of Latin America.

Providing details is one of the simplest yet most effective ways of developing ideas. All it takes on your part is close attention and precise wording to communicate details to readers. If readers were on the scene, what would they see? What would they hear, smell, or feel? Which small details from your reading are most meaningful to you? Would a bit of research turn up just the right fact or statistic? Remember that, to be effective, details must have a specific purpose: they must make your images more evocative or your point more convincing. Every detail should in some way support your main idea.

The Details Checklist offers several questions to consider when you use specific information.

DETAILS CHECKLIST

☐ Do all your details support your point of view, main idea, or thesis?

☐ Do you have details of sight? sound? taste? touch? smell?

☐ Have you included enough details to make your writing clear and interesting?

☐ Have you selected details that will engage and inform your readers?

☐ Have you arranged your details in an order that is easy to follow?

■ **ACTIVITY:** Providing Details

To practice generating and using specific details, brainstorm (see pp. 44–46) with classmates or alone on one of the following subjects. Be sure to include details that appeal to all five senses. Group the details in your list (see pp. 69–73), and write a paragraph or two using your specific details. Begin by stating a main idea that conveys an engaging impression of your subject (not "My grandmother's house was in Topeka, Kansas" but "My grandmother's house was my childhood haven").

the things in my room	a memorable event	my job
my grandmother's house	an unusual person	a classroom
a haunted house	my favorite pet	the cafeteria
my old car	a hospital room	an incident

DRAWING ON EXPERIENCE

Your experience includes whatever has happened to or around you, and telling, or narrating, that story is the way to share its significance with your readers. Your experience can supply evidence to support a statement, illustrate a point, establish the rationale for your point of view, or enhance your credibility as a writer. Even a brief account can bring the authenticity of a real event and the power of personal testimony to your writing.

As you recall experience, you draw on memory, a writer's richest — and handiest — resource. All by itself, memory may not give you enough to write about, and in some situations, readers will expect evidence other than experience. However, you will rarely go wrong if you start by jotting down something you remember, even if it serves primarily as the platform on which you build a research scaffold. As you think back, you're likely to recall an event or a person that is part of a tale you might tell — something memorable that happened, an encounter with someone notable, a situation that provoked a decision, or the struggle necessary to overcome an obstacle.

In "Cheers for Tears" (*Salon.com*, October 18, 2005), Cecelie S. Berry demonstrates how to convey experience powerfully yet briefly. She supports her opening assertion with three experiences, each sketched in a single sentence.

> I discovered early on that crying was controversial. "People will think you're weak," my older sister said, when I came home from a schoolyard fight in tears. "People will think you're unstable," I was told as a summer associate in a big city law firm, when I went crying to a female lawyer after a senior partner obliterated one of my memos. "People will think you're unhappy," my mother warned when I cried at my son's brilliant performance as Charlie Brown in the kindergarten play.

On the other hand, in "Departing Resident Aliens: No Compassion, No Sense" (*America*, February 27, 1999), attorney Ann Carr takes two paragraphs to recount her meeting with a client.

> The young man fidgets as he sits across from me in the prison consulting room. As his immigration lawyer, I have just finished telling him that he is going to have to leave the country and go back to Mexico. The reason: He was guilty of the "crime" of working in the United States without permission, doing work that most Americans won't do, so that he could support his American wife and child. Earning one's living and supporting one's family used to be considered a virtue, last time I checked.
>
> "But my wife is expecting her baby in a few weeks. How is she going to live if I can't work to support her?" His face quivers with the anxiety and stress this thought provokes. I am at a complete loss to explain to him the rationale of the law that mandates such a result—a young American family being deprived of the husband and father figure, and almost certainly being forced onto the welfare rolls to boot. The young man has fallen afoul of the recent legislation that sends people back to their country of origin to apply for an immigrant visa. They usually experience delays of a year or more before they can return. When he asks if there is anything he can do, I suggest that his wife, a U.S. citizen with a vote, call her Congressional representatives to ask them for a solution.

Carr pares her experience down to the essentials that convey to readers its significance to her. She could have begun her account with her walk into the building; instead, she zeroes in on the exchange with her client. She might have described what he wore; instead, she focuses on his quivering face and his concern for his family.

When you recount your experience, you'll need to dig deeply but select carefully so that you stick to what matters. Consider the questions in the Experience Checklist when you recall and write about experience.

EXPERIENCE CHECKLIST

☐ What is your purpose in recalling your experience? Given your writing task, what role would be appropriate for personal experience?

☐ What do you want your readers to grasp? How might you engage their interest?

☐ Have you deepened your account of events by asking the reporter's
   questions: Who? What? Where? When? Why? How?

☐ Do you plan to present events in chronological order, from
   beginning to end, or with flashbacks, jumping from the middle
   or end back to earlier events?

☐ Have you brought your story to life by supplying details that appeal
   to the senses — sight, sound, taste, touch, and smell?

☐ Have you selected what's necessary for your purpose and left out
   what's not?

■ **ACTIVITY:** Drawing on Experience

Think back to an experience that you'd like to share with readers.
Answer the reporter's questions or list events chronologically to establish what happened during the event. Then review your notes about
the experience, highlighting what's relevant to the particular point
you want to make in your writing. Finally, sum up the impact you'd
like your story to have.

OBSERVING A SCENE

Sometimes you can develop your writing simply by observing, using
your senses to notice what's around you. Formal observation is a valuable
research method in education and in the social sciences. Informal observation is a handy resource for compelling eyewitness evidence and concrete details about a scene, activity, or event. Be sure to observe using all
of your senses — sight, sound, taste, touch, and smell — and to record the
details accurately.

   Generally you notice and record far more than you'll be able to use in
your writing, so you'll need to select and group the details. If you want to
share an overall impression of the scene with readers, you may arrange
details in spatial or chronological order, using movement through space or
time to draw readers into the scene. For example, you might begin with the
outermost details and then move closer to the central activity. Or you might
move around a crowded urban classroom, across a polluted skyline, or up
a hiking trail. You might also wish to generalize or summarize, perhaps
based on typical or representative scenes you have observed. Then you
might group your details thematically, clustering them to support each of
your points. (See also pp. 69–73.)

In "To the Singing, to the Drums" (*Natural History,* February 1975),
N. Scott Momaday describes his observations at the Kiowa celebration
of the Gourd Dance on the Fourth of July in Carnegie, Oklahoma.

> The celebration is on the north side. We turn down into a dark depres-
> sion, a large hollow among trees. It is full of camps and cars and people.
> At first there are children. According to some centrifugal social force, chil-
> dren function on the periphery. They run about, making festival noises.
> Firecrackers are snapping all around. We park and I make ready; the girls
> help me with my regalia. I am already wearing white trousers and moc-
> casins. Now I tie the black velvet sash around my waist, placing the
> beaded tassels at my right leg. The bandoleer of red beans, which was my
> grandfather's, goes over my left shoulder, the V at my right hip. I decide
> to carry the blanket over my arm until I join the dancers; no sense in
> wrapping up in this heat. There is deep, brick-red dust on the ground. The
> grass is pale and brittle here and there. We make our way through the
> camps, stepping carefully to avoid the pegs and guy lines that reach about
> the tents. Old people, imperturbable, are lying down on cots and benches
> in the shadows. Smoke hangs in the air. We smell hamburgers, popcorn,
> gunpowder. Later there will be fried bread, boiled meat, Indian corn.

Momaday arranges his vivid details both spatially and chronologically.
Notice his spatial transitions: *on the north side, turn down, on the periph-
ery, all around, on the ground, here and there, through the camps, in the
shadows, in the air.* Look also at the time markers: *At first, Now, until,
Later.* These transitions guide readers through the experience, helping
them approach the celebration alongside Momaday.

Use the following checklist to help you strengthen your observations.

OBSERVATION CHECKLIST

☐ What did you see—landmarks, structures, objects, people, animals,
activities, colors, shapes, or sizes?

☐ What did you hear—conversations, music, other sounds, tones,
pitches, rhythms, or silence?

☐ What did you taste—sweet, salty, spicy, or other flavors?

☐ What did you touch and feel—shapes, textures, movements, or
sensations?

☐ What did you smell—aromas, fragrances, or odors?

☐ Have you selected and organized the details needed to support the overall impression of the scene that you want to share with your audience?

☐ Do you need to sharpen either your overall impression of the scene or your selection of supporting details?

■ ACTIVITY: Observing a Scene

Practice observing by positioning yourself in a rich environment full of activity or sensory detail. Watch carefully, using all of your senses, and record what you notice. Conclude by writing a sentence that sums up your overall impression of the scene highlighting or listing details to support that impression.

CONVERSING AND INTERVIEWING

When you need fresh or timely information to develop your writing, try talking with someone. A simple conversation with a friend can suggest new ideas or details, challenge assumptions, or introduce alternative views. A more formal interview with the right person can supply expert testimony, a valuable form of evidence in either verbal or written form. Select your expert carefully, looking for someone with the appropriate background or professional credentials to convince your readers that his or her knowledge is credible. As reporters know, interviews often capture the flavor of the moment, the passion behind the topic, or the insight of those personally engaged in a situation.

For "Purging the Poor" (*The Nation*, October 10, 2005), Naomi Klein talked with her experts—displaced residents, volunteers, and officials—about the number of available housing units in post-Katrina New Orleans. As the following selection from her article illustrates, Klein varies her presentation of this expert information; she quotes directly and also attributes ideas while integrating facts and statistics from other sources.

The citywide numbers are staggering: In the areas that sustained only minor damage and are on the mayor's repopulation list, there are at least 11,600 empty apartments and houses. If Jefferson Parish is included, that number soars to 23,270. With three people in each unit, that means homes could be found for roughly 70,000 evacuees. With the number of permanently homeless city residents estimated at 200,000, that's a significant dent in the housing crisis. And it's doable. Democratic Representative Sheila Jackson Lee, whose Houston district includes some 150,000 Katrina evacuees, says there are ways to convert vacant apartments into affordable or free housing. After passing an ordinance, cities could issue Section 8 certificates, covering rent until evacuees find jobs. Jackson Lee says she plans to introduce legislation that will call for federal funds to be spent on precisely such rental vouchers. "If opportunity exists to create viable housing options," she says, "they should be explored."

Malcolm Suber, a longtime New Orleans community activist, was shocked to learn that thousands of livable homes were sitting empty. "If there are empty houses in the city," he says, "then working-class and poor people should be able to live in them." According to Suber, taking over vacant units would do more than provide much-needed immediate shelter: It would move the poor back into the city, preventing the key decisions about its future—like whether to turn the Ninth Ward into marshland or how to rebuild Charity Hospital—from being made exclusively by those who can afford land on high ground.

When you want to interview someone, plan ahead: schedule the meeting, write out questions in advance, and gather supplies for recording the conversation. Be prepared to jot down and label direct quotations during the interview and to add notes about your impressions immediately afterward. Then evaluate your material before adding it to your writing. For example, if the person you interviewed is the focus of your paper, you'd select and organize comments that reveal the person's character, passion, or impact. On the other hand, to support your assertions about an issue, you'd integrate information from your interview as it logically fits.

Use the Interview Checklist to help you get started.

INTERVIEW CHECKLIST

☐ Have you selected an appropriate expert for the interview? Have you researched his or her background, experience, publications, or other professional activities?

☐ Have you scheduled the interview at a convenient time and location?

☐ Have you prepared questions, perhaps moving from general background to specifics?

☐ Have you revised your questions, making sure that each one is clear, relevant, and sufficiently open-ended to stimulate a valuable response?

☐ Are you prepared to record the interview (with your subject's permission) and jot notes on paper (as a backup in all cases)?

☐ Did you thank your expert after the interview? If necessary, have you confirmed the accuracy of direct quotations or specific information?

☐ Have you selected and organized your material to speak meaningfully to your readers and to achieve your writing purpose?

■ **ACTIVITY:** Interviewing

Schedule a practice interview with a classmate or friend. In advance, develop a list of questions to help you discover and learn about something at which that person is expert. (That expertise might fall in any area—academic, social, work, sports, hobbies, or activities.) Take notes during the interview, and then evaluate your notes afterward to learn how you might strengthen your interviewing skills.

DEFINING

Define, from the Latin, means "to set bounds to." You define a thing, a word, or a concept by describing it so that it is distinguished from all similar things. If people don't agree on the meaning of a word or an idea, they can't share knowledge about it. Scientists in particular take special care to define their terms precisely. In his article "A Chemist's Definition of pH" from *The Condensed Chemical Dictionary* (New York: Reinhold, 1981), Gessner G. Hawley begins with a brief definition:

> pH is a value taken to represent the acidity or alkalinity of an aqueous solution; it is defined as the logarithm of the reciprocal of the hydrogen-ion concentration of a solution:
>
> $$pH = \ln \frac{1}{[H^+]}$$

If you use a word in a special sense or coin a word, you have to explain it or your readers will be lost. In "The Futile Pursuit of Happiness," (*New York Times*, September 7, 2003), Jon Gertner reports on "affective forecasting," an intriguing area of study by economists and psychologists such as Professors Daniel Gilbert of Harvard and Tim Wilson of the University of Virginia. These researchers are exploring what people expect will bring them happiness and how their expectations pan out. Not surprisingly, this new area of study has generated new terms, as the following paragraph explains.

> Gilbert and his collaborator Tim Wilson call the gap between what we predict and what we ultimately experience the "impact bias" — "impact" meaning the errors we make in estimating both the intensity and duration of our emotions and "bias" our tendency to err. The phrase characterizes how we experience the dimming excitement over not just a BMW but also over any object or event that we presume will make us happy. Would a 20 percent raise or winning the lottery result in a contented life? You may predict it will, but almost surely it won't turn out that way. And a new plasma television? You may have high hopes, but the impact bias suggests that it will almost certainly be less cool, and in a shorter time, than you imagine. Worse, Gilbert has noted that these mistakes of expectation can lead directly to mistakes in choosing what we think will give us pleasure. He calls this "miswanting."

Sometimes you will define an unfamiliar word to save your readers a trip to the dictionary or a familiar but often misunderstood concept to clarify the meaning you intend. For example, what would you mean by *guerilla, liberal,* or *minimum wage*? The more complex or ambiguous an idea, a thing, a movement, a phenomenon, or an organization, the more detailed the definition you will need to clarify the term for your readers.

The Definition Checklist includes questions to consider when you explain a term.

DEFINITION CHECKLIST

☐ Have you used definitions to help your readers understand the subject matter (not to show off your knowledge)?
☐ Have you tailored your definition to the needs of your audience?
☐ Is your definition specific, clear, and accurate?
☐ Would your definition benefit from an example or from details?

■ ACTIVITY: Defining

Write an extended definition (a paragraph or so) of one of the following words. Begin with a one-sentence definition of the word. Then, instead of getting most of your definition from a dictionary or textbook, expand and clarify your ideas using some of the strategies explained in this chapter—examples, details, subject analysis, and so forth. You may also use *negation*, explaining what something is by stating what it is not. Share your definition with your classmates.

education	abuse	exercise	literacy
privacy	jazz	dieting	success
taboo	rap music	gossip	fear
prejudice	bird flu	security	gender

REASONING INDUCTIVELY AND DEDUCTIVELY

As you develop a typical paragraph in a paper, you are likely to rely on both generalizations and particulars. A *generalization* is a broad statement that establishes the point you want to make, the viewpoint you hold, or the conclusion you have reached. A *particular* is an instance, a detail, or an example—some specific that supplies evidence that a general statement is reasonable. Your particulars support your generalizations; by presenting compelling instances, details, and examples, you back up your broader point. At the same time, your generalizations pull together your particulars, identifying patterns or connections that relate individual cases. (See also pp. 37–40 on the statement-support pattern and Ch. 10 on argument.)

To relate particulars and generalizations, you can use an inductive or deductive process. An *inductive process* begins with the particulars—a convincing number of instances, examples, tests, or experiments. Taken together, these particulars substantiate a larger generalization. In this way a number of long-term studies of weight loss can eventually lead to a consensus about the benefits of walking or eating low-fat foods or of some other variable. Less formal inductive reasoning is common as people *infer* or conclude that particulars do or do not support a generalization. For example, if your sister ate strawberries three times and got a rash each time, she might infer that she is allergic to strawberries. Induction breaks down when the particulars are too weak or too few to support a generalization: for example, not enough weight-loss studies have comparable results or not enough clear instances occur when strawberries—and nothing else—trigger a reaction.

A *deductive process* begins with a generalization and applies it to another case. When your sister says no to a piece of strawberry pie, she does so because, based on her assumptions, she *deduces* that it, too, will trigger a rash. Deduction breaks down when the initial generalization is flawed or when a particular case doesn't fit the generalization. For instance, suppose that each time your sister ate strawberries she drizzled them with lemon juice, the real culprit. Or suppose that the various weight-loss studies defined low-fat food so differently that no one could reach a clear conclusion about how the latest study relates to earlier ones.

Once you have reached your conclusions as a writer—either by using particulars to reach generalizations or by applying reliable generalizations to other particulars—you still need to decide how to present your reasoning to your readers. Do you want your readers to follow your own process, perhaps examining numerous cases before reaching a conclusion about them? Or do you want them to learn what you've concluded first and then review the evidence? Because audiences for academic writing tend to expect conclusions first, many writers begin essays with thesis statements and paragraphs with topic sentences. On the other hand, if your readers are likely to reject an unexpected thesis initially, you may need to show them the evidence first and then lead them gently but purposefully to your point.

In "The Good Heart" (*Newsweek*, October 3, 2005), Anne Underwood opens with a paragraph organized inductively: she describes a particular situation that has helped substantiate the broad, even surprising, generalization with which she concludes the paragraph.

> You can call it the Northridge Effect, after the powerful earthquake that struck near Los Angeles at 4:30 on a January morning in 1994. Within an hour, and for the rest of the day, medics responding to people crushed or trapped inside buildings faced a second wave of deaths from heart attacks among people who had survived the tremor unscathed. In the months that followed, researchers at two universities examined coroners' records from Los Angeles County and found an astonishing jump in cardiovascular deaths, from 15.6 on an average day to 51 on the day of the quake itself. Most of these people turned out to have a history of coronary disease or risk factors such as high blood pressure. But those who died were not involved in rescue efforts or trying to dig themselves out of the rubble. Why did they die? In the understated language of *The New England Journal of Medicine*, "emotional stress may precipitate cardiac events in people who are predisposed to such events." To put it simply, they were scared to death.

Underwood goes on to review the impact on heart attack patients of various psychosocial factors such as anxiety, depression, and childhood trauma. Then, in the following passage, she first states and supports a generalization about the effects of common stresses in adult life, citing the results of an inductive study. In the second paragraph, she deductively applies the generalization to a particular case.

> And if stress in childhood can lead to heart disease, what about current stressors—longer work hours, threats of layoffs, collapsing pension funds? A study last year in *The Lancet* examined more than 11,000 heart-attack sufferers from 52 countries and found that in the year before their heart attacks, patients had been under significantly more strains—from work, family, financial troubles, depression, and other causes—than some 13,000 healthy control subjects. "Each of these factors individually was associated with increased risk," says Dr. Salim Yusuf, professor of medicine at Canada's McMaster University and senior investigator on the study. "Together, they accounted for 30 percent of overall heart-attack risk." But people respond differently to high-pressure work situations. The key to whether it produces a coronary seems to be whether you have a sense of control over life, or live at the mercy of circumstances and superiors.
>
> That was the experience of John O'Connell, a Rockford, Illinois, laboratory manager who suffered his first heart attack in 1996, at the age of 56. In the two years before, his mother and two of his children had suffered serious illnesses, and his job had been changed in a reorganization. "My life seemed completely out of control," he says. "I had no idea where I would end up." He ended up on a gurney with a clot blocking his left anterior descending artery—the classic "widowmaker." Two months later he had triple bypass surgery. A second heart attack when he was 58 left his cardiologist shaking his head. There's nothing more we can do for you, doctors told him.

Use the following questions to help you present your reasoning clearly and persuasively.

INDUCTION AND DEDUCTION CHECKLIST

☐ Do your generalizations follow logically from your particulars? Can you substantiate what and how much you claim?

☐ Are your particulars typical, numerous, and relevant enough to support your generalizations? Are your particulars substantial enough to warrant the conclusion you have drawn?

☐ Are both your generalizations and your particulars presented clearly? Have you identified your assumptions for your readers?

☐ How do you expect your reasoning patterns to affect your readers? What are your reasons for opening with generalizations or reserving them until the end of a paragraph or passage?

☐ Is your reasoning in an explanatory paper clear and logical? Is your reasoning in an argumentative paper rigorous enough to withstand the scrutiny of readers? Have you avoided generalizing too broadly or illogically connecting generalizations and particulars?

■ ACTIVITY: Reasoning Inductively and Deductively

Look through a recent magazine for an article that explores a health, environmental, or economic issue. Read the article, looking for paragraphs organized inductively and deductively. Why do you think the writer chose one pattern or the other in the various sections of the article? How well do those patterns work from a reader's point of view?

ANALYZING A SUBJECT

Analyzing a subject means dividing it into its parts and then examining one part at a time. If you have taken a chemistry course, you probably analyzed water: you separated it into hydrogen and oxygen, its two elements. You've heard many a television commentator analyze the news, telling us what made up an event—who participated, where it occurred, what happened. Analyzing a news event may produce results less certain and clear-cut than analyzing a chemical compound, but the principle is similar: by taking something apart, by examining its components, you can understand it better.

Analysis helps readers grasp something complex: they can more readily take in the subject in a series of bites than in one gulp. For this reason, college textbooks do a lot of analyzing. An economics text divides a labor union into its component parts; an anatomy text divides the hand into its bones, muscles, and ligaments. In your college papers, you might analyze and explain to readers anything from a contemporary subculture (What social groups make up the homeless population of Los Angeles?) to an ecosystem (What animals, plants, and minerals coexist in a rainforest?). Analysis is so useful that you can apply it in many situations: separating the stages in a process to see how it works, breaking down the components of a subject to classify them, or identifying the possible results of an event to project consequences. (For more on process analysis, see pp. 122–24. For more on division and classification, see pp. 125–27. For more on cause and effect, see pp. 130–32.)

In *Cultural Anthropology: A Perspective on the Human Condition* (St. Paul: West, 1987), Emily A. Schultz and Robert H. Lavenda briefly but effectively demonstrate by analysis how a metaphor like "the Lord is my shepherd" makes a difficult concept ("the Lord") easy to understand.

The first part of a metaphor, the metaphorical subject, indicates the domain of experience that needs to be clarified (e.g., "the Lord"). The second part of a metaphor, the metaphorical predicate, suggests a domain of experience which is familiar (e.g., sheep-herding) and which may help us understand what "the Lord" is all about.

In much the same way, Lillian Tsu, a government major at Cornell University, uses analysis in her essay "A Woman in the White House" to identify major difficulties faced by female politicians in the United States:

> Although traditionally paternalistic societies like the Philippines and Pakistan and socially conservative states like Great Britain have elected female leaders, particular characteristics of the United States' own electoral system make it unlikely that this country will follow suit and elect a female president. Despite social modernization and the progress of the women's movement, the voters of the United States still lag far behind those of other nations in their willingness to trust in the leadership of a female executive. While the women's movement has succeeded in changing Americans' attitudes as to what roles are socially acceptable for women, female candidates still face a more difficult task in U.S. elections than their male counterparts face. Three factors are responsible for this situation--political socialization, lack of experience, and open discrimination.

Tsu treats the three factors in turn, beginning each section with a transition that emphasizes the difficulties female candidates in the United States face: "One obstacle," "A second obstacle," "A third obstacle." The opening list and the transitions give readers clear direction in a complicated essay, guiding them through the explanation of the three factors to the final section on the implications of the analysis.

When you plan an analysis, you might label slices in a pielike circle or arrange subdivisions in a list running from smallest to largest or from least to most important. Make sure that your analysis has a purpose, that it demonstrates something about your subject or tells your readers something they didn't know before. For example, to show the ethnic composition of New York City, you might divide the city geographically into neighborhoods—Harlem, Spanish Harlem, Yorkville, Chinatown, Little Italy. If you want to explain New York's social classes, however, you might start with homeless people and work up to the wealthy elite. The way you slice your subject into pieces will depend in part on the point you want to make about it. And the point you end up making will depend in part on how you've sliced it up. As you develop your ideas, you may also find that you have a stronger point to make—that New York City's social hierarchy is oppressive and unstable, for example.

How can you help your readers follow your analysis? Some writers like to begin by identifying the subdivisions into which they are going to slice their subject ("The federal government has three branches"). If you name or label each part you mention, define the terms you use, and clarify with examples, you will also help distinguish each part from all the others. You can make your essay as readable as possible by using transitions, leading readers from one part to the next. (For more on transitions, see pp. 97–100.)

Use the Analysis Checklist for questions to consider when you want to analyze a subject.

ANALYSIS CHECKLIST

☐ Exactly what will you try to achieve in your analysis? What is its purpose?

☐ How does your analysis support your main idea or thesis?

☐ How will you break your subject into parts?

☐ How can you make each part clear to your readers?

☐ What definitions, details, and examples would help clarify each part?

■ **ACTIVITY:** Analyzing a Subject

Analyze one of the following subjects by making a list of its basic parts or elements. Be sure to identify the purpose or point of your analysis. Compare your analysis with those of others in your class who chose the same subject.

a college	a choir, orchestra, or other musical group
a newspaper	a computer or other technological device
a reality TV show	a basketball, baseball, hockey, or other team
effective teaching	a family
a healthy lifestyle	leadership

ANALYZING A PROCESS

Analyzing a process means telling step by step how something is, was, or could be done. You can analyze an action or a phenomenon—how a skyscraper is built, how a revolution begins, how sunspots form, how to make chili. This strategy can also explain large, long-ago happenings that a writer couldn't possibly have witnessed and complex technical processes that a writer couldn't personally duplicate. Here, for instance, is a paragraph from "The Case for Cloning" (*Time*, February 9, 1998), in which Madeleine Nash describes the process of cloning cells. Her *informative process analysis* sets forth how something happens:

> Cloning individual human cells . . . is another matter. Biologists are already talking about harnessing for medical purposes the technique that produced the sheep called Dolly. They might, for example, obtain healthy cells from a patient with leukemia or a burn victim and then transfer the nucleus of each cell into an unfertilized egg from which the nucleus has been removed. Coddled in culture dishes, these embryonic clones—each genetically identical to the patient from which the nuclei came—would begin to divide. The cells would not have to grow into a fetus, however. The addition of powerful growth factors could ensure that the clones develop only into specialized cells and tissue. For the leukemia patient, for example, the cloned cells could provide an infusion of fresh bone marrow, and for the burn victim, grafts of brand-new skin. Unlike cells from an unrelated donor, these cloned cells would incur no danger of rejection; patients would be spared the need to take powerful drugs to suppress the immune system.

The *directive* (how-to) *process analysis* tells readers how to do something (how to box, invest for retirement, clean a painting) or how to make something (how to draw a map, blaze a trail, set up a computer). Especially on Web sites, directions may consist of simple step-by-step lists designed for browsers who want quick advice. In essays and articles, however, the basics may be supplemented with advice, encouragement, or relevant experience. In the following example from "How to Catch More Trout" (*Outdoor Life*, May 2006), Joe Brooks identifies the critical stages in the process in his first paragraph:

> Every move you make in trout fishing counts for or against you. The way you approach a pool, how you retrieve, how you strike, how you play the fish, how you land him—all are important factors. If you plan your tactics according to the demands of each situation, you'll catch a lot more trout over a season.

Then Brooks introduces the first stage:

> The first thing you should do is stand by the pool and study it awhile before you fish. Locate the trout that are rising consistently. Choose one (the lowest in the pool, preferably), and work on him. If you rush right in and start casting, you'll probably put down several fish that you haven't seen. And you can scare still more fish by false-casting all over the place. A dozen fish you might have caught with a more careful approach may see the line and go down before you even drop the fly on the surface.

He continues with stages and advice until he reaches the last step:

> The safest way to land a fish is to beach it. If no low bank is handy, you can fight a fish until he is tired and then pull his head against a bank or an upjutting rock and pick him up. Hold him gently. The tighter your grip, the more likely he is to spurt from your fingers, break your leader tippet, and escape. Even if you intend to put him back, you want to feel that he is really yours—a trout you have cast and caught and released because you planned it that way.

Throughout the article, Brooks skillfully addresses his audience—readers of *Outdoor Life,* people who probably already know how to fish, hunt, and enjoy other outdoor recreation. As his title indicates, Brooks isn't explaining how to catch trout but how to catch *more* trout. For this reason, he skips topics for beginners (such as how to cast) and instead urges readers to plan and implement more sophisticated tactics to increase their catch.

Although generally used to supply accurate directions, process analysis can also be turned to humorous ends, as illustrated in this paragraph from "How to Heal a Broken Heart (in One Day)" by student Lindsey Schendel.

> To begin your first day of mourning, you will wake up at 11 a.m., thus banishing any feelings of fatigue. Forget eating a healthy breakfast; toast two waffles, and plaster them with chocolate syrup instead of maple. Then make sure you have a room of serenity so you may cry in peace. It is important that you go through the necessary phases of denial and depression. Call up a friend or family member while you are still in your serious, somber mood. Explain to that person the hardships you are facing and how you don't know if you can go on. Immediately afterwards, turn on any empowering music, get up, and dance.

Like more serious process directions, this paragraph includes steps or stages (sleeping late, eating breakfast, crying and calling, and getting up and dancing). They are arranged in chronological order with transitions marking the movement from one to the other (*To begin, Then, while, Immediately afterwards*).

Process analyses are wonderful ways to show your readers the inside workings of events or systems, but they can be difficult to follow. Be sure to divide the process into logical steps or stages and to put the steps in a sensible chronological order. Add details or examples wherever your description seems ambiguous or abstract, and use transitions to mark the end of one step and the beginning of the next. (For more on transitions, see pp. 97–100.)

The Process Checklist includes questions to consider when you use process analysis.

PROCESS CHECKLIST

☐ Do you thoroughly understand the process you are analyzing?

☐ Do you have a good reason to analyze a process at this point in your writing? How does your analysis support your main idea or thesis?

☐ Have you broken the process down into logical and useful steps? Have you adjusted your explanation of the steps for your audience?

☐ Is the order in which you present these steps the best one possible?

☐ Have you used transitions to guide your readers from one step to the next?

■ **ACTIVITY:** Analyzing a Process

Analyze one of the following processes or procedures as the basis of a paragraph or short essay. Then share your process analysis with classmates. Can they follow your analysis easily? Do they spot anything you left out?

registering for college classes	falling in love
studying for a test	buying a used car
having the flu (or another illness)	moving

DIVIDING AND CLASSIFYING

To *divide* is to break something down, identifying or analyzing its components. (For more on analyzing a subject, see pp. 119–21.) It's far easier to take in a subject, especially a complex one, a piece at a time. The subject divided may be as concrete as a medical center (which a writer might divide into specialty units) or as abstract as a person's knowledge of art (which the writer might divide into knowledge of sculpture, painting, drawing, and other forms). To *classify* is to make sense of a complicated and potentially bewildering array of things—works of literature, this year's movies—by sorting them into categories (*types* or *classes*) that you can deal with one at a time. Literature is customarily arranged by genre—novels, stories, poems, plays; movies might be sorted by audience (movies for children, teenagers, or mature audiences).

Dividing and classifying are like two sides of the same coin. In theory, any broad subject can be *divided* into components, which can then be *classified* into categories. In practice, it's often difficult to tell where division stops and classification begins.

In the following paragraph from his college textbook *Wildlife Management* (San Francisco: Freeman, 1978), Robert H. Giles Jr. uses division to simplify an especially large, abstract subject: the management of forest wildlife in America. To explain which environmentalists assume which duties and responsibilities, Giles divides forest wildlife management into six levels or areas of concern, arranged roughly from large to small, all neatly explained in fewer than two hundred words.

> There are six scales of forest wildlife management: (1) national, (2) regional, (3) state or industrial, (4) county or parish, (5) intra-state region, management unit, or watershed, and (6) forest. Each is different. At the national and regional levels, management includes decisions on timber harvest quotas, grazing policy in forested lands, official stance on forest taxation bills, cutting policy relative to threatened and endangered species, management coordination of migratory species, and research fund allocation. At the state or industrial level, decision types include land acquisition, sale, or trade; season setting; and permit systems and fees. At the county level, plans are made, seasons set, and special fees levied. At the intra-state level, decisions include what seasons to recommend, what stances to take on bills not affecting local conditions, the sequence in which to attempt land acquisition, and the placement of facilities. At the forest level, decisions may include some of those of the larger management unit but typically are those of maintenance schedules, planting stock, cutting rotations, personnel employment and supervision, road closures, equipment use, practices to be attempted or used, and boundaries to be marked.

In a textbook lesson on how babies develop, Kurt W. Fischer and Arlyne Lazerson, writing in *Human Development* (New York: Freeman, 1984), describe a research project that classified individual babies into three types according to temperament:

> The researchers also found that certain of these temperamental qualities tended to occur together. These clusters of characteristics generally fell into three types—the easy baby, the difficult baby, and the baby who was slow to warm up. The *easy infant* has regular patterns of eating and sleeping, readily approaches new objects and people, adapts easily to changes in the environment, generally reacts with low or moderate intensity, and typically is in a cheerful mood. The *difficult infant* usually shows irregular patterns of eating and sleeping, withdraws from new objects or people, adapts slowly to changes, reacts with great intensity, and is frequently cranky. The *slow-to-warm-up infant* typically has a low activity level, tends to withdraw when presented with an unfamiliar object, reacts with a low level of intensity, and adapts slowly to changes in the environment. Fortunately for parents, most healthy infants—40 percent or more—have an easy temperament. Only about 10 percent have a difficult temperament, and about 15 percent are slow to warm up. The remaining 35 percent do not easily fit one of the three types but show some other pattern.

When you divide and classify, your point is to use systematic grouping to make order out of a complex or overwhelming jumble.

- Make sure the components and categories you identify are sensible, given your purpose, and follow the same principle of classification or analysis for all categories. For example, if you're trying to discuss campus relations, it makes sense to divide the school population into *instructors, students,* and *support staff;* it would make less sense to divide it into *people from the South, people from the other states,* and *people from overseas.*
- Try to group apples with apples so that all the components or categories are roughly equivalent. For example, if you're classifying television shows and you've come up with *sitcoms, dramas, talk shows, children's shows, news,* and *cartoons,* then you've got a problem: the last category is probably part of *children's shows.*
- Check that your final system is simple and easy for your readers to understand. Most people can handle only about seven things at once. If you've got more than six or seven components or categories, perhaps you may need to combine or eliminate some.

Use the Division and Classification Checklist when you plan to divide and classify.

DIVISION AND CLASSIFICATION CHECKLIST

☐ How does your division or classification support your main idea or thesis?

☐ Do you use the most logical principle of division or classification for your purpose?

☐ Do you stick to one principle throughout?

☐ Have you identified components or categories that are comparable?

☐ Have you arranged your components or categories in the best order?

☐ Have you given specific examples for each component or category?

☐ Have you made a complex subject more accessible to your readers?

■ **ACTIVITY:** Dividing and Classifying

To practice dividing and classifying, choose two of the following subjects. Brainstorm for five minutes on each, trying to come up with as many components as you can. With your classmates, create one large list by combining items from all students who chose each subject. Working together, take the largest list and try to classify the items on it into logical categories. Feel free to add or change components or categories if you've overlooked something.

students	customers	sports	families
teachers	Web sites	vacations	drivers

COMPARING AND CONTRASTING

Often you can develop ideas by setting a pair of subjects side by side, comparing and contrasting them. When you *compare,* you point out similarities; when you *contrast,* you discuss differences. In daily life, we compare and contrast to decide which menu item to choose, which car (or other product) to buy, which college course to sign up for. A comparison and contrast can lead to a final evaluation and a decision about which thing is better, but it doesn't have to.

Working together, these twin strategies use one subject to clarify another. The dual method works well for a pair similar in nature—two cities, two films, two economic theories. Because this method shows that you have observed and understood both subjects, college instructors will often ask you to compare and contrast on exams ("Discuss the chief similarities and differences between nineteenth-century French and English colonial policies in West Africa").

You can use two basic methods of organization for comparison and contrast: the opposing pattern and the alternating pattern. Using the *opposing pattern*, you discuss all the characteristics or subdivisions of the first subject in the first half of the paragraph or essay and then discuss all the characteristics of the other subject. Using the *alternating pattern*, you move back and forth between the two subjects. This pattern places the specifics close together for immediate comparison and contrast. Whichever pattern you choose, be sure to cover the same subpoints for each subject and to follow the same order in each part.

OPPOSING PATTERN, SUBJECT BY SUBJECT	ALTERNATING PATTERN, POINT BY POINT
Subject A	Point 1
Point 1	Subject A
Point 2	Subject B
Point 3	Point 2
Subject B	Subject A
Point 1	Subject B
Point 2	Point 3
Point 3	Subject A
	Subject B

The following selection opens Chapter One of *Rousseau's Dog* by David Edmonds and John Eidinow (New York: HarperCollins, 2006). The book tells the story of the bitterness that grew between David Hume and Jean-Jacques Rousseau, two eighteenth-century philosophers with very different views and styles.

On the evening of January 10, 1766, the weather in the English Channel was foul—stormy, wet, and cold. That night, after being held in harbor by unfavorable winds, a packet boat beat its way, rolling and plunging, from Calais to Dover. Among the passengers were two men who had met for the first time some three weeks earlier in Paris, a British diplomat and a Swiss refugee. The refugee was accompanied by his beloved dog, Sultan, small and brown with a curly tail. The diplomat stayed below, tormented by seasickness. The refugee remained on deck all night; the frozen sailors marveled at his hardiness.

If the ship had foundered, she would have carried to the bottom of the Channel two of the most influential thinkers of the eighteenth century.

The diplomat was David Hume. His contributions to philosophy on induction, causation, necessity, personal identity, morality, and theism are of such enduring importance that his name belongs in the league of the most elite philosophers, the league that would also include Plato, Aristotle, Descartes, Kant, and Wittgenstein. A contemporary and friend of Adam Smith's, he paved the way to modern economics; he also modernized historiography.

The refugee was Jean-Jacques Rousseau. His intellectual range and achievements were equally staggering. He made epochal contributions to political theory, literature, and education. His autobiography, *The Confessions,* was a stunningly original work, one that has spawned countless successors but still sets the standard for a narrative of self-revelation and artistic development. *Émile,* his educational tract, transformed the debate about the upbringing of children and was instrumental in altering our perceptions of childhood. *On the Social Contract,* his most significant political publication, has been cited as an inspiration for generations of revolutionaries. More fundamentally, Rousseau altered the way we view ourselves, our emotions, and our relationship to society and to the natural world.

In the first paragraph of this selection, the authors use a short form of the alternating pattern to introduce the two men—moving briefly from diplomat to refugee, diplomat to refugee. The next paragraph establishes their significance, providing a transition to the third and fourth paragraphs, which use the opposing pattern to introduce the contributions, stature, and legacy of the two. As the first chapter continues comparing and contrasting, the difference between the temperaments of the two men— and the potential for deep conflict—grows increasingly clear to readers.

Consider the Comparison and Contrast Checklist when you use this strategy for development.

COMPARISON AND CONTRAST CHECKLIST

- ☐ Is your reason for comparing and contrasting unmistakably clear? Does it support or develop your main idea or thesis?
- ☐ Have you chosen to write about *major* similarities and differences?
- ☐ Have you compared or contrasted like things? Have you discussed the same categories or features for each item?
- ☐ Have you used the best possible arrangement, given your subject and the point you're trying to make?

☐ Have you selected points of comparison and supporting details
   that will intrigue, enlighten, and persuade your audience?

☐ If you are making a judgment, have you treated both subjects fairly?

☐ Have you avoided moving mechanically from "On the one hand" to
   "On the other hand"?

■ **ACTIVITY:** Comparing and Contrasting

Write a paragraph or two in which you compare and contrast the
subjects in one of the following pairs:

   baseball and football (or two other sports)
   living in an apartment (or dorm) and living in a house
   two cities or towns you are familiar with
   two musicians
   communication by telephone and e-mail
   watching a sports event on television and in person

IDENTIFYING CAUSES AND EFFECTS

From the time we are children, we ask why. Why can't I go out and play?
Why is the sky blue? Why did my goldfish die? Searching for causes and
effects continues into adulthood, so it's natural that explaining causal
relationships is a common method of development. To use this method
successfully, you must think about the subject critically, gather evidence,
draw judicious conclusions, and clarify relationships.

In the following paragraph from "What Pop Lyrics Say to Us" *(New
York Times,* February 24, 1985), Robert Palmer speculates on the causes
that led young people to turn to rock music for inspiration as well as on
the effects of their expectations on the musicians of the time:

> By the late '60's, the peace and civil rights movements were beginning
> to splinter. The assassinations of the Kennedys and Martin Luther King
> had robbed a generation of its heroes, the Vietnam War was escalating
> despite the protests, and at home, violence was on the rise. Young people
> turned to rock, expecting it to ask the right questions and come up with
> answers, hoping that the music's most visionary artists could somehow
> make sense of things. But rock's most influential artists—Bob Dylan, the
> Beatles, the Rolling Stones—were finding that serving as the conscience
> of a generation exacted a heavy toll. Mr. Dylan, for one, felt the pressures

becoming unbearable, and wrote about his predicament in songs like "All Along the Watchtower."

Instead of focusing on causes *or* effects, often writers trace a *chain* of cause-and-effect relationships. That's what Charles C. Mann and Mark L. Plummer do in "The Butterfly Problem" *(Atlantic Monthly,* January 1992):

> More generally, the web of species around us helps generate soil, regulate freshwater supplies, dispose of waste, and maintain the quality of the atmosphere. Pillaging nature to the point where it cannot perform these functions is dangerously foolish. Simple self-protection is thus a second motive for preserving biodiversity. When DDT was sprayed in Borneo, the biologists Paul and Anne Ehrlich relate in their book *Extinction* (1981), it killed all the houseflies. The gecko lizards that preyed on the flies ate their pesticide-filled corpses and died. House cats consumed the dying lizards; they died too. Rats descended on the villages, bringing bubonic plague. Incredibly, the housefly in this case was part of an intricate system that controlled human disease. To make up for its absence, the government was forced to parachute cats into the area.

Use the following checklist when you investigate causes and effects.

CAUSE-AND-EFFECT CHECKLIST

☐ Is your use of cause and effect clearly tied to your main idea or thesis?

☐ Have you identified actual causes? Have you supplied evidence that will persuade readers to support them?

☐ Have you identified actual effects, or are they conjecture? If conjecture, are they logical possibilities? Can you find persuasive evidence to support them?

☐ Have you judiciously drawn conclusions concerning causes and effects? Have you avoided logical fallacies? (See pp. 198–99.)

☐ Have you presented your points clearly and logically so that your readers can follow them easily?

☐ Have you considered other causes or effects, immediate or long term, that readers might find relevant?

■ ACTIVITY: Identifying Causes and Effects

1. Identify some of the *causes* of five of the following. Then discuss the possible causes with your classmates.

failing an exam	stage fright	losing a job
an automobile accident	losing or winning a game	losing weight arriving late
poor health	stress	going to college
good health	getting a job	getting a scholarship

2. Identify some of the *effects* of five of the following. Then discuss the possible effects with your classmates.

an insult	speeding	traveling to another country
a compliment	winning the lottery	
learning to read	divorce	drinking while driving
dieting	changing jobs	

3. Identify some of the *causes and effects* of one of the following. You may need to do a little research to identify the chain of causes and effects for the event. Discuss your findings with your classmates.

the online shopping boom	the bird flu
the Vietnam War	recycling
the attacks on September 11, 2001	a gay marriage court case
the discovery of atomic energy	the uses of solar energy
a major U.S. Supreme Court decision	global warming racial tension

ADDING VISUAL EVIDENCE

At times you may feel that a project, report, or essay would benefit from visual as well as textual development. Visual evidence—for example, graphs, maps, diagrams, photographs, or other materials—can clarify an explanation or argument. In fact, well-selected visual evidence can do even more—engage the attention of your audience, show directly something that might otherwise require a long explanation, or emphasize relationships or complexities so that readers truly "see" what you are saying.

Sometimes visual materials represent or reflect the same method of development that you are using in your text. For example, a visual might illustrate a procedure, an activity, a set of directions, or the stages in a process, as the "How to Study Model" in Figure 7.1 does.

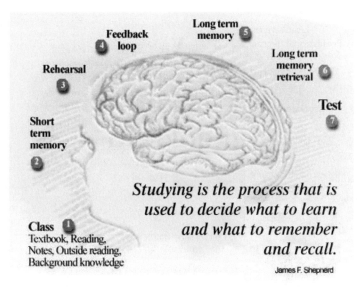

Fig. 1. "How to Study Model," figure from Lucy Tribble MacDonald, *Howtostudy.org.* (Chemeketa Community Coll., 2006; web; 3 May 2006).

Figure 7.1   Using and citing a visual (MLA style)

Visuals can also present complex information in an especially clear, attractive, or persuasive manner. A straightforward pie chart or bar graph, like the graph on educational attainment in Figure 7.2, can help readers grasp information, as can a map like the one on rental costs in Figure 7.3.

Carefully selected visuals reinforce or supplement your text; they function as evidence, not decoration. For example, color effectively highlights key information, perhaps distinguishing slices in a pie chart. However, too much color can overload readers as can hard-to-see colors on a white page or a tinted screen. Providing a context for a visual also helps your readers make sense of it. In an introductory sentence, identify the number or letter of the visual (for example, Figure 6), its content, and the point that it helps you make. Place the visual close to the related discussion, and size it so that it supports, not overshadows, the text.

If you have never before created charts, graphs, or tables, try your software's special tools for making them. Typically, tables clearly label

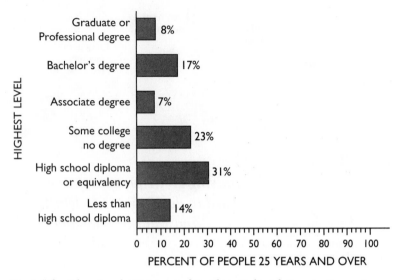

Fig. 2. "The Educational Attainment of People in Sedgwick County, Kansas in 2004," bar graph from United States, Census Bureau, *2004 American Community Survey* (US Census Bureau, 2005; web; 22 May 2006).

Figure 7.2   Using and citing a graph (MLA style)

both the columns (running up and down) and the rows (running across). Within this grid, they can display numerical findings, group items in categories, or align information for comparison or contrast. Besides creating your own visuals, you also can use an image editor to add digital photos or a scanner to integrate printed material from sources. If you are unfamiliar with these options, ask for advice at the computer lab.

Whenever you adapt or borrow visuals from another source, printed or electronic, credit that source in your paper. If you download an image from the Web, check the site for its guidelines for using images; follow them, requesting permission when required and giving credit to the copyright owner. If you are uncertain about whether you can use an image from a source, check with your instructor.

The Visual Evidence Checklist on page 136 can help you add visual evidence to your text.

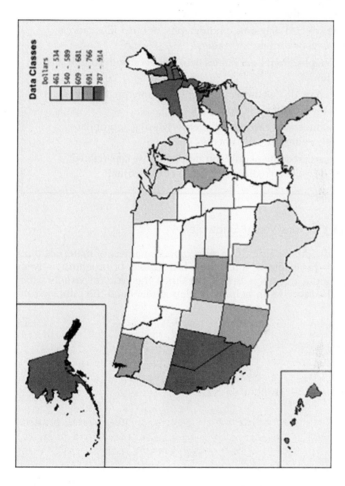

Fig. 3. "Median Monthly Housing Costs for Renter-occupied Housing Units (Dollars): 2004," map from United States, Census Bureau, *2004 American Community Survey* (US Census Bureau, 2005; web; 22 May 2006).

Figure 7.3   Using and citing a map (MLA style)

135

VISUAL EVIDENCE CHECKLIST

☐ Have you mentioned all the visuals in your text so that readers can easily connect them to your discussion? Have you labeled all the visuals so that they are easy to identify?

☐ Have you selected diagrams, photographs, or other illustrations that clarify your content for readers?

☐ Do your graphs, charts, and tables help readers absorb complicated information?

☐ Have you provided whatever explanation or interpretation readers might need to understand your visuals?

☐ Have you integrated each visual effectively using appropriate placement, sizing, and alignment?

☐ Have you secured any permission needed to use copyrighted material? Have you credited the source of each visual?

■ ACTIVITY: Using Visual Evidence

Working individually or with a group, gather a variety of materials that use visuals—for example, a textbook, a pamphlet or brochure, a flyer, a catalog, and a magazine article. Evaluate the types of visuals used and their effectiveness in helping readers understand the information presented.

8

Strategies for Revising

Good writing is rewriting. When Ernest Hemingway was asked what made him rewrite the last page of the novel A *Farewell to Arms* thirty-nine times, he replied, "Getting the words right." His comment reflects the care that serious writers take in revising their work. In this chapter we provide strategies for revising—ways to rethink muddy ideas and emphasize

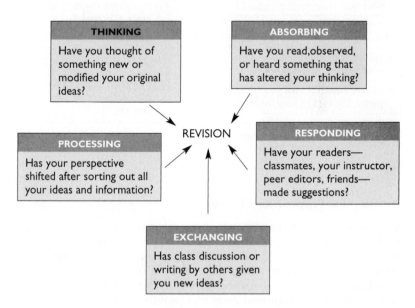

THINKING
Have you thought of something new or modified your original ideas?

ABSORBING
Have you read, observed, or heard something that has altered your thinking?

REVISION

PROCESSING
Has your perspective shifted after sorting out all your ideas and information?

RESPONDING
Have your readers—classmates, your instructor, peer editors, friends—made suggestions?

EXCHANGING
Has class discussion or writing by others given you new ideas?

important ones, to rephrase obscure passages and restructure garbled
sentences whether you are rewriting a whole essay or specific sentences
and paragraphs. Revision is your opportunity to make adjustments based
on changes in your thinking and responses from others, as illustrated on
page 137.

RE-VIEWING AND REVISING

Revision means "seeing again"—discovering again, conceiving again,
shaping again. As an integral aspect of the writing process, it can occur
at any and all stages of the process, and most writers do a lot of it. *Macro
revising* is making large, global, or fundamental changes that affect the
overall direction or impact of writing—its purpose, organization, or
audience. Its companion is *microrevising,* paying attention to the language aspects of writing—sentences, words, grammar—including ways
to create emphasis, eliminate wordiness, and increase clarity.

MACROREVISING	MICROREVISING
• **PURPOSE:** How might you refine what you want to accomplish?	• **EMPHASIS:** How might you position your ideas more effectively?
• **THESIS:** How could you state your main point more accurately?	• **CONCISENESS:** Can you spot extra words that you might cut?
• **AUDIENCE:** Should you address your readers differently?	• **CLARITY:** Can you make any sentences and words clearer?
• **STRUCTURE:** Should you reorganize any part of your writing?	
• **SUPPORT:** Do you need to add, drop, or rework your support?	

Revising for Purpose and Thesis

When you revise for purpose, you make sure that your writing accomplishes what you want it to do. If your goal is to create an interesting
profile of a person, have you done so? If you want to persuade your readers to take a certain course of action, have you succeeded? Of course, if
your complex project has evolved or your assignment is now clearer to
you, the purpose of your final essay may be different from your purpose

when you began. To revise for purpose, try to step back and see your writing as other readers will. Concentrate on what's actually in your paper, not what you assume is there.

At this point you'll probably want to revise your working thesis statement (if you've developed one) or create a thesis sentence (if you haven't). (See pp. 62–68.) First scrutinize your working thesis statement. Reconsider how it is worded:

- Is it stated exactly in concise yet detailed language?
- Is it focused on only one main idea?
- Is it stated positively rather than negatively?
- Is it limited to a demonstrable statement?

Then consider how accurately your thesis now represents your main idea and your draft as a whole:

- Does each part of your essay relate directly to your thesis?
- Does each part of your essay develop and support your thesis?
- Does your essay deliver everything your thesis promises?

If you find unrelated or contradictory passages, you have two options: revise the thesis, or revise the essay.

You may find that your ideas have deepened, your topic has become more complex, or your essay has developed along new lines during the process of writing. If so, you may want to refine or expand your thesis statement so that it accurately represents this evolution.

WORKING THESIS	The *Herald's* coverage of the Senate elections was more thorough than the *Courier's.*
REVISED THESIS	The *Herald's* coverage of the Senate elections was less timely but more thorough and fairer than the *Courier's.*
WORKING THESIS	As the roles of men and women have changed in our society, old-fashioned formal courtesy has declined.
REVISED THESIS	As the roles of men and women have changed in our society, old-fashioned formal courtesy has declined not only toward women but also toward men.

See the Revision Checklist for Purpose and Thesis on page 140 for helpful questions about revising for purpose and thesis.

REVISION CHECKLIST FOR PURPOSE AND THESIS

☐ Do you know exactly what you want your essay to accomplish? Can you put it in one sentence: "In this paper I want to . . ."?

☐ Is your thesis stated outright in the essay? If not, have you provided clues so that your readers will know precisely what it is?

☐ Does every part of the essay work to achieve the same goal?

☐ Have you tried to do too much? Does your coverage of the topic seem too thin? If so, how might you reduce the scope of your thesis?

☐ Does your essay say all that needs to be said? Is everything — ideas, connections, supporting evidence — on paper, not just in your head?

☐ In writing the essay, have you changed your mind, rethought your assumptions, made a discovery? Does anything now need to be recast?

☐ Do you have enough evidence? Is every point developed fully enough to be clear and convincing?

Revising for Audience

An essay is effective only if it succeeds with its particular audience. What works with one audience can fall flat with another. Visualize one of your readers poring over the essay, sentence by sentence, reacting to what you have written. What expressions do you see on that reader's face? Where does he or she have trouble understanding? Where have you hit the mark? Your organization, your selection of details, your word choice, and your tone all affect your readers, so pay special attention to these aspects.

Use the Revision Checklist for Audience to revise for your readers.

REVISION CHECKLIST FOR AUDIENCE

☐ Who will read this essay? What will they expect of it?

☐ Does the essay tell your readers what they want to know rather than what they probably know already?

☐ Are there any places where readers might fall asleep? If so, can you shorten, delete, or liven up those passages?

☐ Does the opening of the essay mislead your readers by promising something that the essay never delivers?

☐ Do you unfold each idea in enough detail to make it both clear and interesting? Would readers appreciate more detailed evidence?

☐ Have you anticipated questions readers might ask?

☐ Where might readers raise serious objections? How might you anticipate their objections and answer them?

☐ Have you used any specialized or technical language that your readers might not understand? If so, have you worked in brief definitions?

☐ What is your attitude toward your readers? Are you chummy, angry, superior, apologetic, condescending, preachy? Should you revise to improve your attitude? Ask your peers for an opinion.

☐ Will your readers be convinced that you have told them something worth knowing?

Revising for Structure and Support

When you revise for structure and support, you make sure that the order of your ideas and your selection and arrangement of supporting material are as effective as possible. You may have all the ingredients of a successful essay, but your essay won't succeed if those ingredients are in a jumbled, confusing mess.

In a well-structured essay, each paragraph, sentence, and phrase serves a clear function. Are your opening and closing paragraphs relevant, concise, and interesting? Is everything in each paragraph on the same topic? Are all of your ideas adequately developed? Are the paragraphs arranged in the best possible order? Finally, have you reviewed each place where you lead readers from one idea to the next to be certain that the transition is clear and painless?

A revision outline can be useful for diagnosing a draft that you suspect doesn't quite make sense. Instead of using outlining to plan, now you want to show what you've succeeded in getting on paper. Start by finding the topic sentence of each paragraph in your draft (or creating one, if necessary) and listing them in order. Label the sentences *I, II, A, B,* and so on to indicate the logical relationships of ideas in your essay. Do the same with the supporting details under each topic sentence, labeling them also with letters and numbers and indenting appropriately. (For more on outline format, see pp. 73–82.)

Now look at the outline. Does it make sense on its own, without the essay to explain it? Would a different order or arrangement be more effective? Do any sections look thin, in need of more evidence? Are the connections between parts in your head but not on paper? Maybe too many ideas are jammed into too few paragraphs. Maybe you haven't included as many specific details and examples as you need, or maybe you need stronger ones. Work on the outline until you get it into good shape, and then rewrite the essay to follow it.

You'll find helpful questions on this topic in the Revision Checklist for Structure and Support.

REVISION CHECKLIST FOR STRUCTURE AND SUPPORT

- ☐ Does your introduction set up the whole essay? Does it both grab readers' attention and hint at what is to follow?
- ☐ Does the essay deliver all that you promise in your opening?
- ☐ Would any later passage make a better beginning?
- ☐ Is your thesis clear early in the essay? If explicit, is it positioned prominently?
- ☐ Do the paragraph breaks seem logical?
- ☐ Is the main idea of each paragraph clear? Have you used a topic sentence in every paragraph?
- ☐ Is the main idea of each paragraph fully developed? Where might you need more details or better evidence to be convincing?
- ☐ Within each paragraph, is each detail or piece of evidence relevant to the topic sentence? If you find a stray bit, should you move it to another paragraph or omit it altogether?
- ☐ Are all the ideas directly relevant to the main point of the essay?
- ☐ Would any paragraphs make more sense in a different order?
- ☐ Does everything follow clearly? Does one point smoothly lead to the next? Would transitions help make the connections clearer?
- ☐ Does the conclusion follow from what has gone before, or does it seem tacked on?

■ ACTIVITY: Tackling Macro Revision

Even if you don't know exactly what needs to be changed in a draft, this activity will help you get started making productive changes.

Select a draft that would benefit from revision. Then, based on your sense of the draft's greatest need, choose one of the revision checklists, and use it to guide a first revision. Let the draft sit for a few hours or a day or so. Then consider what else you'd like to do to improve the draft, and select one of the remaining checklists to work with.

WORKING WITH A PEER EDITOR

Of course, there's no substitute for having someone else go over your writing. Many college assignments ask you to write for an audience of classmates, but even if your essay is written for a different group—the town council or readers of *Newsweek*, for example—having a classmate read over your essay is a worthwhile revision strategy.

To gain all you can as a writer from a peer review, you need to play an active part in the discussion of your work.

- Ask your reader questions. (If this prospect seems difficult, write a "Dear Editor" letter or memo ahead of time, and bring it to your meeting.)
- Be open to new ideas about your focus, organization, details, or material.
- Use what's helpful, but trust yourself as the author.

To be a helpful, supportive peer editor, try to offer honest, intelligent feedback, not judgment.

- Look at the big picture: purpose, focus, clarity, coherence, organization, support.
- When you spot strengths or weaknesses, be specific. Note examples.
- Answer the writer's questions, and also use the questions supplied throughout this book to concentrate on essentials, not details.

As a writer, you can ask your peer editor to begin with your specific questions or to select applicable questions from the following list.

QUESTIONS FOR A PEER EDITOR

Overall Questions

What is your first reaction to this paper?
What is this writer trying to tell you?

What are this paper's greatest strengths?

Does the paper have any major weaknesses?

What one change would most improve the paper?

Questions on Meaning

Do you understand everything? Is the draft missing any information that you need to know?

Does this paper tell you anything you didn't know before?

Is the writer trying to cover too much territory? Too little?

Does any point need to be explained or illustrated more fully?

When you come to the end, has the paper delivered what it promised?

Could this paper use a down-to-the-ground revision?

Questions on Organization

Has the writer begun in a way that grabs your interest and quickly draws you in? Or can you suggest a better beginning at some later point?

Does the paper have one main idea, or does it juggle more than one?

Would the main idea stand out better if anything were removed or added?

Might the ideas in the paper be more effectively arranged? Do any ideas belong together that now seem too far apart?

Can you follow the ideas easily? Are transitions needed? If so, where?

Does the writer keep to one point of view, one angle of seeing?

Does the ending seem deliberate, as if the writer meant to conclude? Or does it seem as though the writer ran out of gas? How might the writer strengthen the conclusion?

Questions on Writing Strategies

Do you feel that this paper addresses you personally?

Do you dislike or object to any statement the writer makes or any wording the writer uses? Is the problem word choice, tone, or inadequate support? Should the writer keep or change this part?

Does the draft contain anything that distracts you or seems unnecessary?

Do you get bored at any point? How might the writer keep you reading?

Is the language of this paper too lofty and abstract? If so, where does the writer need to come down to earth and get specific?

Do you understand all the words used? Do any specialized words need clearer definition?

E-mail can be an efficient way for writers and readers to exchange drafts. You can simply copy and paste a draft into an e-mail message. This process may remove some formatting — italics or bold, for example — but it usually works well and avoids spreading computer viruses. You can also attach a document to an e-mail message. Use the Save As option (usually in the File menu) to create a duplicate version of your file in Rich Text Format (RTF) or another format that can be opened with any word-processing software. Add a new title or simply a plus sign (+) and your peer's initials to the file name to help you keep track of different drafts.

When you and a peer respond to each other's texts, you may want to use all capitals for your comments within each other's drafts. Capitalized comments generally are easy to distinguish from the original text. You might also agree to use an editing tool, such as Track Changes (in the Tools menu). This resource automatically highlights suggested changes in a draft with color, underlining, and strikeouts. It also allows you to track suggestions from several readers.

Although e-mail is convenient for sending drafts back and forth, a face-to-face meeting can be an inspiration. When the peer editing is finished, try to meet with your peer editor or editing group to talk through your drafts. During the meeting, you can return the drafts with comments, ask questions about and respond to suggestions, and add your own notes to your draft.

■ ACTIVITY: Exchanging Drafts with a Group

Working with a partner or a small editing group, have everyone exchange drafts. Let each writer select one of the sets of peer editing questions (see pp. 143–45) for his or her reader, based on the type of revision that the draft probably needs most. Read each other's drafts, add suggestions, and meet to discuss everyone's revision suggestions.

REVISING FOR EMPHASIS, CONCISENESS, AND CLARITY

After you've revised for the large issues in your draft—purpose, thesis, audience, structure, and support—you're ready to turn your attention to micro revising. Now is the time to emphasize what matters most and communicate it concisely and clearly.

Stressing What Counts

An ineffective writer treats all ideas as equals. An effective writer decides what matters most and shines a bright light on it. You can't emphasize merely by *italicizing*, putting words in "quotation marks," or throwing them into CAPITAL LETTERS. These devices soon grow monotonous, stressing nothing at all. In this section we suggest how to emphasize what counts using the most emphatic positions in an essay, a paragraph, or a sentence—the beginning and the end.

Stating It First.   In an essay, you might start with what matters most. For an economics paper on import quotas, student Donna Waite first summed up her conclusion.

> Although an import quota has many effects, both for the nation imposing the quota and for the nation whose industries must suffer from it, I believe that the most important effect is generally felt at home. A native industry gains a chance to thrive in a marketplace of lessened competition.

A paper that takes a stand or makes a proposal might open with the writer's position:

> Our state's antiquated system of justices of the peace is inefficient.

> The United States should orbit a human observer around Mars.

In a single sentence, you can also stress a point at the start. Consider the following unemphatic (and confusing) sentence:

> When Congress debates the Hall-Hayes Act removing existing protections for endangered species, as now seems likely to occur on May 12, it will be a considerable misfortune if this bill should pass because the extinction of many rare birds and animals would certainly result.

The debate and its likely timing consume the start of the sentence. Here's a better use of this emphatic position:

> The extinction of many rare birds and animals would certainly follow passage of the Hall-Hayes Act.

Now the writer is stressing what he most fears—the consequences of the act. In a later sentence, he can add the date and his opinion about the likelihood of passage.

Stating It Last.   Placing an idea last also can give it weight. Emphatic order, proceeding from least important to most, is dramatic: it builds up and up. In a paper on import quotas, a dramatic buildup might look contrived. However, in an essay on how city parks can attract visitors to a city, the thesis sentence—summing up the point of the essay—might stand at the very end:

> For the urban core, improved parks could bring about a new era of prosperity.

Giving the evidence first and leading up to the thesis at the end is particularly effective in editorials and informal persuasive essays.

A sentence that uses climactic order, suspending its point until the end, is called a *periodic sentence*. Notice how novelist Julian Green builds to his point of emphasis:

> Amid chaos of illusions into which we are cast headlong, there is one thing that stands out as true, and that is—love.

Cutting and Whittling

Like pea pickers who throw out dirt and pebbles, good writers remove unnecessary words that clog their prose. One of the chief joys of revising is to watch 200 paunchy words shrink to a svelte 150. To see how saving words helps, let's first look at some wordiness. In what she imagined to be a gracious style, a New York socialite once sent this dinner invitation to Hu Shi, the Chinese ambassador:

> O learned sage and distinguished representative of the numerous Chinese nation, pray deign to honor my humble abode with your noble presence at a pouring of libations, to be followed by a modest evening repast, on the forthcoming Friday, June Eighteenth, in this Year of the Pig, at the approximate hour of eight o'clock, Eastern Standard Time.

Kindly be assured furthermore, O most illustrious sire, that a favorable reply at your earliest convenience will be received most humbly and gratefully by the undersigned unworthy suppliant.

In reply, the witty diplomat sent this telegram:

CAN DO. HU SHI.

Hu Shi's reply disputes a common assumption — that the more words an idea takes, the more impressive it will seem. Most good contemporary writers know that the more succinctly they can state an idea, the clearer and more forceful it will be.

Cutting the Fanfare.   Why bother to announce that you're going to say something? Cut the fanfare. We aren't, by the way, attacking the usefulness of transitions that lead readers along. (For more on transitions, see pp. 97–100.)

WORDY	As far as getting ready for winter is concerned, I put antifreeze in my car.
REVISED	To get ready for winter, I put antifreeze in my car.
WORDY	The point should be made that . . . Let me make it perfectly clear that . . . In this paper I intend to . . . In conclusion I would like to say that . . .

Beginning Directly.   Words also tend to abound after *There is* or *There are*.

| WORDY | There are many people who dislike flying. |
| REVISED | Many people dislike flying. |

Using Strong Verbs.   Forms of the verb *be* (*am, is, are, was, were*) followed by a noun or an adjective can make a statement wordy. These weak verbs can almost always be replaced by active verbs.

| WORDY | The Akron game was a disappointment to the fans. |
| REVISED | The Akron game disappointed the fans. |

Using Relative Pronouns with Caution.   When a clause begins with a relative pronoun (*who, which, that*), you often can whittle it to a phrase.

| WORDY | Venus, which is the second planet of the solar system, is called the evening star. |

REVISED   Venus, the second planet of the solar system, is called the evening star.

Cutting Out Deadwood.   The more you revise, the more shortcuts you'll discover. Try reading the sentences below without the words in italics.

Howell spoke for the sophomores, and Janet *also spoke* for the seniors.

He is *something of* a clown but *sort of the* lovable *type.*

As a major in *the field of* economics, I plan to concentrate on *the area of* international banking.

The decision as to whether *or not* to go is up to you.

Cutting Descriptors.   Adjectives and adverbs are often dispensable. Contrast these two versions.

WORDY   Johnson's extremely significant research led to highly important major discoveries.

REVISED   Johnson's research led to major discoveries.

Selecting Short Words.   Although a long word may convey a shade of meaning that a shorter synonym doesn't, in general shun a long word when you can pick a short one. Instead of *the remainder,* write *the rest;* instead of *activate, start* or *begin;* instead of *adequate* or *sufficient, enough.* Look for the right word, one that wraps an idea in a smaller package.

WORDY   Andy has a left fist that has a lot of power in it.

REVISED   Andy has a potent left.

By the way, it pays to read. From reading, you absorb words like *potent* and set them to work for you.

Keeping It Clear

Finally, recall what you want to achieve—clear communication with your readers using specific, unambiguous words arranged in logical order. Aim for direct, forceful expression.

WORDY   He is more or less a pretty outstanding person in regard to good looks.

REVISED   He is strikingly handsome.

Try to read your draft as a first-time reader would. Be sure to return, after a break, to passages that you have struggled to write; heal any battle scars by focusing on clarity.

UNCLEAR   Thus, after a lot of thought, it should be approved by the board even though the federal funding for all the cow tagging may not be approved yet because it has wide support from local cattle ranchers.

CLEAR   In anticipation of federal funding, the Livestock Board should approve the cow-tagging proposal widely supported by local cattle ranchers.

The Microrevision Checklist includes questions to use in emphasizing, slimming, and clarifying your writing.

MICROREVISION CHECKLIST

☐ Have you positioned what counts at the beginning or the end?

☐ Are you direct, straightforward, and clear?

☐ Can you recast any sentence that begins *There is* or *There are*?

☐ Can you substitute an active verb wherever you use a form of the verb *be* (*is, was, were*)?

☐ Can you reduce to a phrase any clause beginning with *which, who,* or *that*?

☐ Have you used too much deadwood or too many adjectives and adverbs?

☐ Do you see any long words where short words would do?

☐ Do you announce an idea before you explain it? If so, consider chopping out the announcement.

■ **ACTIVITY:** Tackling Microrevision

Think back over the revisions you've already made to your draft and the advice you've received from peer editors or other readers. Consider whether your paper is more likely to seem bland (because it lacks emphasis), wordy (because it needs a good trimming), or foggy (because it needs to be more clear, direct, and logical). Pick one issue as your focus for the moment, and concentrate on adding emphasis, cutting extra words, or expressing ideas clearly using the advice in this section.

A SAMPLE STUDENT REVISION

John Martin, a business administration major, wrote the following economics paper to fulfill the assignment "Briefly discuss a current problem in international trade. Venture an opinion or propose a solution." You can see the thoughtful cuts and condensations that Martin made with the help of his English instructor and his peer editor. His large changes—macrorevisions—are highlighted in the margin. Both these macrorevisions and his smaller microrevisions are marked in the text. Following the draft you'll find the paper as he revised it—in fewer words.

FIRST DRAFT

Japan's Closed Doors: Should the U.S. Retaliate?

State problems more clearly for readers

~~There is currently a~~ *A* serious problem *is* brewing in ~~the world of~~ international trade ~~which may turn out to be a real temptest in a~~

a cliché to cut

~~teapot, so to speak.~~ According to the latest National Trade Estimates report, several ~~of the countries that the~~ U.S. ~~has been~~ *trading partners* ~~doing business with~~ deserve to be condemned for ~~what the report has characterized as~~ "unfair trade practices." The government has said it will use the report to single out ~~specific~~ countries ~~which it is then going to go ahead and~~ *to* punish under the Super 301 provisions of the trade law.

Rework paragraph to move more directly to point about Japan

The Super 301 section ~~of the trade law~~ requires Carla Hills, ~~who is~~ the U.S. trade representative, to ~~try to get rid of~~ *attack* what she *calls* ~~has officially designated to be~~ "priority unfair practices." She will ~~be~~ slashing at the ~~whole~~ web of impediments ~~and obstacles~~ that

same as impediments

have ~~slowed down or~~ denied ~~the various products of the many~~ *American* ~~United States~~ firms ~~much~~ *fast* access to Japanese markets.

Move paragraph to follow background

Some American businesspeople would ~~like to~~ take aim at Japan immediately. However, Clyde Prestowitz, ~~who is~~ a former Commerce Department official, ~~seriously~~ doubts that ~~in the last analysis~~ it would be ~~a good idea to come out and~~ *wise to* name Japan ~~to~~ *for* ~~feel the terrible effects of~~ retaliation under Super 301 *:* ~~in view of the fact that in his opinion,~~ "It's hard to negotiate with guys you are calling cheats." No doubt ~~there are~~ many other observers ~~who~~ share his view.

Strengthen paragraph focus by opening with the point

~~It is important for the reader to note here that for a long time, longer than anyone can remember,~~ Japan has *long* been the ~~leading~~ prime candidate for a dose of Super 301. Over the past decade, ~~there have been many years of negotiations and battering by different~~ *have battered* industry groups at the unyielding doors of ~~the~~ Japanese markets, ~~which have yielded~~ *with* some success~~es~~/ but have ~~pretty much~~ failed ~~miserably~~ to ~~dent the invisible trade barriers~~ *make them swing wide.* ~~that stand looming between us and the Japanese markets,~~ ~~preventing the free access of U.S. goods to Japanese consumers.~~ ~~As far as the~~ *The* U.S. trade deficit with Japan, ~~is concerned, it was somewhat~~ more than $50 billion last year, ~~and it~~ shows ~~very~~ little sign of ~~getting significantly much better~~ *improving* this year.

State opinion more clearly to achieve paper's purpose

~~Evidently it is the task of the~~ **The** administration **has** to try to **help** ~~pave the way for~~ U.S. exports ~~to~~ wedge their way into ~~the~~ protected Japanese markets while keeping ~~it firmly~~ in mind that the interests of both ~~the United States and Japan~~ **nations** call for ~~strengthening of the~~ **stronger** economic and military ties.~~that bind both countries into a sphere of friendly relationship. It is my personal conclusion that~~ **If** ~~if~~ the administration goes ahead,~~with this,~~ it will ~~certainly~~ need to plan ~~ahead for the future~~ carefully.

REVISED VERSION

Japan's Closed Doors: Should the U.S. Retaliate?

A serious problem is brewing in international trade. According to the latest National Trade Estimates report, several U.S. trading partners deserve to be condemned for "unfair trade practices." The government has said it will use the report to single out countries to punish under the Super 301 provisions of the trade law.

The Super 301 section requires Carla Hills, the U.S. trade representative, to attack what she calls "priority unfair practices." She will slash at the web of impediments that have denied American firms fast access to Japanese markets.

Japan has long been the prime candidate for a dose of Super 301. Over the past decade, industry groups have battered at the unyielding doors of Japanese markets with some success but have failed to make them swing wide. The U.S. trade deficit with Japan, more than $50 billion last year, shows little sign of improving this year.

Some American businesspeople would take aim at Japan immediately. However, Clyde Prestowitz, a former Commerce Department official, doubts that it would be wise to name Japan for retaliation under Super 301: "It's hard to negotiate with guys you are calling cheats." No doubt many other observers share his view.

The administration has to try to help U.S. exports wedge their way into protected Japanese markets while keeping in mind that the interests of both nations call for stronger economic and military ties. If the administration goes ahead, it will need to plan carefully.

John Martin's revision is both shorter and more forceful than his original draft. Next he edited and proofread his paper (see Ch. 9), making his final refinements. He also added citations to identify his sources (see Ch. 11) as he prepared the final version to submit.

9

Strategies for Editing and Proofreading

Editing means correcting and refining wording, grammar, punctuation, and mechanics. Proofreading means taking a final look at your paper to check correctness and to catch spelling and word-processing errors. Both activities allow you to refine your paper based on your own efforts and the advice of others, as illustrated in the graphic on the following page. Don't edit and proofread too soon. In your early drafting, don't fret over the correct spelling of an unfamiliar word; it may be revised in a later version. If the word stays in, you'll have time to check it later. After you have revised, however, you are ready to refine and correct. In college, good editing and proofreading can make the difference between a C and an A. On the job, they may help you get a promotion. Readers, teachers, and bosses like careful writers who take time to edit and proofread.

EDITING

As you edit, whenever you doubt whether a word or construction is correct, consult a good handbook. Learn the grammar conventions you don't understand so you can spot and eliminate problems in your own writing. Practice until you easily recognize major errors such as fragments and comma splices. Ask for help from a peer editor or a tutor in the writing center if your campus has one.

 If you use a grammar-checker to help you edit, you'll discover that it is a handy tool but not foolproof. A grammar-checker can alert you to many types of sentence problems. For example, it probably will spot

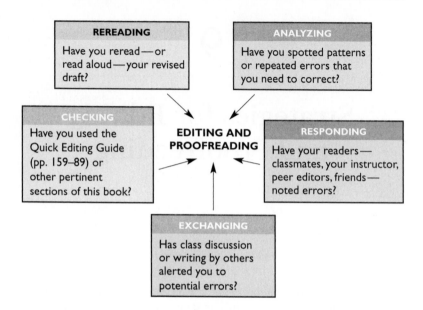

problems with adjectives and adverbs, such as confusing *good* and *well*. However, it also may question long sentences and unusual constructions that are perfectly correct. Because it will not always correctly identify the subject or verb in a sentence, it may question whether a correct sentence is complete or the subject and verb agree. It also is likely to miss faulty parallelism, misplaced modifiers, possessives without apostrophes, and commas in the wrong places. For these reasons, you always need to consider the grammar-checker's suggestions carefully before accepting them. As the writer, you, not your software, should have the final word.

Use the "Quick Editing Guide" that begins on page 160 of this chapter to get you started. It briefly reviews grammar, style, punctuation, and mechanics problems typically found in college writing. For each problem, it supplies definitions, examples, and a checklist to help you tackle the problem. The Quick Editing Guide Directory on page 159 provides a checklist for the problems identified there, along with the relevant section letter and number.

EDITING	PROOFREADING
• **WORDING:** Are your words correct and well chosen?	• **SPELLING:** Have you spell-checked and reread attentively?
• **GRAMMAR:** Are your sentences and their parts correct?	
• **SENTENCES:** Are your sentences clear and effective?	• **INCORRECT WORDS:** Have you used any words by mistake?
• **PUNCTUATION:** Do you need to add, correct, or drop any marks?	• **MISSING WORDS:** Have you left out any words?
• **MECHANICS:** Do you need to correct capitals, italics, or other matters?	• **MINOR ERRORS:** Can you find any small mistakes?
• **FORMAT:** Do you need to adjust margins, spacing, or headings?	• **MINOR DETAILS:** Can you see any incorrect details?

PROOFREADING

Careful proofreading is especially important because many errors in writing occur unconsciously and easily become habits. If you have never looked closely at the spelling of *environment,* you may never have noticed the second *n*. A moment's break in concentration can also lead to errors. Because the mind works faster than the pencil (or the word processor), when you are distracted by someone talking or a telephone ringing, you may leave out a word or put in the wrong punctuation.

The very way our eyes work also leads to errors. When you read normally, you usually see only the shells of words — the first and last letters. You fix your eyes on the print only about three or four times per line. To proofread effectively, you must look at the letters in each word and the punctuation marks between words without sliding over them. Proofreading requires time and patience, but it is a skill you can develop. Here are some proofreading tips:

- All writers make mistakes when they put ideas on paper. Making mistakes isn't bad; you simply need to take the time to find and correct them.
- Let a paper sit several days, overnight, or at least a few hours before proofreading it.
- Budget enough time to proofread thoroughly.

- Read what you have written very slowly, looking at every word and letter. See what you have actually written, not what you think is there.
- Read your paper aloud. Speaking forces you to slow down and see more, and sometimes you will hear a mistake you haven't seen.
- Read the essay backward. This will force you to look at each word because you won't get caught up in the flow of ideas.
- Use a dictionary or a spell-checker whenever you can. Watch for common errors: misspellings, incorrect words, missing words, and other minor errors.
- Double-check for your habitual errors (such as leaving off -*s* or -*ed* or putting in unnecessary commas).
- Read your essay several times, focusing each time on a specific area of difficulty (once for spelling, once for punctuation, once for a problem that recurs in your writing).
- Ask someone else to read your paper and tell you if it is free of errors. But take pride in your own work. Don't let someone else do it for you.

■ ACTIVITY: Editing and Proofreading

Read the following passage carefully. Assume that its organization is fine, but look for more than ten errors in the paragraph. Find these mistakes in sentence structure, grammar, spelling, punctuation, and capitalization, and correct them. After you have corrected the passage, discuss with your classmates the changes you have made and your reasons for making them.

Robert Frost, one of the most popular American poets. He was born in San Francisco in 1874, and died in Boston in 1963. His family moved to new England when his father died in 1885. There he completed highschool and attended colledge but never graduate. Poverty and problems filled his life. He worked in a woolen mill, on a newspaper, and at varous odd jobs. Because of ill health, he settled on a farm and began to teach school to support his wife and children. Throughout his life he dedicated himself to writing poetry, by 1915 he was in demand for public readings and speaking engagements. He was awarded the Pulitzer Prize for poetry four times-in 1924, 1931, 1937, and 1943. The popularity of his poetry rests in his use of common themes and images, expressed in everyday language. Everyone can relate to his universal poems, such as "Birches" and "Stopping by Woods on a Snowy Evening." Students read his poetry from seventh grade through graduate school, so almost everyone recognize lines from his best-loved poems. America is proud of it's son, the homespun poet Robert Frost.

■ **ACTIVITY:** Proofreading in Pairs

Select a passage from this textbook or elsewhere that is about one hundred words long. Type up the passage, intentionally adding ten errors in grammar, spelling, punctuation, or capitalization. Swap passages with a classmate; proofread, and then check each other's work against the original. Share your proofreading strategies.

QUICK EDITING GUIDE DIRECTORY: CHECKLIST FOR COMMON AND SERIOUS PROBLEMS

Grammar Problems — Section

☐ Are any of your sentences actually fragments? — A1
☐ Are any of your sentences comma splices or fused sentences? — A2
☐ Have you used the correct form for all verbs in the past tense? — A3
☐ Do all verbs agree with their subjects? — A4
☐ Have you used the correct case for all pronouns? — A5
☐ Do all pronouns agree with their antecedents? — A6
☐ Have you used adjectives and adverbs correctly? — A7

Sentence Problems

☐ Does each modifier clearly modify the appropriate sentence element? — B1
☐ Have you used parallel structure where necessary? — B2

Punctuation Problems

☐ Have you used commas correctly? — C1
☐ Have you used apostrophes correctly? — C2
☐ Have you punctuated quotations correctly? — C3

Mechanics and Format Problems

☐ Have you used capital letters correctly? — D1
☐ Have you spelled all words correctly? — D2
☐ Have you used correct manuscript form? — D3

Quick Editing Guide

Editing and proofreading are needed at the end of the writing process because writers—all writers—find it difficult to write error-free sentences the first time they try. Sometimes as a writer you pay more attention to what you want to say than to how you say it. Sometimes you forget spelling or grammar or punctuation conventions. At other times you are distracted by events around you, or you simply make keyboarding errors. Once you are satisfied that you have expressed your ideas, you should make sure that each sentence, and word is concise, clear, and correct.

This Quick Editing Guide provides an overview of grammar, style, punctuation, and mechanics problems typical of college writing. Certain common errors in Standard Written English are like red flags to careful readers: they signal that the writer is either ignorant or careless. Use the Editing Checklist to check your paper for these problems; then use the editing checklists in each section to help you focus on and correct specific errors.

A   EDITING FOR COMMON GRAMMAR PROBLEMS

A1   Check for sentence fragments.

A complete sentence is one that has a subject,° has a predicate,° and can stand on its own. A *sentence fragment* lacks a subject, a predicate, or both, or for some other reason fails to convey a complete thought. It cannot stand on its own as a sentence.

Although they are common in advertising and fiction, fragments are usually ineffective in college writing because they do not communicate coherent thoughts. To edit for fragments, examine each sentence carefully to make sure that it has a subject and a verb and that it expresses a complete thought. To correct a fragment, you can make it into a complete sentence by adding a missing part, dropping an unnecessary subordinating conjunction,° or joining it to a complete sentence nearby, if that would make more sense.

subject: The part of a sentence that names something—a person, an object, an idea, a situation—about which the predicate makes an assertion: The *king* lives.   predicate: The part of a sentence that makes an assertion about the subject involving an action (Birds *fly*), a relationship (Birds *have feathers*), or a state of being (Birds *are warm-blooded*)   subordinating conjunction: A word (such as *because, although, if, when*) used to make one clause dependent on, or subordinate to, another: *Unless* you have a key, we are locked out.

FRAGMENT	Roberto has two sisters. Maya and Leeza.
CORRECT	Roberto has two sisters, Maya and Leeza.

FRAGMENT	The children going to the zoo.
CORRECT	The children were going to the zoo.
CORRECT	The children going to the zoo were caught in a traffic jam.

FRAGMENT	Last night when we saw Cameron Diaz's most recent movie.
CORRECT	Last night we saw Cameron Diaz's most recent movie.

EDITING CHECKLIST FOR FRAGMENTS

☐ Does the sentence have a subject?

☐ Does the sentence have a complete verb?

☐ If the sentence contains a subordinate clause, does it contain a clause that is a complete sentence too?

☐ If you find a fragment, can you link it to an adjoining sentence, eliminate its subordinating conjunction, or add a missing element?

A2   Check for comma splices or fused sentences.

A complete sentence has a subject and a predicate and can stand on its own. When two sentences are joined together to form one sentence, each sentence within the larger one is called a main clause.° However, there are rules for joining main clauses. When writers fail to follow these rules, they create serious sentence errors—comma splices or fused sentences. A *comma splice* is two main clauses joined with only a comma. A *fused sentence* is two main clauses joined with no punctuation at all.

COMMA SPLICE	I went to the mall, I bought a CD by a new group.
FUSED SENTENCE	I went to the mall I bought a CD by a new group.

---

main clause: A group of words that has both a subject and a verb and can stand alone as a complete sentence: *My sister has a car.*

To find comma splices and fused sentences, examine each sentence to be sure it is complete. If it has two main clauses, make sure they are joined correctly. If you find a comma splice or fused sentence, correct it in one of these four ways, depending on which makes the best sense:

ADD A PERIOD	I went to the mall. I bought a CD by a new group.
ADD A COMMA AND A COORDINATING CONJUNCTION°	I went to the mall, and I bought a CD by a new group.
ADD A SEMICOLON	I went to the mall; I bought a CD by a new group.
ADD A SUBORDINATING CONJUNCTION°	I went to the mall before I bought a CD by a new group.

EDITING CHECKLIST FOR COMMA SPLICES AND FUSED SENTENCES

☐ Can you make each main clause a separate sentence?

☐ Can you link the two main clauses with a comma and a coordinating conjunction?

☐ Can you link the two main clauses with a semicolon or, if appropriate, a colon?

☐ Can you subordinate one clause to the other?

A3 Check for correct past-tense verb forms.

The *form* of a verb,° the way it is spelled and pronounced, can change to show its *tense* — the time when its action did, does, or will occur (in the past, present, or future). A verb about something in the present often is spelled and pronounced differently than a verb about something in the past.

PRESENT	Right now, I *watch* only a few minutes of television each day.
PAST	Last month, I *watched* television every evening.

---

coordinating conjunction: A one-syllable linking word (*and, but, for, or, nor, so, yet*) that joins elements with equal or near-equal importance: Jack *and* Jill, sink *or* swim
subordinating conjunction: A word (such as *because, although, if, when*) used to make one clause dependent on, or subordinate to, another: *Unless* you have a key, we are locked out   **verb:** A word that shows action (The cow *jumped* over the moon) or a state of being (The cow *is* brown).

Many writers fail to use the correct form for a verb in the past tense because they leave off the past tense ending on a regular verb or forget the past tense form of an irregular verb.

Regular verbs are verbs that form the past tense following the standard rule, by adding -ed or -d to the end of the present tense form: *watch/watched, look/looked, hope/hoped.* Check all regular verbs in the past tense to be sure you have used one of these endings.

FAULTY   I *ask* my brother for a loan yesterday.
CORRECT   I *asked* my brother for a loan yesterday.

FAULTY   Nicole *race* in the track meet last week.
CORRECT   Nicole *raced* in the track meet last week.

TIP: If you say the final -d sound when you talk, you may find it easier to remember add the final -d or -ed when you write past tense regular verbs.

Irregular verbs do not follow the standard rules to form the past tense, as Table 9.1 shows. Instead, their unpredictable past tense forms are different from their base forms and thus have to be memorized: *eat/ate, see/saw, get/got.* In addition, the past tense form may differ from the past participle:° "She *ate* the whole pie; she *has eaten* two pies this week." The most troublesome irregular verbs are actually very common, so if you make the effort to learn the correct forms, you will quickly improve your writing.

FAULTY   My cat *laid* on the tile floor to take her nap.
CORRECT   My cat *lay* on the tile floor to take her nap.

FAULTY   I *have swam* twenty laps every day this month.
CORRECT   I *have swum* twenty laps every day this month.

TIP: In your college papers, follow convention by using the present tense, not the past, to describe the work of an author or the events in a literary work.

FAULTY   In "The Lottery," Shirley Jackson *revealed* the power of tradition. As the story *opened,* the villagers *gathered* in the square.
CORRECT   In "The Lottery," Shirley Jackson *reveals* the power of tradition. As the story *opens,* the villagers *gather* in the square.

---

participle: A form of a verb that cannot function alone as a main verb, including present participles, which end in -ing *(dancing),* and past participles, which often end in -ed or -d *(danced)*

EDITING CHECKLIST FOR PAST TENSE VERB FORMS

☐ Have you identified the main verb in the sentence?

☐ Is the sentence about the past, the present, or the future? Does the verb reflect this sense of time?

☐ Is the verb regular or irregular?

☐ Have you used the correct form to express your meaning?

TABLE 9.1   Principal Parts of Common Irregular Verbs

Base Form	Past Tense	Past Participle
be	was	been
become	became	become
begin	began	begun
blow	blew	blown
break	broke	broken
bring	brought	brought
burst	burst	burst
catch	caught	caught
choose	chose	chosen
come	came	come
do	did	done
draw	drew	drawn
drink	drank	drunk
drive	drove	driven
eat	ate	eaten
fall	fell	fallen
fight	fought	fought
freeze	froze	frozen
get	got	got, gotten
give	gave	given
go	went	gone
grow	grew	grown
have	had	had
hear	heard	heard

Base Form	Past Tense	Past Participle
hide	hid	hidden
know	knew	known
lay	laid	laid
lead	led	led
let	let	let
lie	lay	lain
make	made	made
raise	raised	raised
ride	rode	ridden
ring	rang	rung
rise	rose	risen
run	ran	run
say	said	said
see	saw	seen
set	set	set
sing	sang	sung
sit	sat	sat
slay	slew	slain
slide	slid	slid
speak	spoke	spoken
spin	spun	spun
stand	stood	stood
steal	stole	stolen
swim	swam	swum
swing	swung	swung
teach	taught	taught
tear	tore	torn
think	thought	thought
throw	threw	thrown
wake	woke, waked	woken, waked
write	wrote	written

For the forms of irregular verbs not in this table, consult your dictionary. (Some dictionaries list principal parts for all verbs, some just for irregular verbs.)

A4   Check for subject-verb agreement.

The **form** of a verb,° the way it is spelled and pronounced, can change to show **number**—whether the subject° is singular (one) or plural (more than one). It can also show **person**—whether the subject is *you* or *she,* for example.

SINGULAR	Our instructor *grades* every paper carefully.
PLURAL	Most instructors *grade* tests using a standard scale.
SECOND PERSON	You *write* well-documented research papers.
THIRD PERSON	She *writes* good research papers, too.

A verb must match, or *agree with,* its subject in terms of number and person. Regular verbs (those that follow a standard rule to make the different forms) are problems only in the present tense, where they have two forms: one that ends in *-s* or *-es* and one that does not. Only the subjects *he, she, it,* and singular nouns use the verb form that ends in *-s* or *-es.*

I like	we like	Dan like**s**
you like	you like	the child like**s**
he/she/it like**s**	they like	the children like

The verbs *be* and *have* do not follow the *-s/no -s* pattern to form the present tense; they are irregular verbs, so their forms must be memorized. The verb *be* is also irregular in the past tense (Table 9.2).

Problems in agreement often occur when the subject is difficult to find, is an indefinite pronoun° or is confusing for some other reason. In particular, make sure that you have not left off any *-s* or *-es* endings and that you have used the correct form for irregular verbs (see Table 9.1).

FAULTY	Jim *write* his research papers on a computer.
CORRECT	Jim *writes* his research papers on a computer.

FAULTY	The students *has* difficulty with the assignment.
CORRECT	The students *have* difficulty with the assignment.

FAULTY	Every one of the cakes *were* sold at the church bazaar.
CORRECT	Every one of the cakes *was* sold at the church bazaar.

verb: A word that shows action (The cow *jumped* over the moon) or a state of being (The cow *is* brown)   **subject:** The part of a sentence that names something—a person, an object, an idea, a situation—about which the predicate makes an assertion: The *king* lives.   **indefinite pronoun:** A pronoun that stands for an unspecified person or thing, including singular forms (*each, everyone, no one*) and plural forms (*both, few*): *Everyone* is soaking wet.

TABLE 9.2   Forms of *be* and *have*

Verb	Present Tense	Past Tense
be	I am	I was
	you are	you were
	he/she/it is	he/she/it was
	we are	we were
	you are	you were
	they are	they were
have	I have	I had
	you have	you had
	he/she/it has	he/she/it had
	we have	we had
	you have	you had
	they have	they had

EDITING CHECKLIST FOR SUBJECT-VERB AGREEMENT

☐ Have you correctly identified the subject and the verb in the sentence?

☐ Is the subject singular or plural? Does the verb match?

☐ Have you used the correct form of the verb?

A5   Check for correct pronoun case.

Depending on the role a pronoun° plays in a sentence, it is said to be in the *subjective case, objective case*, or *possessive case*. Use the subjective case if the pronoun is the subject° of a sentence, the subject of a subordinate clause, or a subject complement° (after a linking verb). Use the objective case if the pronoun is a direct or indirect object° of a verb or the object of a preposition. Use the possessive case to show possession.

---

pronoun: A word that stands in place of a noun (*he, him,* or *his* for *Nate*)   **subject:** The part of a sentence that names something—a person, an object, an idea, a situation—about which the predicate makes an assertion: The *king* lives.   **subject complement:** A noun, an adjective, or a group of words that follows a linking verb (*is, become, feel, seem,* or another verb that shows a state of being) and that renames or describes the subject: This plum tastes *ripe*.   **object:** The target or recipient of the action of a verb: Some geese bite *people*.

TABLE 9.3   Pronoun Cases

Subjective	Objective	Possessive
I	me	my, mine
you	you	your, yours
he	him	his
she	her	hers
it	it	its
we	us	our, ours
they	them	their, theirs
who	whom	whose

SUBJECTIVE   *I* will argue that our campus needs more parking.

OBJECTIVE   This issue is important to *me.*

POSSESSIVE   *My* argument will be quite persuasive.

There are many types of pronouns, but only some change form to show case. The personal pronouns *I, you, he, she, it, we,* and *they* and the relative pronoun *who* each have at least two forms (Table 9.3).

There are two common errors in pronoun case. First, writers often use the subjective case when they should use the objective case—sometimes because they are trying to sound formal and correct. Instead, choose the correct form for a personal pronoun based on its function in the sentence. If the sentence pairs a noun and a pronoun, try the sentence with the pronoun alone.

FAULTY   My company gave my husband and *I* a trip to Hawaii.

TRIAL   My company gave I a trip?

CORRECT   My company gave my husband and *me* a trip to Hawaii.

FAULTY   The argument occurred because my uncle and *me* had different expectations.

TRIAL   Me had different expectations?

CORRECT   The argument occurred because my uncle and *I* had different expectations.

If the sentence leaves out implied words, try filling them in.

FAULTY	Jack ran faster than *me.*
TRIAL	Jack ran faster than me ran.
CORRECT	Jack ran faster than *I.*

The second common error with pronoun case involves gerunds.° Whenever you need a pronoun to modify a gerund, use the possessive case.

FAULTY	Our supervisor disapproves of *us* talking in the hallway.
CORRECT	Our supervisor disapproves of *our* talking in the hallway.

EDITING CHECKLIST FOR PRONOUN CASE

☐ Have you identified all the pronouns in the sentence?
☐ Does each one function as a subject, an object, or a possessive?
☐ Given the function of each pronoun, have you used the correct form?

A6   Check for pronoun-antecedent agreement.

The *form* of a pronoun,° the way it is spelled and pronounced, changes depending on its use in a particular sentence. The form can change to show *number*—whether the subject is singular (one) or plural (more than one). It can change to show *gender*—masculine, feminine, or neuter. It can also change to show *person*—first (*I, we*), second (*you*), or third (*he, she, it, they*).

SINGULAR	My brother took *his* coat and left.
PLURAL	My brothers took *their* coats and left.

MASCULINE	I talked to Steven before *he* had a chance to leave.
FEMININE	I talked to Stephanie before *she* had a chance to leave.

FIRST PERSON	*I* ordered a sandwich.
THIRD PERSON	*She* ordered a sandwich.

---

gerund: A form of a verb, ending in *-ing,* that functions as a noun: Lacey likes *playing* in the steel band.   **pronoun:** A word that stands in place of a noun (*he, him,* or *his* for *Nate*).

In most cases, a pronoun refers to a specific noun or pronoun mentioned nearby; that word is called the pronoun's ***antecedent.*** The connection between the pronoun and the antecedent must be clear so that readers know what the pronoun means in the sentence. One way to make this connection clear is to be sure that the pronoun and the antecedent match (or *agree*) in number and gender.

A common error in pronoun agreement is using a plural pronoun to refer to a singular antecedent. This error often crops up when the antecedent is difficult to find, when the antecedent is an indefinite pronoun, or when the antecedent is confusing for some other reason. When editing for pronoun-antecedent agreement, look carefully to find the correct antecedent, and then make sure you know whether it is singular or plural. Then make the pronoun match its antecedent.

FAULTY   Each of the boys in the Classic Club has *their* own rebuilt car.

CORRECT   Each of the boys in the Classic Club has *his* own rebuilt car.

[The word *each,* not *boys,* is the antecedent. *Each* is an indefinite pronoun and is always singular, so any pronoun referring to it must be singular as well.]

FAULTY   Everyone in the meeting had *their* own cell phone.

CORRECT   Everyone in the meeting had *his or her* own cell phone.

[*Everyone* is an indefinite pronoun that is always singular, so any pronoun referring to it must be singular as well.]

FAULTY   Neither Juanita nor Paula has received approval of *their* financial aid yet.

CORRECT   Neither Juanita nor Paula has received approval of *her* financial aid yet.

[*Neither Juanita nor Paula* is a compound subject joined by *nor.* Any pronoun referring to it must agree with only the nearer part of the compound. In other words, *her* needs to agree with *Paula,* which is singular.]

Indefinite pronouns as antecedents are troublesome when they are grammatically singular but create a plural image in the writer's mind. Fortunately, most indefinite pronouns are either always singular or always plural (Table 9.4). A few (such as *some* or *all*) can vary in number to fit the noun represented.

SINGULAR   *Some* of the stew lost *its* flavor.

PLURAL   *Some* of the players lost *their* equipment.

TABLE 9.4   Indefinite Pronouns

Always Singular			Always Plural
anybody	everyone	nothing	both
anyone	everything	one (of)	few
anything	much	somebody	many
each (of)	neither (of)	someone	several
either (of)	nobody	something	
everybody	no one		

EDITING CHECKLIST FOR PRONOUN-ANTECEDENT AGREEMENT

☐ Have you identified the antecedent for each pronoun?

☐ Is the antecedent singular or plural? Does the pronoun match?

☐ Is the antecedent masculine, feminine, or neuter? Does the pronoun match?

☐ Is the antecedent in the first, second, or third person? Does the pronoun match?

A7   Check for correct adjectives and adverbs.

Adjectives and **adverbs** are modifiers° that describe or give more information about (*modify*) other words in a sentence. Many adverbs are formed by adding *-ly* to adjectives: *simple/simply; quiet/quietly.* Because adjectives and adverbs resemble each other, writers sometimes mistakenly use one instead of the other. To edit, find the word that the adjective or adverb modifies. If that word is a noun or pronoun, use an adjective. (An adjective typically describes which or what kind.) If that word is a verb, adjective, or another adverb, use an adverb. (An adverb typically describes how, when, where, or why.)

FAULTY	Kelly ran into the house *quick.*
CORRECT	Kelly ran into the house *quickly.*

FAULTY	Gabriela looked *terribly* after her bout with the flu.
CORRECT	Gabriela looked *terrible* after her bout with the flu.

modifier: A word (such as an adjective or adverb), phrase, or clause that provides more information about another part of a sentence: Plays *staged by the drama class* are *always successful.*

TABLE 9.5   Comparison of Irregular Adjectives and Adverbs

Modifier	Positive	Comparative	Superlative
ADJECTIVES	good	better	best
	bad	worse	worst
	little	less, littler	least, littlest
	many, some, much	more	most
ADVERBS	well	better	best
	badly	worse	worst
	little	less	least

FAULTY   His scar healed so *good* that it was barely visible.
CORRECT   His scar healed so *well* that it was barely visible.

Adjectives and adverbs that have similar comparative and superlative forms can also cause trouble. Always ask whether you need an adjective or an adverb in the sentence, and then use the correct word.

EDITING CHECKLIST FOR ADJECTIVES AND ADVERBS

☐ Have you identified which word the adjective or adverb modifies?

☐ If the word modified is a noun or pronoun, have you used an adjective?

☐ If the word modified is a verb, adjective, or adverb, have you used an adverb?

☐ Have you used the correct comparative or superlative form?

B   EDITING TO ENSURE EFFECTIVE SENTENCES

B1   Check for misplaced and dangling modifiers.

For a sentence to be clear, the connection between a modifier° and the thing it modifies must be obvious. Usually a modifier should be placed right before or right after the sentence element it modifies. If the modifier is placed too close to some other sentence element, it is a ***misplaced modifier.*** If there is nothing in the sentence that the modifier can logically

---

modifier: A word (such as an adjective or adverb), phrase, or clause that provides more information about another part of a sentence: Plays *staged by the drama class* are *always successful.*

modify, it is a **_dangling modifier._** Both of these errors cause confusion for readers—and they sometimes create unintentionally humorous images. As you edit, be sure that a modifier is placed directly before or after the word being modified and that the connection between the two is clear.

MISPLACED   George found the leftovers when he visited in the refrigerator.

CORRECT   George found the leftovers in the refrigerator when he visited.

[In the faulty sentence, *in the refrigerator* seems to modify George's visit. Obviously the leftovers are in the refrigerator, not George.]

DANGLING   Looking out the window, the clouds were beautiful.

CORRECT   Looking out the window, I saw that the clouds were beautiful.

CORRECT   When I looked out the window, the clouds were beautiful.

[In the faulty sentence, *looking out the window* should modify *I,* not *the clouds,* but *I* is not in the sentence. The modifier is left without anything logical to modify—a dangling modifier. To correct this, the writer has to edit so that *I* is in the sentence.]

EDITING CHECKLIST FOR MISPLACED AND DANGLING MODIFIERS

☐ What is each modifier meant to modify? Is the modifier as close as possible to that sentence element? Is any misreading possible?

☐ If a modifier is misplaced, can you move it to clarify the meaning?

☐ What noun or pronoun is a dangling modifier meant to modify? Can you make that word or phrase the subject of the main clause? Or can you turn the dangling modifier into a clause that includes the missing noun or pronoun?

B2   Check for parallel structure.

A series of words, phrases, clauses, or sentences with the same grammatical form is said to be **_parallel._** Using parallel form for elements that are parallel in meaning or function helps readers grasp the meaning of a sentence more easily. A lack of parallelism can distract, annoy, or even confuse readers.

To use parallelism, put nouns with nouns, verbs with verbs, and phrases with phrases. Parallelism is particularly important in a series, with correlative conjunctions,° and in comparisons using *than* or *as.*

FAULTY I like to go to Estes Park for skiing, ice skating, and to meet interesting people.

CORRECT I like to go to Estes Park to ski, to ice skate, and to meet interesting people.

FAULTY The proposal is neither practical, nor is it innovative.
CORRECT The proposal is neither practical nor innovative.

FAULTY A parent should have a few firm rules rather than having many flimsy ones.

CORRECT A parent should have a few firm rules rather than many flimsy ones.

Take special care to reinforce parallel structures by repeating articles, conjunctions, prepositions, or lead-in words as needed.

AWKWARD His dream was that he would never have to give up his routine but he would still find time to explore new frontiers.

PARALLEL His dream was that he would never have to give up his routine but *that* he would still find time to explore new frontiers.

EDITING CHECKLIST FOR PARALLEL STRUCTURE

☐ Are all the elements in a series in the same grammatical form?
☐ Are the elements in a comparison parallel in form?
☐ Are the articles, conjunctions, or prepositions between elements repeated rather than mixed or omitted?
☐ Are lead-in words repeated as needed?

correlative conjunction: A pair of linking words (such as *either/or, not only/but also*) that appear separately but work together to join elements of a sentence: *Neither* his friends *nor* hers like pizza.

C   EDITING FOR COMMON PUNCTUATION PROBLEMS

C1   Check for correct use of commas.

The *comma* is a punctuation mark that indicates a pause. By setting some words apart from others, commas help clarify relationships; they prevent the words on a page and the ideas they represent from becoming a jumble. Here are some of the most important conventional uses of commas:

- Use a comma before a coordinating conjunction *(and, but, for, or, so, yet, nor)* that joins two main clauses° in a compound sentence.

  The discussion was brief, *so* the meeting was adjourned early.

- Use a comma after an introductory word or word group unless it is short and cannot be misread.

  After the war, the North's economy developed rapidly.

- Use commas to separate the items in a series of three or more items.

  The chief advantages will be *speed, durability,* and *longevity.*

- Use commas to set off a modifying clause or phrase if it is nonrestrictive° rather than restrictive.°

  Good childcare, *which is difficult to find,* should be provided by the employer.

  Good childcare *that is reliable and inexpensive* is the right of every employee.

- Use commas to set off an appositive,° an expression that comes directly after a noun or pronoun and renames it, if it is nonrestrictive° rather than restrictive.°

  Sheri, my sister, has a new job as an events coordinator.

  My dog, Rover, is better trained than my cat, Sheba.

  My dog Rover is better trained than my dog Homer.

---

main clause: A group of words that has both a subject and a verb and can stand alone as a complete sentence: *My sister has a car.*   **nonrestrictive modifier:** an expression (set off by commas) that adds nonessential, though perhaps interesting or valuable, information that could be left out   **restrictive modifier:** an expression (not set off by commas) that adds limiting information, essential to specify what it modifies   **appositive:** A word or group of words that adds information about a subject or object by identifying it in a different way: my dog *Rover,* Hal's brother *Fred*

- Use commas to set off parenthetical expressions,° conjunctive adverbs,° and other interrupters.

  The proposal from the mayor's commission, however, is not feasible.

EDITING CHECKLIST FOR COMMAS

☐ Have you added a comma between two main clauses joined by a coordinating conjunction?

☐ Have you added the commas needed after introductory words or word groups?

☐ Have you separated items in a series with commas?

☐ Have you avoided putting commas before the first item in a series or after the last?

☐ Have you used commas before and after each nonrestrictive phrase or clause?

☐ Have you avoided using commas around a restrictive word, phrase, or clause?

☐ Have you used commas to set off parenthetical expressions, conjunctive adverbs, and other interrupters?

C2 Check for correct use of apostrophes.

An **apostrophe** is a punctuation mark that either shows possession *(Sylvia's)* or indicates that one or more letters have intentionally been left out to form a contraction *(didn't)*. Because apostrophes are easy to overlook, writers often omit a necessary apostrophe. They also may use an apostrophe where it is not needed or put one in the wrong place. An apostrophe is never used to create the possessive form of a personal pronoun; use the possessive pronoun form (Table 9.6) instead.

FAULTY   *Mikes* car was totaled in the accident.

CORRECT   *Mike's* car was totaled in the accident.

FAULTY   The principles of the *womens'* movement are still controversial to some people.

CORRECT   The principles of the *women's* movement are still controversial to some people.

parenthetical expression: An aside to readers or a transitional expression such as *for example* or *in contrast*   conjunctive adverb: A linking word that can connect independent clauses and show a relationship between two ideas: Armando is a serious student; *therefore,* he studies every day.

TABLE 9.6   Possessive Personal Pronouns

Personal Pronoun	Possessive Case
I	my, mine
you	your, yours (*not* your's)
he	his
she	her, hers (*not* her's)
it	its (*not* it's)
we	our, ours (*not* our's)
they	their, theirs (*not* their's)
who	whose (*not* who's)

FAULTY   Che *did'nt* want to stay home and study.
CORRECT   Che *didn't* want to stay home and study.

FAULTY   The dog wagged *it's* tail happily.
CORRECT   The dog wagged *its* tail happily.

FAULTY   *Its* raining.
CORRECT   *It's* raining. [it's = it is]

EDITING CHECKLIST FOR APOSTROPHES

☐ Have you used an apostrophe to create the possessive form of a noun?

☐ Have you used an apostrophe to show that letters have been left out in a contraction?

☐ Have you used the possessive case—rather than an apostrophe—to show that a pronoun is possessive?

☐ Have you used *it's* correctly (to mean *it is*)?

C3   Check for correct punctuation of quotations.

When you quote the exact words of a person you have interviewed or a source you have read, be sure to enclose those words in *quotation marks*. Notice how student Betsy Buffo presents the words of her subject in this excerpt from "Interview with an Artist."

> Derek is straightforward when asked about how his work is received in
> the local community: "My work is outside the mainstream. Because it's
> controversial, it's not easy for me to get exposure."

If your source is quoting someone else (a quotation within a quotation),
put your subject's words in quotation marks and the words he or she is
quoting in single quotation marks. Always put commas and periods inside
the quotation marks; put semicolons and colons outside.

Substitute an *ellipsis mark* (. . .) — three spaced dots — for any words
you have omitted from the middle of a direct quotation. If you are following MLA style, you may place ellipsis marks inside brackets ([. . .])
when necessary to avoid confusing your ellipsis marks with those of the
original writer. If an ellipsis mark comes at the end of a sentence, add
another period to conclude the sentence. You don't need an ellipsis mark
to show the beginning or ending of a quotation that is clearly incomplete. In this selection from "Playing Games with Women's Sports," student Kelly Grecian indicates two omissions from her quotation.

> "The importance of what women athletes wear can't be underestimated,"
> Rounds claims. "Beach volleyball, which is played . . . by bikini-clad women,
> rates network coverage. . . ." (44).

Common errors in punctuating quotations include leaving out
necessary punctuation marks or putting them in the incorrect place or
sequence. Each source-citation guide, such as MLA and APA, also recom-
mends its own preferences for presenting quotations. (See pp. 215–17 and
pp. 232–44.)

EDITING CHECKLIST FOR PUNCTUATION WITH QUOTATIONS

☐ Are the exact words quoted from your source enclosed in
quotation marks?

☐ Are commas and periods placed inside closing quotation
marks?

☐ Are colons and semicolons placed outside closing quotation
marks?

☐ Have you used an ellipsis mark to show where any words
have been omitted from the middle of a quotation?

D   EDITING FOR COMMON MECHANICS AND FORMAT PROBLEMS

D1   Check for correct use of capital letters.

Capital letters are used in three general situations: to begin a new sentence; to begin names of specific people, places, dates, and things (proper nouns); and to begin main words in titles. Writers sometimes use capital letters where they are not needed—for emphasis, for example—or fail to use them where they are needed.

> FAULTY   During my Sophomore year in College, I took World Literature, Biology, History, Psychology, and French—courses required for a Humanities Major.

> CORRECT   During my sophomore year in college, I took world literature, biology, history, psychology, and French—courses required for a humanities major.

EDITING CHECKLIST FOR CAPITALIZATION

☐ Have you used a capital letter at the beginning of each complete sentence, including sentences that are quoted?

☐ Have you used capital letters for proper nouns and pronouns?

☐ Have you avoided using capital letters for emphasis?

☐ Have you used a capital letter for each main word in a title, including the first word and the last word?

CAPITALIZATION AT A GLANCE

Capitalize the following cases.

THE FIRST LETTER OF A SENTENCE, INCLUDING A QUOTED SENTENCE

She called out, "Come in! The water's not cold."

PROPER NAMES AND ADJECTIVES MADE FROM THEM

| Marie Curie | Smithsonian Institution | a Freudian reading |

A RANK OR TITLE BEFORE A PROPER NAME

| Ms. Olson | Professor Santocolon | the president |

A FAMILY RELATIONSHIP ONLY WHEN IT SUBSTITUTES
FOR OR IS PART OF A PROPER NAME

| Grandma Jones | Father Time | my father |

RELIGIONS, THEIR FOLLOWERS, AND DEITIES

| Islam | Orthodox Jew | Buddha |

PLACES, REGIONS, AND GEOGRAPHIC FEATURES

| Palo Alto | the Midwest | the Berkshire Mountains |

DAYS OF THE WEEK, MONTHS, AND HOLIDAYS

| Wednesday | July | Labor Day |

HISTORICAL EVENTS, PERIODS, AND DOCUMENTS

| the Boston Tea Party | the Middle Ages | the Constitution |

SCHOOLS, COLLEGES, UNIVERSITIES, AND SPECIFIC COURSES

| Temple University | Introduction to Psychology | a psychology course |

FIRST, LAST, AND MAIN WORDS IN TITLES OF PAPERS, BOOKS,
ARTICLES, WORKS OF ART, TELEVISION SHOWS, POEMS, AND
PERFORMANCES

| *The Decline and Fall of the Roman Empire* | "The Road Not Taken" | *King Lear* |

D2   Check spelling.

Misspelled words are difficult to spot in your own writing. You usually
see what you think you wrote, and often pronunciation or faulty memory
interferes with correct spelling. When you proofread for spelling, check
especially for *homonyms,* words that sound alike but are spelled differently (Table 9.7); words that are spelled differently than they are pronounced; words that do not follow the basic rules for spelling English
words (Table 9.8); and words that you habitually confuse and misspell.

If you know the words you habitually misspell, you can use your software's Search or Find functions to locate all instances and check the spelling. Consider keeping track of misspelled words in your papers for a few weeks so you can take advantage of this feature to simplify your editing.

Spell-checkers offer a handy alternative to the dictionary, but you need to be aware of their limitations. A spell-checker compares the words in your text with the words listed in its dictionary, and it highlights words that do not appear there. (The size of computer spelling dictionaries varies greatly, but most contain fewer entries than a typical college-level dictionary in book form.) A spell-checker cannot help you spell words that its dictionary does not contain, including most proper nouns. Spell-checkers also ignore one-letter words: For example, they will not flag a typographical error such as *s truck* for *a truck*. Nor will they highlight words that are misspelled as different words—*their* for *there*, *to* for *too*, or *own* for *won*. Always check the spelling in your text by eye after you've used your spell-checker.

EDITING CHECKLIST FOR SPELLING

☐ Have you checked for the words you habitually misspell?

☐ Have you checked for commonly confused or misspelled words?

☐ Have you used any standard spelling rules, including their exceptions?

☐ Have you checked a dictionary for any words you are unsure about?

☐ Have you run your spell-checker? Have you read your paper carefully for errors that it would miss?

TABLE 9.7   Commonly Confused Homonyms

---

accept (v., receive willingly); **except** (prep., other than)

> Mimi could *accept* all of Lefty's gifts *except* his ring.

affect (v., influence); **effect** (n., result)

> If the new rules *affect* us, what will be their *effect*?

allusion (n., reference); **illusion** (n., fantasy)

> Any *allusion* to Norman's mother may revive his *illusion* that she is upstairs, alive, in her rocking chair.

(Continued)

TABLE 9.7 *(Continued)*

capital (adj., uppercase; n., seat of government); **capitol** (n., government building)

> The *Capitol* building in our nation's *capital* is spelled with a *capital C.*

cite (v., refer to); **sight** (n., vision or tourist attraction); site (n., place)

> Did you *cite* Aunt Peggy as your authority on which *sites* feature the most interesting *sights?*

complement (v., complete; n., counterpart); **compliment** (v. or n., praise)

> For Lee to say that Sheila's beauty *complements* her intelligence may or may not be a *compliment.*

desert (v., abandon; n., hot, dry region); **dessert** (n., end-of-meal sweet)

> Don't *desert* us by leaving for the *desert* before *dessert.*

elicit (v., bring out); **illicit** (adj., illegal)

> By going undercover, Sonny should *elicit* some offers of *illicit* drugs.

formally (adv., officially); **formerly** (adv., in the past)

> Jane and John Doe-Smith, *formerly* Jane Doe and John Smith, sent cards *formally* announcing their marriage.

led (v., past tense of *lead*); **lead** (n., a metal)

> Gil's heart was heavy as *lead* when he *led* the mourners to the grave.

principal (n. or adj., chief); **principle** (n., rule or standard)

> The *principal* problem is convincing the media that our school *principal* is a person of high *principles.*

stationary (adj., motionless); **stationery** (n., writing paper)

> Hubert's *stationery* shop stood *stationary* until a flood swept it away.

their (pron., belonging to them); **there** (adv., in that place); **they're** (contraction of *they are)*

> Sue said *they're* going over *there* to visit *their* aunt.

to (prep., toward); **too** (adv., also or excessively); **two** (n. or adj., numeral: one more than one)

> Let's not take *two* cars *to* town—that's *too* many unless Lucille and Harry are coming *too.*

who's (contraction of *who is*); **whose** (pron., belonging to whom)

> *Who's* going to tell me *whose* dog this is?

your (pron., belonging to you); **you're** (contraction of *you are)*

> *You're* not getting *your* own way this time!

Table 9.8   Commonly Misspelled Words

a lot	association	conscience
absence	athlete	conscientious
academic	athletics	conscious
acceptable	attendance	consistent
accessible	audience	controlled
accidentally	average	criticism
accommodate	awkward	criticize
achievement	basically	curiosity
acknowledgment	beginning	curious
acquaintance	believe	deceive
acquire	beneficial	decision
address	benefited	defendant
advertisement	breath (noun)	deficient
advice	breathe (verb)	definite
advise	bureaucracy	dependent
aggravate	business	descendant
aggressive	calendar	describe
aging	careful	description
all right	casualties	desirable
all together (in one group)	category	despair
allege	cemetery	desperate
already	certain	develop
although	changeable	development
altogether (entirely)	changing	device (noun)
amateur	characteristic	devise (verb)
analysis	chief	diary
analyze	choose (present tense)	difference
answer	chose (past tense)	dilemma
anxiety	climbed	dining
appearance	column	disappear
appetite	coming	disappoint
appreciate	commitment	disastrous
appropriate	committed	discipline
arctic	comparative	discussion
argument	competition	disease
ascent	conceive	dissatisfied
assassinate	condemn	
assistance	congratulate	*(Continued)*

TABLE 9.8 (Continued)

divide	fulfill	jealousy
doesn't	gaiety	judgment
dominant	genealogy	knowledge
don't	generally	laboratory
drunkenness	genuine	led (past tense of *lead*)
efficiency	government	library
eighth	grammar	license
either	grief	lightning
embarrass	guarantee	literature
entirety	guard	loneliness
environment	guidance	loose (adjective)
equipped	harass	lose (verb)
especially	height	lying
exaggerate	heroes	magazine
exceed	herring	maintenance
excel	humorous	marriage
excellence	illiterate	mathematics
exercise	illogical	medicine
exhaust	imitation	miniature
existence	immediately	mischievous
experience	incredible	misspell
explanation	indefinite	muscle
extremely	independence	mysterious
familiar	indispensable	necessary
fascinate	infinite	neither
February	influential	niece
fiery	intelligence	ninety
financial	intentionally	ninth
foreign	interest	noticeable
foresee	interpret	notorious
forth	interrupt	nuclear
forty	irrelevant	nucleus
forward	irresistible	numerous
fourth (number four)	irritable	obstacle
frantically	island	occasionally
fraternities	it's (it is, it has)	occur
friend	its (possessive)	occurrence

official

omission

omitted

opinion

opportunity

originally

outrageous

paid

pamphlet

panicky

parallel

particularly

pastime

peaceable

perceive

performance

permanent

permissible

persistence

personnel

persuade

physical

playwright

possession

possibly

practically

precede (go before)

predominant

preferred

prejudice

prevalent

privilege

probably

procedure

proceed (continue)

professor

prominent

pronounce

pronunciation

pursue

quantity

quiet

quite

quizzes

realize

rebelled

recede

receipt

receive

recipe

recommend

reference

referring

regrettable

relevance

relief

relieve

religious

remembrance

reminisce

reminiscence

repetition

representative

resistance

restaurant

review

rhythm

ridiculous

roommate

sacrifice

safety

scarcely

schedule

secretary

seize

separate

siege

similar

sincerely

sophomore

source

specifically

sponsor

strategy

strength

stretch

succeed

successful

suddenness

supersede

suppress

surprise

suspicious

technical

technique

temperature

tendency

therefore

thorough

thoroughbred

though

thought

throughout

tragedy

transferred

traveling

truly

twelfth

tyranny

unanimous

unnecessary

unnoticed

until

useful

(Continued)

TABLE 9.8 *(Continued)*

usually	warrant	whose (possessive of
valuable	weather	*who*)
vengeance	Wednesday	withhold
vicious	weird	woman
view	whether	women
villain	who's (who is)	

D3   Check for correct manuscript form.

In case you have received no particular instructions for the form of your paper, here are some general, all-purpose specifications.

General Manuscript Style for College Essays, Articles, and Reports

1. Pick a conventional, easy-to-read typeface such as Courier, Times New Roman, Helvetica, or Palatino. Make sure you have a fresh cartridge in your printer. If you handwrite your paper, make sure your handwriting is legible.
2. Print in black ink. Use dark blue or black ink if you write by hand.
3. Write or print on just one side of standard letter-size bond paper (8½ by 11 inches). If you handwrite your paper, use 8½-by-11-inch paper with smooth edges (not torn from a spiral-bound notebook).
4. For a paper without a separate title page, place your name, your instructor's name, the number and section of the course, and the date in the upper left or right corner of the first page, each item on a new line. (Ask whether your instructor has a preference for which side.) Double-space and center your title. Don't underline the title, don't put it in quotation marks or use all capital letters, and don't put a period after it. Capitalize the first and last words, the first word after a colon or semicolon, and all other words except prepositions,° coordinating conjunctions,° and articles.° Double-space between the title and the first line of your text. (Most instructors do not require a title page for short college papers. If your instructor asks for one but doesn't give you any guidelines, see the first item under Additional Suggestions for Research Papers, below.)

---

preposition: A word (such as *in, on, at, of, from*) that shows a connection and leads into a phrase   **coordinating conjunction:** A one-syllable linking word (*and, but, for, or, nor, so, yet*) that joins elements with equal or near-equal importance   **article:** The word *a, an,* or *the*

5. Number your pages consecutively, including the first page. For a paper of two or more pages, use a running header to put your last name in the upper right corner of each sheet along with the page number. (Use the Header option under View or Edit.) Do not type the word *page* or the letter *p* before the page number, and do not follow the number with a period or parenthesis.

6. Leave ample margins—at least an inch—left, right, top, and bottom.

7. If you use a word processor, double-space your manuscript; if you handwrite, use wide-ruled paper or skip every other line.

8. Indent each new paragraph five spaces or one-half inch.

9. Long quotations should be double-spaced like the rest of your paper but indented from the left margin—ten spaces (one inch) if you're following MLA (Modern Language Association) guidelines, five spaces (one-half inch) if you're using APA (American Psychological Association) guidelines. Put the source citation in parentheses immediately after the final punctuation mark of the block quotation. (See the examples on pp. 222–23 and pp. 236–37.)

10. Label all illustrations. Make sure any insertions are bound securely to the paper.

11. Staple the paper in the top left corner, or use a paper clip as MLA advises. Don't use any other method to secure the pages unless one is recommended by your instructor.

12. For safety's sake and peace of mind, make a copy of your paper, and back up your file.

Additional Suggestions for Research Papers

For research papers, the format is the same as recommended in the previous section, with the following additional specifications.

1. The MLA guidelines do not recommend a title page. If your instructor wants one, type the title of your paper, centered and double-spaced, about a third of the way down the page. Go down two to four more lines and type your name, the instructor's name, the number and section of the course, and the date, each on a separate line and double-spaced.

2. Do not number your title page; number your outline, if you submit one with your paper, with small roman numerals (i, ii, iii, and so on). Number consecutively all subsequent pages in the essay, including your works cited or references pages, using arabic numerals (1, 2, 3, and so on) in the upper right corner of the page.

3. Double-space your works cited or references list, if you have one.

How to Make a Correction

Before you produce your final copy, make any large changes in your draft, edit and proofread carefully, and run your spell-checker. When you give your paper a last once-over, however, don't be afraid to make small corrections in pen. In making last-minute corrections, you may find it handy to use these symbols and marks used by proofreaders. (See the last page of this book for a list of correction symbols.)

- A transposition mark ($\cap\cup$) reverses the positions of two words or two letters:

  The nearby star Tau Ceti closely resmebles our sun.

- Close-up marks ($\bigcirc$) bring together the parts of a word accidentally split. A separation mark (|) inserts a space where one is needed:

  The nearby star Tau Ceti closely re sembles our|sun.

- To delete a letter or punctuation mark, draw a line with a curlicue through it:

  The nearby star Tau Ceti closely ressembles our sun.

- Use a caret ($\wedge$) to indicate where to insert a word or letter:

  The nearby star Tau Ceti closely resemble our sun.
  ^s

- The symbol ¶ before a word or a line means "start a new paragraph":

  Recently, astronomers have reduced their efforts to study dark nebulae. ¶ That other solar systems may also support life makes for another fascinating speculation.

- To make a letter lowercase, draw a slanted line through it. To make a letter uppercase, put three short lines under it:

  i read it for my History class.

- You can always cross out a word neatly, with a single horizontal line, and write a better one above it:

  closely
  The nearby star Tau Ceti somewhat resembles our sun.

- Finally, if a page has many handwritten corrections on it, print or write it over again.

■ ACTIVITY: Editing with a Computer

Use your computer to help you read your draft more closely. For example, you can automatically isolate each sentence so that you are less likely to skip over sentence errors. After making a copy of the draft, select the Replace function in your software's Edit menu. Then ask the software to find every period in the file and replace it with a period and two returns. This change will create a version with every sentence separated by several spaces so that you can easily check each one for fragments, comma splices, and other problems. This draft also will reveal other characteristics of your sentences. For instance, should you see that most of your sentences are of the same length or begin in much the same way, you can edit to relieve the monotony.

You also may be able to search for your personal editing problems. Begin by keeping track of your mistakes or reviewing comments on past papers so that you can develop an "error hit list." Then use your software's Find and Replace function (probably in the Edit menu) to check quickly for some of these problems. For instance, you might search for *each* (always singular) or *few* (always plural) to see if all the verbs agree, for *its* and *it's* to turn up apostrophe errors, or for *There* to discover whether you have overused sentences beginning with *There is* or *There are*.

10

Strategies for Arguing

Both in class and outside of class, you'll hear controversial issues discussed—immigration policy, standardized testing, disaster preparedness, prayer in the schools, health insurance, global outsourcing of jobs, regulations to protect endangered species. In many fields of study, experts don't always agree, and some academic issues remain controversies for years. On the surface, these issues often are simplified, presented as either/or debates between two battling opponents. In reality, most civic discussions encompass multiple points of view, and most responses to problems need to incorporate multiple ideas and compromises. Whatever the issue or type of argument you tackle, you'll want to argue effectively as you acknowledge the exchanges around you.

DEVELOPING AN ARGUMENT

The strategies you have used for developing other papers may also be useful for an argument. (See Chs. 7 and 11.) However, readers typically expect an argument to be both logical and persuasive, and those expectations set the standard for your thesis, your reasons, and your supporting evidence. The following strategies should help you write powerful arguments that successfully appeal to readers.

Beginning with an Issue and a Thesis

A solid argument begins with a specific issue about which people hold different opinions. The issue might be a widely debated civic controversy (such as immigration policy) or a local matter (such as a zoning dispute). It might be a disagreement among researchers about the likely effects of a food additive or among readers about interpretations of a short story. Your working thesis states your initial position on an issue, usually a perspective you will refine as you gain understanding of the issue. (For more on thesis statements, see pp. 62–68.)

WORKING THESIS We should expect advertisers to fight rather than reinforce stereotypes of people with disabilities.

REVISED THESIS Consumers should spend their shopping dollars thoughtfully, holding advertisers accountable for feeding rather than fighting stereotypes of people with disabilities.

When you draft your argument paper, you will probably want to open with enough background about the issue to justify your concern about it and to help your readers appreciate the controversy. You'll need to define key terms, especially the words and expressions on which your points hinge. As you investigate the issue, you'll also identify or develop substantial reasons for agreeing with your thesis (and perhaps recognize a valid point or two that you'll need to counter). Your reasons will help you focus and build persuasive supporting paragraphs where you present the evidence to support your thesis.

Because a thesis identifies and states your position, it generally forms the basis of a strong argument. Use the following questions to help you improve yours.

THESIS CHECKLIST

☐ Have you stated your thesis clearly? Could you sharpen any vague or imprecise wording?

☐ Does your thesis stick to one main idea? Is it focused?

☐ Is your thesis stated positively, not negatively?

☐ Is your thesis limited? Can you support it with enough evidence in a short essay?

☐ Does your thesis need any other revision to attract your readers' attention?

Making a Claim

As you plan an argument, consider three general types of claims: those that require substantiation, endorse policy, and provide evaluation. Although these three categories overlap somewhat and often can be made about the same topic, you should develop the claim that is most likely to speak to your audience. Suppose, for example, that the local school board is examining a proposal for an early childhood center at South High for students' babies. High school students, their parents, school administrators, counselors, and early childhood specialists might all agree that an on-site facility would benefit the babies and their teen parents. They might disagree, however, about whether district policies allow the use of funds to support this kind of project or whether the facility's presence would be a good or bad influence on South High students who do not have children. Different claims and different evidence might appeal to each group in the effort to reach consensus.

Claims of Substantiation.   Claims of substantiation require examining and interpreting information to resolve disputes over facts, circumstances, causes or effects, definitions, or even the extent of a problem.

> Certain types of cigarette advertisements, such as the once-popular Joe Camel ads, significantly encourage smoking among teenagers.

> Despite a few well-publicized exceptions to the rule, police brutality is not a major problem in this country.

> On the whole, bilingual education programs help students learn English more quickly and more effectively than immersion programs do.

Claims of Policy.   Claims of policy challenge or defend methods of achieving generally accepted goals.

> The federal government should support the distribution of clean needles to reduce the rate of HIV infection among intravenous drug users.

> Denying illegal immigrant children enrollment in U.S. public schools will reduce the problem of illegal immigration.

> Any teenager accused of murder should be tried as an adult.

Claims of Evaluation.   Claims of evaluation consider the rightness, appropriateness, or worth of an issue.

> Research using fetal tissue is unethical in a civilized society.

> English-only legislation promotes cultural intolerance in our society.

> Allowing gays and lesbians to adopt children is immoral.

■ ACTIVITY: Making a Claim with a Group

Have each member of your group write out a one-sentence claim or position. Ask the group to suggest possible supporting evidence, opposing evidence, and arguments to counter the opposing evidence. When you are finished, have each writer reconsider his or her position based on the group's discussion.

Selecting Persuasive Evidence

Gather facts, statistics, expert testimony, firsthand observations, and other kinds of evidence to support your position and the type of claim you are making. Credible evidence is accurate, reliable, up-to-date, relevant, and representative. It also needs to be complex, not oversimplified, so that it is sufficient and strong enough to support your thesis and persuade your readers. Cluster and organize the evidence to back up your reasons for thinking as you do.

Besides hunting for evidence to support your stand, look carefully at the stands others take. Your evidence may easily persuade those who already agree with you; the challenge is to engage or persuade those who are undecided or who see things differently. Be sure to consider your own assumptions about both the nature of the issue and the authority of your view. What you assume, readers may question. Your best answer to such questions is compelling evidence. (For a checklist for testing evidence, see pp. 35–36. For criteria for research sources, see pp. 205–07.)

Use the following questions as a guide to building strong and persuasive evidence.

PERSUASIVE EVIDENCE CHECKLIST

☐ What do you assume about the issue and your stand? What seems unquestionably logical or true to you?

☐ What evidence supports your assumptions? How logical and relevant is that evidence?

☐ How can you integrate your evidence so that readers understand and perhaps come to share your assumptions?

☐ What are your readers likely to think about the issue? Which of their opinions or claims differ from yours?

☐ What evidence supports those other views? How logical and relevant is that evidence?

☐ What evidence can you use to show why those views are weak, only partially true, misguided, or just plain wrong?

☐ Which alternative views might you want to recognize, concede, or even integrate into your position?

☐ Which other views or evidence might you want to question or challenge?

Using Evidence to Support an Appeal

One way to select evidence and to judge whether it is appropriate and sufficient is to consider the types of appeal—logical, emotional, and ethical. Most effective arguments work on all three levels, using evidence that supports each type of appeal.

Logical Appeals (Logos).   When writers use a logical appeal (*logos* or "word" in Greek), they appeal to the reader's mind or intellect. This appeal relies on evidence that is factual, objective, clear, and relevant. Critical readers expect to find logical evidence supporting major claims and statements. For example, if a writer were arguing for term limits for legislators, she wouldn't want to base her argument on evidence that some long-term legislators weren't reelected last term (irrelevant) or that the current system is unfair to young people who want to get into politics (not logical). Instead she might argue that the absence of term limits encourages corruption, using evidence of legislators who repaid lobbyists for campaign contributions with key votes.

Emotional Appeals (Pathos).   When writers use an emotional appeal (*pathos* or "suffering" in Greek), they appeal to the reader's heart. They choose language, facts, quotations, examples, and images that evoke an emotional response. Of course, convincing writing does touch readers' hearts as well as their minds. Without this heartfelt tug, a strict logical appeal may seem cold and dehumanized. If a writer opposed hunting seals for their fur, he might combine statistics about the number of seals killed each year and the overall population decrease with a vivid description of baby seals being slaughtered. Some writers use emotional words and sentimental examples to manipulate readers—to arouse their sympathy, pity, or anger in order to convert them without much logical evidence—but dishonest emotional appeals may alienate readers. Instead of basing an argument against a political candidate on pitiful images of scrawny children living in roach-infested squalor, a good writer would report the candidate's voting record on issues that affect children.

Ethical Appeals (Ethos).   When writers use an ethical appeal (*ethos* or "character" in Greek), they call on the reader's sense of fairness and trust. They select and present evidence in a way that will make the audience trust them, respect their judgment, and believe what they have to say. The best logical argument in the world falls flat when readers don't take the writer seriously. How can you use an ethical appeal to establish your credibility as a writer? First, you need to establish your credentials in the field through experience, reading, or interviews that help you learn about the subject. If you are writing about environmental pollution, tell your readers that your allergies have been irritated by chemicals in the air. Identify medical or environmental experts you have contacted or whose publications you have read. Demonstrate your knowledge through the information you present, the experts and sources you cite, and the depth of understanding you convey. Establish a rapport with readers by pointing to values and attitudes you share with them and by responding seriously to opposing arguments. Finally, use language that is precise, clear, and appropriate in tone.

The logical appeal engages readers' intellect; the emotional appeal touches their hearts; the ethical appeal draws on their sense of fairness and reasonableness. A persuasive argument usually operates on all three levels. For example, you might develop a thesis about the need to curb accidental gunshot deaths in your county, as Table 10.1 illustrates.

TABLE 10.1   Appeals and Evidence: Curbing Accidental Gunshot Deaths

Type of Appeal	Ways of Making the Appeal	Possible Supporting Evidence
Logical (logos)	• Rely on clear reasoning and sound evidence to influence your readers' thinking. • Demonstrate what you claim, and don't claim what you can't demonstrate. • Test and select your evidence.	• Supply current and reliable statistics about gun ownership and accidental shootings. • Prepare a bar graph that shows the number of incidents during the past ten years, using data from the county records. • Describe the immediate and long-term consequences of a typical shooting accident.
Emotional (pathos)	• Choose examples and language that will influence your readers' feelings. • Include effective images, but don't overdo them. • Complement logical appeals, but don't replace them.	• Describe the wrenching scenario of a father whose college-age son unexpectedly returns home at 3:00 A.M. The father mistakes his son for an intruder and shoots him, throwing the family into turmoil.

(Continued)

TABLE 10.1   (Continued)

Type of Appeal	Ways of Making the Appeal	Possible Supporting Evidence
Emotional (pathos) cont.		• Use quotations and descriptions from newspaper accounts to show the reactions of family members and neighbors.
Ethical (ethos)	• Use a tone and approach that appeal to your readers' sense of fairness and reasonableness. • Spell out your values and beliefs, and acknowledge the values and beliefs of others with different opinions. • Establish your credentials, if any, and the credentials of experts you cite. • Instill confidence in your readers so that they see you as a caring, trustworthy person with reliable views.	• Establish your reasonableness by acknowledging the views of hunters and others who store guns at home and follow recommended safety procedures. • Supply the credentials or affiliation of experts ("Raymond Fontaine, public safety director for the county"). • Note ways in which experts have established their authority ("During my interview with Ms. Dutton, she related several recent incidents involving gun accidents in the home, testifying to her extensive knowledge of this issue in our community.").

■ **ACTIVITY:** Identifying Types of Appeals

Bring to class the editorial or opinion page from a newspaper or newsmagazine. Read some of the letters or articles. Identify the types of appeals each author uses to support his or her point.

Reasoning Logically

Why do you have to be logical? Isn't it enough just to tell everybody else what you think? That tactic probably works fine when you and your friends are solving the problems of the world at two in the morning. After all, your friends already know you, your opinions, and the way you typically think. They may even find your occasional rant entertaining. Whether they agree or disagree with you, they probably tolerate your ideas because they are your friends.

When you write an argument paper in college, however, you face a different type of audience, one that needs to learn what you assume, what you advocate, and why you hold to that position. Your readers also want to learn the specifics of your argument—the reasons you find compelling, the evidence that supports your views, and the connections that relate each point to your position. Finally, they expect reasoning, not pleading or bullying. How you reason—and how you present your reasoning—is an important part of gaining readers' confidence, acknowledgment, and eventual agreement.

As you plan a particular college paper, read the assignment carefully. It may suggest the kind of reasoning or evidence that your instructor will find logical. The readings that accompany the assignment may do the same, acting as strong or weak examples of the kind of argument assigned or as reliable sources for supporting evidence. In addition, a college writing assignment often assumes that you are contributing to an exchange of knowledge. It expects you to draw on the opinions and supporting evidence of others. Your argument, however, needs to integrate the work of others with your own views and to supply logical transitions that connect each idea or bit of evidence with the next. Use the following questions as you plan your draft or revise it, refining your reasoning and demonstrating it to others.

LOGICAL REASONING CHECKLIST

☐ Have you built your argument on a solid foundation? Are your premises, your initial assumptions, sound?

☐ Is your thesis or claim clearly stated? Are its terms explained or defined?

☐ What are your reasons or supporting arguments for thinking that your thesis is sound? Have you identified and arranged them in a sequence that will persuade your audience? Have you used transitions to introduce them so that readers can't miss them?

☐ Have you located and identified credible evidence to support each reason you present? Have you favored objective, research-based evidence (facts, statistics, and expert testimony) rather than personal experiences or beliefs?

☐ Have you explained and connected your evidence so that your audience can see how it applies or relates to your argument? Have you added transitions to clarify those relationships for readers?

☐ Have you enhanced your own credibility by acknowledging other points of view? Have you effectively integrated or countered those views?

☐ Have you adjusted your tone and style so that you come across as reasonable and fair-minded? Have you avoided arrogant claims about proving (rather than showing) points? Have you avoided wishy-washy evasions?

☐ Have you credited all your sources?

Avoiding Logical Fallacies

Logical fallacies are common mistakes in thinking that may lead to faulty conclusions or distort evidence. Table 10.2 describes a few of the most familiar logical fallacies.

TABLE 10.2   Recognizing Logical Fallacies

Term and Explanation	Example
Non sequitur: Stating a claim that doesn't follow from your first premise or statement; Latin for "It does not follow"	Liza should marry Mateo. In college he got all A's.
Oversimplification: Offering easy solutions for complicated problems	If we want to end substance abuse, let's send every drug user to prison for life. [Even aspirin users?]
Post hoc, ergo propter hoc: Assuming a cause-and-effect relationship where none exists even though one event preceded another; Latin for "after this, therefore because of this"	After Jenny's black cat crossed my path, everything went wrong, and I failed my midterm.
Allness: Stating or implying that something is true of an entire class of things, often using *all, everyone, no one, always,* or *never*	Students enjoy studying. [All students? All subjects? All the time?]
Proof by example or too few examples: Presenting an example as proof rather than as illustration or clarification; overgeneralizing (the basis of much prejudice)	Armenians are great chefs. My neighbor is Armenian, and can he cook!

Term and Explanation	Example
Begging the question: Proving a statement already taken for granted, often by repeating it in different words or by defining a word in terms of itself	Rapists are dangerous because they are menaces. Happiness is the state of being happy.
Circular reasoning: Supporting a statement with itself; a form of begging the question	He is a liar because he simply isn't telling the truth.
Either/or reasoning: Oversimplifying by assuming that an issue has only two sides, a statement must be true or false, a question demands a yes or no answer, or a problem has only two possible solutions (and one that's acceptable)	What are we going to do about acid rain? Either we shut down all the factories that cause it, or we just learn to live with it.
Argument from dubious authority: Using an unidentified authority to shore up a weak argument or an authority whose expertise lies outside the issue, such as a TV personality selling insurance	According to some of the most knowledgeable scientists in America, smoking two packs a day is as harmless as eating oatmeal cookies.
Argument ad hominem: Attacking an individual's opinion by attacking his or her character, thus deflecting attention from the merit of a proposal; Latin for "against the man"	Carruthers may argue that we need to save the whales, but he's the type who gets emotional over everything.
Argument from ignorance: Maintaining that a claim has to be accepted because it hasn't been disproved or that it has to be rejected because it hasn't been proved	Despite years of effort, no one has proved that ghosts don't exist; therefore, we should expect to see them at any time. No one has ever shown that life exists on any other planet; clearly the notion of other living things in the universe is absurd.
Argument by analogy: Showing the similarities between familiar and unfamiliar items (while ignoring differences) as evidence rather than as a useful way of explaining	People are born free as the birds; it's cruel to expect them to work.
Bandwagon argument: Suggesting that everyone is joining the group and that readers who don't may miss out on happiness, success, or a reward	Purchasing the new Swallowtail admits you to the nation's most elite group of drivers.

■ **ACTIVITY:** Checking for Logical Reasoning

Gather a small collection of print or online editorials and letters to the editor. (Consider your campus or community newspaper as well as big-city or national publications.) Working with a partner from your class, sort through these examples, looking for both reasonable and flawed arguments. Analyze several of these by identifying the claims and appeals, outlining the sequence of points, and evaluating the supporting evidence. Present to classmates your conclusions about what strengthens or weakens an argument.

PRESENTING YOUR ARGUMENT

After you have worked out your argument and found evidence to substantiate it, you need to shape it into final form for readers. To influence your audience as you hope, you will need a carefully crafted argument. Many arguments follow this long-established pattern:

1. Introduce your topic in a way that will interest your readers.
2. State your thesis.
3. Provide an overview of the situation along with any necessary or useful background.
4. Present the reasons that support your thesis or the points that justify it, along with persuasive supporting evidence.
5. Acknowledge opposing points of view, conceding or challenging them as appropriate.
6. Reaffirm your main point.

Argument assignments, like civic and academic exchanges, may take many forms. Common types include taking a stand on an issue, proposing a solution to a problem, and evaluating something according to specific criteria. The purposes and challenges of these typical arguments are briefly reviewed in this section.

Taking a Stand

A common argument assignment is to take a stand on a controversy that engages your interest. Taking a stand on an issue will help you understand the controversy and clarify what you believe. Writing of this kind serves a twofold purpose: (1) to state an opinion and (2) to win your readers' respect for it. To do so effectively, you must first know exactly where you stand and why. You will need to state what you believe, give reasons with evidence to support your position, enlist your readers' trust, respect what your readers are likely to think and feel, and choose strategies that will garner their support.

Your major challenge will be gathering enough relevant evidence to support your position. Without that evidence, you'll convince only those who agreed with you in the first place. You also won't persuade readers by ranting, insulting those who disagree with you, or being wishy-washy. Instead, build respect—yours for the views of your readers and theirs for you—by anticipating their objections, showing awareness of alternate views, and presenting evidence that both addresses the concerns of others and strengthens your argument.

TAKING A STAND CHECKLIST

☐ Have you selected an issue or controversy that you know and care about?

☐ Have you settled on your position and identified alternative or opposing views?

☐ Have you identified the main reasons for your view or the main persuasive points that justify it?

☐ Have you gathered enough relevant evidence to support your position?

☐ Have you defined all the critical or potentially ambiguous key terms that you plan to use in your argument?

☐ Have you respectfully anticipated the objections and arguments that your skeptical readers are likely to make?

☐ Have you sustained a suitable tone—that is, a tone neither hostile nor weakly apologetic?

Proposing a Solution

Sometimes when you learn about a problem—global warming, homelessness, or famine, for example—you say to yourself, "Something should be done about that." You can do something constructive yourself by writing powerfully and persuasively. Your purpose in this type of writing, as politicians and advertisers well know, is to rouse your audience to action. That's what Thomas Jefferson and the others who wrote the Declaration of Independence did, and it's what you can do even in your daily life at college. Does some school policy irk you? Do you think students should attend a rally for a cause or an organization? Do you want to encourage members of your college community to volunteer for a worthy effort? You can write a letter to your college newspaper or to someone in authority in order to stir your readers to action. The major challenge writers face in a proposal is developing a detailed and convincing solution. Finding problems is much easier than finding solutions. To generate a viable solution, begin with a close analysis of the problem. Try to understand how it might affect different groups of people—conservatives and liberals, parents and children, men and women, for example. Your task then is to propose a realistic way to solve or alleviate the problem while addressing readers' concerns about all aspects of the problem.

PROPOSING A SOLUTION CHECKLIST

☐ Have you identified a problem or a condition in need of improvement?

☐ Have you analyzed the problem to determine its impact?

☐ Have you included background information and evidence to substantiate the nature and severity of the problem?

☐ Have you noted any experiences or beliefs that qualify you to recommend a solution to the problem?

☐ Have you proposed a realistic solution that would solve the problem in ways that make sense to your audience? Have you supplied logical and persuasive reasons in support of your solution?

☐ Have you conveyed the practicality of your solution by estimating the resources and time needed for implementation, outlining step-by-step actions for implementation, and anticipating possible difficulties?

Writing an Evaluation

Evaluating means judging. You evaluate when you decide which candidate gets your vote, pick which digital camera to buy, watch a game and size up a team's prowess, or recommend a new restaurant to your friends. In everyday situations, people often make snap judgments, but writing an evaluation calls for critical thinking. (See Ch. 3.) A written evaluation begins with a specific subject. Then you must decide on criteria, or standards for judging, and apply them to your subject. You inspect the subject carefully and come to a considered opinion based on evidence that backs up your judgment.

In writing an evaluation, your purpose is twofold: (1) to set forth your assessment of the quality of your subject and (2) to convince your readers that your judgment is reasonable. Your major challenge is to make clear to readers your criteria for arriving at your opinion. Identify the features or standards you'll use for evaluating your topic, briefly explain each of them, and then consider what judgment or evaluation the criteria support. Doing so will help you move from an unsubstantiated opinion or a neutral summary to a judgment that you can justify to your readers.

MAKING A JUDGMENT CHECKLIST

☐ Have you selected something to evaluate that deserves thoughtful consideration?

☐ What criteria do you plan to use in making your evaluation? Are they clear and reasonably easy to apply?

☐ Have you reached a clear judgment? Have you supplied evidence to support each of the reasons for your evaluation?

☐ Have you been fair and reasonable? Have you acknowledged the disadvantages or faults of something you champion? Have you acknowledged any virtues of something you condemn?

☐ Have you anticipated and answered any possible objections of your audience?

■ ACTIVITY: Responding to an Argument with a Group

Working with a small group, exchange the drafts of your argument papers. Ask each reader to identify the writer's thesis and most persuasive evidence and then to present them to the group. Let the group suggest additional logical reasons or points and evidence that might make the argument more compelling.

11

Strategies for Integrating Sources

College assignments often require you to find and use sources in your writing. This requirement is generally intended to guide, lead, or tug you into the intellectual exchange that underlies college writing, reading, and thinking. Whether you plan to use only a few sources or to conduct substantial research, you'll need to read, evaluate, and integrate your evidence ethically and effectively. You're probably wondering exactly how to do that. How can you tell if you've found a source of reliable support for your ideas? How can you record useful information so that it's easy to integrate in your writing? How can you smoothly add information from a source to your own writing? How should you identify where you found the information? This chapter will help you get started answering those questions.

SELECTING SUPPORTING EVIDENCE FOR YOUR WRITING

The value of every source remains potential until you capture its facts, statistics, expert testimony, examples, or other information in a form that you can incorporate into your paper. In addition, you must accurately credit, both in the text of your paper and in a final list, each source whose words or ideas you use. (Follow the advice of the Modern Language Association or the American Psychological Association, both illustrated here, or use whatever other system your instructor requires.) If you add source information skillfully and credit each source conscientiously, your research will probably accomplish its purpose: supporting your thesis so that your paper satisfies you and meets your readers' standards.

Evaluating Sources for Reliable and Appropriate Evidence

When you use evidence from sources to support the points you make in a college paper, both you and your readers are likely to hold two simple expectations:

- That your sources are reliable so that you can trust their information
- That the information you select from your sources is appropriate for your paper

After all, how could an unreliable source successfully support your ideas? And what could unsuitable or mismatched information contribute to your paper? The difficult task, of course, is learning how to judge what is reliable and appropriate. The following checklist suggests how you can use the time-tested reporter's questions—who, what, where, when, why, and how—to evaluate each print or electronic source you consider using.

SOURCE EVALUATION CHECKLIST

Who?

☐ Who is the author of the source? What are the author's credentials and profession? What seems to be the author's point of view?

☐ Who is the intended audience of the source? Experts in the field? Professionals? People with a special interest? General readers? In what ways does the source's tone or evidence appeal to this audience?

☐ Who is the publisher of the source or the sponsor of the site? A corporation? A scholarly organization? A professional association? A government agency? An issue-oriented group? Have you heard of this publisher or sponsor before? Is it well regarded? Does it seem reputable and responsible? Does it take an academic or popular approach?

☐ Who has reviewed the source prior to publication? Only the author? Peer reviewers who are experts in the area? An editorial staff?

What?

- [ ] What is the purpose of the publication or Web site? To sell a product or service? To entertain? To supply information? To publish new research? To shape opinion about an issue or cause?
- [ ] What bias or point of view might affect the reliability of the source?
- [ ] What kind of information does the source supply? Is it a primary source (a firsthand account) or a secondary source (an analysis of primary material)? If it is a secondary source, does it rely on evidence from sound primary sources?
- [ ] What evidence does the source present? Does it seem trustworthy, sufficient, and relevant given what you know about the subject? Does its argument or analysis seem logical and complete, or does it leave important questions unanswered? Does it identify its sources? If it is electronic, does it supply appropriate, active links?

Where?

- [ ] Where did you find the source? Is it a prescreened source available through your campus library? Is it a Web site that popped up during a general search?
- [ ] Where has the source been recommended? On an instructor's syllabus or Web page? On a library list? In another reliable source? During a conference with an instructor or librarian?

When?

- [ ] When was the source published or created? Is its information current?
- [ ] When was the source last revised or updated? Is its information up-to-date?

Why?

- [ ] Why should you use this source rather than others?
- [ ] Why is the information in this source directly relevant to your research question?

How?

☐ How does the selection of evidence in the source reflect the interests and expertise of its author, publisher or sponsor, and intended audience? How might you need to qualify its use in your paper?

☐ How would the source's information add to your paper? How would it support your thesis and provide compelling evidence to persuade your readers?

Reading Your Sources Critically

Size up each source to decide what it covers and what it offers to you. If you can't understand a source because you lack the necessary background, don't use it in your paper. If its ideas, facts, claims, or viewpoints seem unusual, incorporate only what you can substantiate in other unrelated sources. On the other hand, if the source seems enlightening and pertinent, examine it carefully to determine what evidence it might offer in support of your thesis.

Targeting Your Reading.   If you can predict what you're likely to need from a certain source, you might focus your reading on finding information of a certain type or emphasis:

- Facts and statistics that substantiate a situation
- Examples that illustrate comparable or possible situations
- Examples that you observed or identified through your fieldwork
- Analytical systems that may help you classify or organize
- Similar or contrasting viewpoints or research findings
- Historical events that provide background or suggest trends
- Expert opinions, including reasons, for predicting certain outcomes
- Unexpected views that may make you reconsider your assumptions
- Novel solutions that may stimulate your creativity

Reading Actively.   Instead of simply hoping for brilliant insights as you read, try reading actively. This approach can help you search more deeply for reasons and evidence to support your thesis or answer your questions. It can challenge you to think more deeply and more creatively about just which answers are possible. Record your own thoughts in a special reading notebook so that they aren't overwhelmed by your source notes, and try active reading strategies like these:

- Jot down your own notes relating one reading to others or combining ideas from several sources.
- Look for strengths and weaknesses, especially if they challenge your preconceptions.
- Try to figure out what a persuasive writer takes for granted or what a dull writer doesn't express effectively; then reassess the merits of each view.
- Write out your own views, passionately or calmly.
- Sum up the changes in your thinking as you have researched your thesis. Where did you begin? Where are you now? How and why have your views changed?

Avoiding Plagiarism in Academic Writing

Discussions of research ethics sometimes reduce that issue to one topic: plagiarism. Plagiarists intentionally present someone else's work as their own—whether they dishonestly submit a paper purchased from the Web, pretend that passages copied from an article are their own writing, appropriate the ideas or theories of others without identifying their sources, or use someone else's graphics without acknowledgment or permission. Plagiarism is an especially serious offense in college because it shows a deep disrespect for the intellectual work of the academic world—analyzing, comparing, interpreting, creating, investigating, and assessing ideas.

Even if you do not intend to plagiarize—to use another writer's words or ideas without appropriately crediting them—a paper full of sloppy or careless shortcuts can look just like a paper deliberately copied from unacknowledged sources. Instead, borrow carefully and honestly, fully acknowledging your debt to writers from whom you borrow anything. Be sure to allow enough time to add information from sources skillfully and correctly. Find out exactly how your instructor expects you to credit sources.

Identify the source of information, an idea, a summary, a paraphrase, or a quotation right away, as soon as you write it in your notes. Carry that acknowledgment into your first draft and all that follow. You generally do not need to identify a source if you use what is called *common knowledge*—quotations, expressions, or information widely known and widely accepted. If you are uncertain about whether you need to cite a source, ask your instructor, or simply provide the citation.

Table 11.1 reviews accepted methods of adding source material and identifies good research practices. These practices will help prevent common errors that may call into question your integrity or your attentiveness as a research writer.

TABLE 11.1   Accepted Methods of Adding and Crediting Source Material

Method and Its Objectives	Good Practices to Avoid Errors
Quotation: Select and identify the exact words of a source in order to capture its vitality, authority, or incisiveness for your paper.	• Supply complete identification of the source. • Provide the page number or other location of the quotation in the source. • Use both opening and closing quotation marks. • Repeat the exact words of the source or properly indicate changes.
Paraphrase: Reword the detailed ideas of a source in your own words and sentences, giving credit to the original, in order to capture the content of a passage.	• Read carefully so that you can paraphrase accurately without distorting the source. • Supply complete identification of the source. • Provide the page number or other location of the original passage in the source. • Rephrase or add quotation marks to identify words or phrases from the source that creep into your paraphrase. • Apart from brief quotations, use your own words and sentences to avoid following the pattern, sequence, or wording of the original. • Clearly distinguish between the paraphrase and your own ideas to avoid confusing switches.
Summary: Very briefly express the main point or key ideas of a source or passage in your own words, giving credit to the original source, in order to capture its essential ideas or conclusion in your paper.	• Read carefully so that you can summarize accurately without distorting the source. • Supply complete identification of the source. • Rephrase or add quotation marks to identify words or phrases from the source that creep into your summary. • Give specific credit to the source for ideas that you include in your discussion. • Clearly distinguish between the summary and your own ideas to avoid confusing switches. *(Continued)*

TABLE 11.1   (Continued)

Method and Its Objectives	Good Practices to Avoid Errors
In-text citation: Credit each quotation, paraphrase, summary, or other reference to a source in short form by giving the author's last name in the text of the paper or in parentheses—adding the page number, date, or other details required by your citation style.	• Supply consistent citations without forgetting or carelessly omitting sources. • Spell names of authors and titles correctly. • Provide accurate page or other location references, especially for direct quotations, paraphrases, or other specific information. • Add any other information such as dates or note numbers required by your citation style.
Concluding list of works cited or references: Credit each source cited in the text with a corresponding full entry in a list of sources at the end of the paper.	• Provide consistent entries without forgetting or carelessly omitting sources. • Match each source citation in the text with an entry in the final list. • Supply every detail expected in an entry, even if you must return to the library or go back online to complete your source notes. • Follow the exact sequence, capitalization, punctuation, indentation pattern, and other details required by the style you are using. • Check that each entry in your final list appears in the expected alphabetical or numerical order.

Ask yourself the following questions as you consider how to meet college research standards.

RESEARCH ETHICS CHECKLIST

☐ Have you reviewed your school's standards for ethical academic conduct? Do your syllabus and course handouts explain how those standards apply in your class?

☐ Do you have any paper-writing habits, such as procrastination, that might create ethical problems for you? How might you change those habits to avoid problems?

☐ Have you found the section in this chapter that explains the documentation style you'll use in your paper?

☐ Are you keeping track of the author, title, and publication information for every source you use? (For more advice about identifying sources, see pp. 217–44.)

☐ Are you carefully distinguishing your own ideas from those of your sources when you record notes or gather research material?

☐ Have you become aware of any research skills—for example, quoting, paraphrasing, or summarizing—that you need to master or polish?

☐ Have you recorded contact information so that you can request permission to include any visual materials from sources in your paper?

☐ Have you asked your instructor's advice about any other ethical issues that have come up in the course of your research?

CAPTURING, LAUNCHING, AND CITING SOURCE MATERIAL

Before you pop any source material into your paper, think about the reliability and suitability of the source. If its evidence seems accurate, logical, and relevant, consider exactly how you might want to capture it for your paper—by quoting, paraphrasing, or summarizing.

Quoting Accurately

When an author expresses an idea so memorably that you want to reproduce those words exactly, quote them word for word. Direct quotations can add life, color, and authority to a paper. Be sure to quote accurately, including punctuation and capitalization (though APA allows adjusting the capitalization of the first word to fit its placement in a sentence). Use an ellipsis mark—three dots (. . .) midsentence or four dots (. . . .) counting the period concluding a sentence—to show where you leave out any original wording. (For more on punctuating quotations and using ellipsis marks, see pp. 177–78. For examples of specific formats for quotations, see pp. 218–32 on MLA and pp. 232–44 on APA.)

Select what you quote carefully; leave out wording that doesn't relate to your point, but don't distort the original meaning. For example, if a reviewer calls a movie "a perfect example of poor directing and inept acting," you can't quote this comment as "perfect . . . directing and . . . acting."

Limit your direct quotations to compelling selections. A quotation in itself is not necessarily effective evidence, and too many quotations suggest that your writing is padded or lacks original thoughts.

QUOTATION CHECKLIST

☐ Have you limited your quotations to impressive, persuasive passages that might strengthen your paper?

☐ Have you checked the quotation against the original to be sure that it repeats the source word for word?

☐ Have you marked the beginning and the ending of the quotation with quotation marks?

☐ Have you used ellipsis (. . .) marks to indicate where you have left out words in the original?

☐ Have you identified the source of the quotation in a launch statement (see p. 216) or in parentheses?

☐ Have you specified the page number or numbers where the quotation appears in the source?

Paraphrasing Carefully

Paraphrasing involves restating an author's ideas in your own language. A paraphrase is generally about the same length as the original; it expresses the ideas and emphasis of the original using your words and sentences. A sloppy paraphrase — one that sounds too much like the language of the source — will stick out in your paper, resulting in awkward jumps between your style and that of your source. On the other hand, a fresh and creative paraphrase not only avoids plagiarism but also expresses your own style and helps your paper read smoothly.

Be careful to avoid slipping in the author's words or shadowing the original sentence structures too closely. If a source says, "President Wilson called an emergency meeting of his cabinet to discuss the new crisis," and you say, "The president called his cabinet to hold an emergency meeting to discuss the new crisis," your words are too close to those of the source. One option is to quote the original, though it doesn't seem worth quoting word for word in this case. Or, better, you could write: "Summoning his cabinet to an emergency session, Wilson laid out the challenge before them."

PARAPHRASE CHECKLIST

☐ Have you read the passage critically to be sure that you fully understand it?

☐ Have you paraphrased accurately, reflecting both the main points and the supporting details in the original?

☐ Does your paraphrase use your own words without repeating or echoing the words or the sentence structure of the original?

☐ Does your paraphrase stick to the ideas of the original without tucking in your own thoughts?

☐ Have you reread and revised your paraphrase so that it reads smoothly and clearly?

☐ Have you identified the source of the paraphrase in a launch statement (see p. 216) or in parentheses?

☐ Have you specified the page number or numbers where the passage appears in the source?

Summarizing Fairly

Summarizing is a useful way of incorporating the general point of a whole paragraph or section of a work. You briefly state the main sense of the original in your own words and tell where you got the idea. A summary is generally much shorter than the original; it expresses only the most important ideas — the essence — of the original.

In your text, a summary can efficiently present a key idea from a source; a pair of summaries can simplify comparing, contrasting, or merging the central ideas from two different sources. In addition, research assignments may require an annotated bibliography that supplies for each source a full citation followed by a sentence or paragraph annotation that summarizes the source, evaluates its reliability or relevance, or interprets its significance.

Using Summary with Evaluation in an Annotated Bibliography. When Stephanie Hawkins prepared her APA-style paper "Japanese: Linguistic Diversity" for an independent study, she added an annotated bibliography including these entries.

Abe, H. (1995). From stereotype to context: The study of Japanese women's language. *Feminist Study 21*(3). Retrieved from EBSCOhost database.

Abe discusses the roots of Japanese women's language, beginning in ancient Japan and continuing into modern times. I was able to use this peer-reviewed source to expand on the format of women's language and the consequences of its use.

Kristof, N. (1995, September 24). On language: Too polite for words. *New York Times Magazine,* pp. SM22-SM23.

Kristof, a regular columnist for the *New York Times Magazine,* briefly describes the use of honorifics as an outlet for sarcasm and insults. Although the article discusses cultures other than Japanese, it provides insight into the polite vulgarity of the Japanese language.

Using Summary with Interpretation in an Annotated Bibliography. In "Coming of Age under Sputnik: Teenage Male Anxiety and Uncertainty in 1958 America," Alan Espenlaub included this summary and interpretation of a visual source in his annotated bibliography (in MLA style).

Ford Motor Company. "This is the EDSEL. The Emphasis Is on Engneering, But the Accent Is on Elegance." *Life* 28 Oct. 1957.

This double-page full-color advertisement contains a shopping mall parking lot full of shining new Edsel cars and happy shoppers. Palm trees in the background suggest that the southern California lifestyle goes along with the new Edsel lifestyle (1958 was the first year for the Edsel). In the center of the ad is a two-toned blue Edsel Citation two-door hardtop with a poodle in the front seat, even though the windows are rolled down. The ratio of male to female shoppers pictured at the mall is one in ten. Many dyads appear to be mother and daughter. No boys are in the picture. Since the ad's target audience was most probably adult male providers, it is possible that including a teenage son in a picture of a new car would be a negative signal in the potential purchaser's mind. On the other hand, males would feel good about being able to provide a new car for "the little woman," Mrs. Consumer.

SUMMARY CHECKLIST

☐ Have you fairly stated the author's thesis or main point in your own words in a sentence or two?

☐ Have you briefly stated any supporting ideas that you want to summarize?

☐ Have you stuck to the overall point without getting bogged down in details or examples?

☐ Has your summary remained respectful of the ideas and opinions of others, even if you disagree with them?

☐ Have you revised your summary so that it reads smoothly and clearly?

☐ Have you identified the source of the summary in a launch statement (see p. 216) or in parentheses?

☐ Have you specified the page number or numbers where any specific passage appears in the source?

SAMPLE QUOTATIONS, PARAPHRASE, AND SUMMARY

Passage from Original Source

Obesity is a major issue because (1) vast numbers of people are affected; (2) the prevalence is growing; (3) rates are increasing in children; (4) the medical, psychological, and social effects are severe; (5) the behaviors that cause it (poor diet and inactivity) are themselves major contributors to ill health; and (6) treatment is expensive, rarely effective, and impractical to use on a large scale.

Biology and environment conspire to promote obesity. Biology is an enabling factor, but the obesity epidemic, and the consequent human tragedy, is a function of the worsening food and physical activity environment. Governments and societies have come to this conclusion very late. There is much catching up to do.

Sample Quotations from Second Paragraph

Although human biology has contributed to the pudgy American society, everyone now faces the powerful challenge of a "worsening food and physical activity environment" (Brownell and Horgen 51).

As Brownell and Horgen conclude, "There is much catching up to do" (51).

Sample Paraphrase of First Paragraph

The current concern with increasing American weight has developed for half a dozen reasons, according to Brownell and Horgen. They attribute the shift in awareness to the number of obese people and the increase in this number, especially among youngsters. In addition, excess weight carries harsh consequences for individual physical and mental health and for society's welfare. Lack of exercise and unhealthy food choices worsen the health consequences, especially because there's no cheap and easy cure for the effects of eating too much and exercising too little (51).

Sample Summary

After outlining six reasons why obesity is a critical issue, Brownell and Horgen urge Americans to eat less and become more active (51).

Works Cited Entry (MLA Style)

Brownell, Kelly D., and Katherine Battle Horgen. *Food Fight: The Inside Story of the Food Industry, America's Obesity Crisis, and What We Can Do about It.* Chicago: Contemporary-McGraw, 2004. Print.

Launching Each Quotation, Paraphrase, and Summary

Instead of dropping ideas from sources into your paper as if they had just arrived by flying saucer, weave them in so that they effectively support the point you want to make. Launch each quotation, paraphrase, summary, or other reference to a source with an introduction that tells readers who wrote it or why it's in your paper. College instructors tend to favor launch statements that comment on the source, establish its authority, connect it to the paper's thesis, or relate it to other sources. Use strategies such as these, illustrated in MLA style.

- Identify the name of the author in the sentence that introduces the source:

    As Wood explains, the goal of American education continues to fluctuate between gaining knowledge and applying it (58).

- Add the author's name in the middle of the source material:

    In *Romeo and Juliet,* "That which we call a rose," Shakespeare claims, "By any other word would smell as sweet" (2.2.43–44).

- Name the author only in the parenthetical source citation if you want to keep your focus on the topic:

   A second march on Washington followed the first (Whitlock 83).

- Mention the professional title, affiliation, or experience of an author or person you've interviewed to add authority or credibility.

- Explain for the reader why you have selected and included the material.

- Interpret what you see as the point or relevance of the material.

- Relate the source clearly to the paper's thesis or to the specific point it supports.

- Compare or contrast the point of view or evidence of one source with that of another source.

- Supply transitions to connect several sources mentioned in a sentence or paragraph.

- Vary your introductory language (*says, claims, observes, emphasizes, studies,analyzes, interprets*) to portray the contribution of the source accurately.

- Lead smoothly from your launch statement into the source material instead of tossing a stand-alone quotation into your paragraph without any introduction.

Citing Each Source Accurately

Identify the source of your material following whatever style you are using. Although MLA and APA styles have their own conventions (see pp. 218–32 on MLA style and pp. 232–44 on APA style), both expect you to accomplish the following things:

- Acknowledge all material from a source—words directly quoted, information or opinions recast in your own words, summaries of ideas or theories, references to research studies and findings, specific reasons or examples, and anything else drawn from that source.

- Identify the source material at the exact point where you add it to your text, generally by identifying the author (in MLA style) or the author and year of publication (in APA style) in parentheses (unless already identified in your launch statement).

- Begin the citation with the first words of the title if a source has no author.

- Add the page number (or another specific location) for each quotation or paraphrase so that a reader could easily locate the original passage.

- Link the short identification of each source in your paper—supplied in your text wording or in parentheses—to the full description of your sources in a list of works cited or reference list at the end of your paper.
- Follow the conventional patterns for identifying sources, supplying the same details in the same order with the same capitalization and punctuation.

The following sections explain how to cite a source in the text and how to list it at the end of a paper in MLA style or APA style. The core of each source entry is the author's name, recorded first in both styles. Next, the type of source determines the pattern you should follow in the rest of the full entry identifying the source. To help you focus on the information needed to credit your sources, both the MLA and APA sections are organized around these two questions: Who wrote it? What type of source is it?

CITING AND LISTING SOURCES IN MLA STYLE

In MLA style (the format recommended by the Modern Language Association and often required in English classes), your sources need to be identified twice in your paper: first, briefly, in the text where you draw upon the source material and later, in full, at the end of your paper. The short citation includes the name of the author of the source (or a short form of the title if the source does not name an author), so it's easy for a reader to connect the short entry in your text with the related full entry in the final alphabetical list. Because instructors expect source references to be formatted carefully, follow the style guidelines and any special directions supplied by your instructor. For more extensive advice, turn to the *MLA Handbook for Writers of Research Papers* (7th ed.; New York: MLA, 2009), usually available in your campus bookstore and library.

MLA DIRECTORY

CITING SOURCES IN YOUR TEXT

LISTING SOURCES AT THE END

Citing Sources in Your Text

Right in the text, at the precise point where you insert a quotation, a paraphrase, or a summary, you need to identify the source. Your citation often follows a simple pattern: name the author, and note the page or pages in the original where the material is located.

(Last Name of Author ##)   (Talia 35)   (Smitt and Gilbert 152–53)

This basic form applies whatever the type of source—article, book, or Web page—though your purposes as a writer, the nature of the material, and the type of source will influence exactly how you integrate a citation into your discussion. (See the checklist on p. 223.) Keep in mind these two key questions: Who wrote it? What type of source is it?

Who Wrote It?

The core of an MLA citation is the author of the source. Crediting that author is part of your ethical obligation as a researcher. Whether you decide to integrate the author's name in your discussion or in parentheses will vary with your purpose as a writer and the type of material or source you have used.

INDIVIDUAL AUTHOR NOT NAMED IN SENTENCE

Place this citation immediately after a direct quotation or paraphrase.

> When "The Lottery" begins, the reader thinks of the "great pile of stones" (Jackson 191) as children's entertainment.

INDIVIDUAL AUTHOR NAMED IN SENTENCE

When the author is named in your launch statement, the citation can be even simpler.

> According to Hunt, the city faced "deficits and drought" (54) for ten more years.

TWO OR THREE AUTHORS

Include each author's last name either in your text or in the citation.

> Taylor and Wheeler present yet another view (25).

FOUR OR MORE AUTHORS

Give the names of all the authors, or use only the last name of the first author listed, followed by the abbreviation *et al.* (Latin for "and others"). Present the source the same way in your list of works cited.

> In the years between 1870 and 1900, the nation's cities grew at an
> astonishing rate, mostly as a result of internal and international
> movement of people (Roark et al. 422).

UNIDENTIFIED AUTHOR

For a source with an unknown author, use the complete title in your
sentence or a word or two from the title in parentheses. If a source is
sponsored by a corporation or other group, name the sponsor as the
author.

> According to a recent study, drivers are 42% more likely to get into an
> accident if they are using a wireless phone while driving ("Driving
> Dangerously" 32).

What Type of Source Is It?

Because naming the author is the core of your citation, the basic form
applies to any type of source though a few types present complications.

MULTIVOLUME WORK

For a work with multiple volumes, provide the author's name and the
volume number, followed by a colon and the page number.

> In ancient times, astrological predictions were sometimes used as a kind of
> black magic (Sarton 2: 319).

INDIRECT SOURCE

Whenever possible, cite the original source. If that source is not available
to you (as often happens with published accounts of spoken remarks),
use the abbreviation *qtd. in* (for "quoted in") before citing the secondary
source.

> Zill says that, psychologically, children in stepfamilies most resemble
> children in single-parent families, even if they live in a two-parent
> household (qtd. in Derber 119).

NOVEL OR SHORT STORY

Give the page number from your own copy first. If possible, include further identifying information, such as the section or chapter where the
passage can be found in any edition.

> In *A Tale of Two Cities*, Dickens describes the aptly named Stryver as
> "shouldering himself (morally and physically) into companies and
> conversations" (110; bk. 2, ch. 4).

PLAY

For a verse play, list the act, scene, and line numbers, separated by periods.

> "Love," Iago says, "is merely a lust of the blood and a permission of the
> will" (*Oth*. 1.3.326).

POETRY

When quoting poetry, add a slash mark to show where each new line begins. Use the word "line" or "lines" in the first reference but only numbers in subsequent references, as in the following examples from William Wordsworth's "The World Is Too Much with Us." Here is the first reference:

> "The world is too much with us; late and soon / Getting and spending, we
> lay waste our powers" (lines 1–2).

Here is the subsequent reference:

> "Or hear old Triton blow his wreathed horn" (14).

If a poem has multiple parts, cite the part and line numbers, separated by a period. Do not include the word "line."

> In "Ode: Intimations of Immortality," Wordsworth ponders the truths of
> human existence, "Which we are toiling all our lives to find, / In darkness
> lost, the darkness of the grave" (8.116–17).

WORK IN AN ANTHOLOGY

For works in an anthology, cite the author of the selection—not the editor of the collection. (See p. 226 for entries for Tan's essay in Martin's anthology.)

> Amy Tan explains the "Englishes" of her childhood and family (32).

LONG QUOTATION

When a quotation is longer than four typed lines, indent the entire quotation one inch, or ten spaces. Double-space it, but don't place quotation marks around it. If the quotation is one paragraph or less, begin the first line without any extra paragraph indentation. Use ellipsis marks (. . .) to show where you omit anything from the middle of the quotation. Place your citation in parentheses after the punctuation that ends the quotation.

Cynthia Griffin Wolff comments on Emily Dickinson's incisive use of language:

> Language, of course, was a far subtler weapon than a hammer. Dickinson's verbal maneuvers would increasingly reveal immense skill in avoiding a frontal attack; she preferred the silent knife of irony to the strident battering of loud complaint. She had never suffered fools gladly. . . . Scarcely submissive, she had acquired the cool calculation of an assassin. (170–71)

MLA CITATION CHECKLIST

☐ Have you double-checked to be sure that you have acknowledged all material from a source?

☐ Have you placed your citation right after your quotation, paraphrase, summary, or other reference to the source?

☐ Have you identified the author of each source in your text or in parentheses?

☐ Have you used the first few words of the title to cite a work without an identified author?

☐ Have you noted a page number or other specific location whenever needed?

☐ Have you added any necessary extras, whether volume numbers or poetry lines?

☐ Have you checked your final draft to be sure that every source cited in your text also appears in your list of works cited?

Listing Sources at the End

On a new page at the end of your paper, add a list of your sources called Works Cited. For each source mentioned in the text, supply a corresponding full entry here. Arrange the entries alphabetically by author's last name or, for works with no author, by title.

The secret to figuring out what to include in a Works Cited entry generally comes down to two questions about your source: Who wrote it? What is it? Once you identify the number and type of authors, and the type of source you have used, you can find a general pattern for the entry in this book or in the MLA style guide. Then you can examine the title page or other parts of your source to find the details needed to complete the pattern. Using the following examples as guides, supply the same details in the same order with the same punctuation and other features. (See the checklist on p. 232.)

Who Wrote It?

INDIVIDUAL AUTHOR

Hazzard, Shirley. *The Great Fire*. New York: Farrar, 2003. Print.

TWO OR THREE AUTHORS

Name the authors in the order in which they are listed on the title page.

Phelan, James R., and Lewis Chester. *The Money: The Battle for Howard Hughes's Billions*. New York: Random, 1997. Print.

FOUR OR MORE AUTHORS

Name all the authors, or follow the name of the first author with the abbreviation "et al." (Latin for "and others"). Identify the source in the same way you cite it in the text.

Roark, James L., et al. *The American Promise*. Boston: Bedford, 1998. Print.

SAME AUTHOR WITH MULTIPLE WORKS

Arrange the author's works alphabetically by title. Use the author's name for the first entry only, then replace the name with three hyphens.

Gould, Stephen Jay. *Full House: The Spread of Excellence from Plato to Darwin*. New York: Harmony, 1996. Print.

---. *Triumph and Tragedy in Mudville: A Lifelong Passion for Baseball*. New York: Norton, 2003. Print.

ORGANIZATION AUTHOR

Name the organization as author, omitting any initial article ("a," "an," or "the"). (The name may reappear as the publisher.)

Student Conservation Association. *The Guide to Graduate Environmental Programs*. Washington: Island, 1997. Print.

UNIDENTIFIED AUTHOR

"Showtime at Amazon." *Newsweek*. Newsweek, 29 Nov. 2004. Web.

17 Feb. 2005.

What Type of Source Is It?

Once you have found the format that fits the author, look for the type of source and the specific entry that best matches yours. Mix and match the patterns shown here as needed.

Printed or Electronic Book

PRINTED BOOK

Volti, Rudi. *Society and Technological Change*. 4th ed. New York:

Worth, 2001. Print.

ONLINE BOOK

For an online book, supply what you would for a printed book. Then add the name of the site (italicized), the medium of publication, and your access date.

Wharton, Edith. *The Age of Innocence*. New York: Appleton, 1920.

Bartleby.com: Great Books Online. Web. 8 May 2004.

MULTIVOLUME WORK

To cite the full work, include the number of volumes ("vols.") after the title.

Who Built America? Working People and the Nation's Economy, Politics,

Culture, and Society. 2 vols. New York: Worth, 2000. Print.

To cite only one volume, give its number after the title. If you wish, you then can add the total number of volumes after the medium.

Who Built America? Working People and the Nation's Economy, Politics,

Culture, and Society. Vol. 1. New York: Worth, 2000. Print. 2 vols.

ESSAY, SHORT STORY, OR POEM FROM AN EDITED COLLECTION

Rothman, Rodney. "My Fake Job." *The Best American Nonrequired Reading*.

Ed. Dave Eggers. Boston: Houghton, 2002. 117–32. Print.

TWO OR MORE WORKS FROM THE SAME EDITED COLLECTION

If you list more than one selection from an anthology, you can prepare an entry for the collection (instead of repeating it for each selection). Then you can simply refer to it from the entries for the separate readings.

> Cisneros, Sandra. "Only Daughter." Martin 10–13.
>
> Martin, Wendy, ed. *The Beacon Book of Essays by Contemporary American Women*. Boston: Beacon, 1996. Print.
>
> Tan, Amy. "Mother Tongue." Martin 32–37.

SELECTION FROM AN ONLINE BOOK

> Webster, Augusta. "Not Love." *A Book of Rhyme*. London, 1881. N. pag. *Victorian Women Writers Project*. Ed. Perry Willett. Indiana U. Web. 28 Jan. 2005.

ARTICLE FROM A PRINTED REFERENCE WORK

It is not necessary to supply the editor, publisher, or place of publication for well-known references. No volume and page numbers are needed when a reference book is organized alphabetically. If an article's author is identified by initials, check the book's list of contributors, which should supply the full name.

> Leach, Edmund. "Magic." *A Dictionary of the Social Sciences*. Ed. Julius Gould and William L. Kolb. New York: Free, 1964. Print.

ARTICLE FROM AN ONLINE REFERENCE WORK

> "Harlem Renaissance." *Encyclopaedia Britannica*. Encyclopaedia Britannica, 2005. Web. 23 June 2005.

Article in a Printed or Electronic Periodical

ARTICLE FROM A PRINTED JOURNAL PAGINATED BY VOLUME

For an article from a journal in which page numbers run continuously through all issues of a volume, give only the volume number, year (in parentheses), and page numbers.

> Daly, Mary E. "Recent Writing on Modern Irish History: The Interaction between Past and Present." *Journal of Modern History* 69.3 (1997): 512–33. Print.

ARTICLE FROM A PRINTED JOURNAL PAGINATED BY ISSUE

For an article from a journal that starts each issue with page 1, provide the same information as above: the volume number, issue number, year, page numbers, and medium.

> Ferris, Lucy. "'Never Truly Members': Andre Dubus's Patriarchal Catholicism."
> *South Atlantic Review* 62.2 (1997): 39–55. Print.

ARTICLE FROM AN ONLINE JOURNAL

Supply the information you would for a printed article, using "n. pag." if the source does not provide page numbers. If you are citing an abstract, add "Abstract" before the access date.

> Eagleton, Mary B. "Making Text Come to Life on the Computer: Toward
> an Understanding of Hypermedia Literacy." *Reading Online* 6.1
> (2002): n. pag. Web. 25 Feb. 2005.

ARTICLE ACCESSED THROUGH AN ONLINE LIBRARY
OR SUBSCRIPTION SERVICE

If you find a source through a library subscription service, include the name of the service, the medium, and your access date.

> Sataline, Suzanne. "Charter Schools Could Hit Ceiling." *Boston Globe*
> 31 Mar. 2004: B1. *NewsBank*. Web. 5 May 2004.

If you search using a personal subscription service such as *AOL*, use that as the name of the database.

> Curry, Andrew. "Climate Change: Sites in Peril." *Archaeology* Mar.-Apr.
> 2009: n. pag. *America Online*. Web. 17 Apr. 2009.

ARTICLE FROM A PRINTED MAGAZINE

Give the month and year of the issue, or its specific date, after the title of the magazine. If the article's pages are not consecutive, add a + (plus sign) after the initial page.

> Hooper, Joseph. "The New Diet Danger." *Self* July 2003: 128+. Print.

ARTICLE FROM AN ONLINE MAGAZINE

> Douthat, Ross. "The Truth about Harvard." *Atlantic.* Atlantic Monthly Group,
>   Mar. 2007. Web. 8 Mar. 2007.

ARTICLE FROM A PRINTED NEWSPAPER

If the newspaper has different editions, indicate the one where the article can be found.

> Kolata, Gina. "Men and Women Use Brain Differently, Study Discovers."
>   *New York Times* 16 Feb. 1995, natl. ed.: A1+. Print.

ARTICLE FROM AN ONLINE NEWSPAPER

> Austen, Ian. "Internet: It's the New TV." *New York Times.* New York Times,
>   24 Feb. 2005. Web. 8 Mar. 2007.

EDITORIAL FROM A PRINTED PERIODICAL

> Jacoby, Jeff. "When Jerusalem Was Divided." Editorial. *Boston Globe*
>   8 Jan. 2001: A11. Print.
>
> "Taking the Initiatives." Editorial. *Nation* 13 Nov. 2000: 3–4. Print.

EDITORIAL FROM AN ONLINE PERIODICAL

> "Two Messages on Education." Editorial. *Washington Post.* Washington Post,
>   7 Mar. 2007. Web. 8 Mar. 2007.

LETTER TO THE EDITOR

> Cohen, Irving M. Letter. *Atlantic Monthly* Mar. 2004: 14. Print.

Other Printed or Electronic Document

PRINTED GOVERNMENT DOCUMENT

If the document names an author or editor, that name may be provided either before the title or after it, if you identify the agency as author.

> United States. Bureau of the Census. *Statistical Abstract of the United*
>   *States.* 123rd ed. Washington: GPO, 2003. Print.

ONLINE GOVERNMENT DOCUMENT

> United States. National Institute of Child Health and Human Development. National Institutes of Health. "Why Are the Tween and Teen Years So Critical?" *Milk Matters.* NICHD, 21 Aug. 2006. Web. 8 Mar. 2007.

ONLINE DOCUMENT

> Carter, Jimmy. "Inaugural Address of Jimmy Carter." 20 Jan. 1977. *The Avalon Project.* Yale Law School. Web. 14 Feb. 2005.

Internet or Electronic Source

See the directory on pp. 218–19 for entries for other electronic sources, including books and articles.

PERSONAL WEB PAGE

If no title is available, include an identification such as "Home page."

> Tannen, Deborah. Home page. Georgetown U and Deborah Tannen, 1997. Web. 8 Mar. 2007.

ORGANIZATION WEB PAGE

> "Research & Statistics." *American Library Association.* ALA, 2005. Web. 19 June 2005.

HOME PAGE FOR A CAMPUS DEPARTMENT OR COURSE

> *UCLA Department of Sociology.* UCLA, n.d. Web. 8 Mar. 2007.

BLOG OR BLOG ENTRY

If there is no apparent sponsor of the blog you are citing, use "N.p" for no publisher.

> Finnerty, Erin. *Verbs of Leisure.* N.p., 10 Feb. 2008. Web. 14 Feb. 2008.

To cite a blog entry, give the title of the entry in quotation marks. If a blog comment does not have a title, use a label such as "Blog comment."

> Owazny, Kit. Blog comment. *Culture Monster.* Los Angeles Times, 31 May 2009. Web. 31 May 2009.

Visual or Audio Source

ADVERTISEMENT

A. G. Edwards. Advertisement. *Scientific American* Mar. 2004: 17. Print.

COMIC OR CARTOON

Supply the cartoonist's name, and identify the work as a comic strip or cartoon.

McDonnell, Patrick. "Mutts." Comic strip. *Atlanta Journal Constitution*
2 Feb. 2005: F5. Print.

PHOTOGRAPH OR WORK OF ART

Supply the place (museum or gallery and city) where the item is housed. If you are citing it from a publication, identify that source. For a family or personal photograph, identify who took the photograph and when.

Stieglitz, Alfred. *Self-Portrait*. J. Paul Getty Museum, Los Angeles. *Stieglitz: A Beginning Light*. By Katherine Hoffman. New Haven: Yale UP, 2004, 251. Print.

AUDIOTAPE OR RECORDING

Begin with the name of the artist, composer, speaker, writer, or other contributor, based on your interest in the recording. Include the medium using a designation such as "Audiocassette," "CD," or "LP."

Byrne, Gabriel. *The James Joyce Collection*. Dove Audio, 1996. Audiocassette.

PROGRAM ON TELEVISION OR RADIO

"A Dangerous Man: Lawrence after Arabia." *Great Performances*. Perf. Ralph Fiennes and Siddig el Fadil. PBS. WNET, New York. 6 May 1992. Television.

FILM

Start with the title unless you want to emphasize the work of a person connected with the film.

Lord of the Rings: The Return of the King. Dir. Peter Jackson. New Line Cinema, 2003. Film.

PERFORMANCE

> *Whale Music*. By Anthony Minghella. Dir. Anthony Minghella. Perf. Francie
> Swift. Theater Off Park, New York. 23 Mar. 1998. Performance.

Conversation or Field Artifact

PERSONAL, TELEPHONE, OR E-MAIL INTERVIEW

Indicate whether you conducted the interview in person, by telephone, or by e-mail.

> Boyd, Dierdre. Personal interview. 5 Feb. 2005.

BROADCAST INTERVIEW

Identify the source by the person interviewed; if you want, you may also identify the interviewer.

> Bernstein, Richard. Interview by Terry Gross. *Fresh Air*. Natl. Public Radio.
> WBUR, Boston. 3 Apr. 2001. Radio.

PUBLISHED INTERVIEW

> Kerry, John. Interview. *Newsweek* 8 Mar. 2004: 26. Print.

E-MAIL

Use the subject line as a title to identify the message, or describe it as shown below.

> Moore, Jack. Message to the author. 11 Nov. 2005. E-mail.

ONLINE POSTING

Use the subject line as the title. Use the label "Online posting" if the posting has no title.

> Robinson, Meena. "Mansfield Park." *PBS Discussions*. PBS, 28 Jan. 2008.
> Web. 18 May 2008.

MLA WORKS CITED CHECKLIST

☐ Have you begun each entry with the appropriate pattern for the author's name?

☐ Have you figured out what type of source you've used? Have you followed the sample pattern for that type as closely as possible?

☐ Have you used quotation marks and italicizing correctly for titles?

☐ Have you used the conventional punctuation—periods, commas, colons, parentheses—in each entry?

☐ Have you accurately recorded the name of the author, title, publisher, and so on?

☐ Have you checked the accuracy of the numbers in your entry—pages, volume, and dates?

☐ Have you correctly identified the medium of publication or reception, using a label such as Print, Web, CD, DVD, Film, Lecture, Performance, Radio, Television, or E-mail?

☐ Have you arranged your entries in alphabetical order?

☐ Have you checked your final list against your text citations to be sure that every source appears in both places?

☐ Have you double-spaced your list, like the rest of your paper, and allowed an inch margin on all sides?

☐ Have you begun the first line of each entry at the left margin and indented each additional line one-half inch? (Check your software for a "hanging" indentation option, usually in the Format/Paragraph Indentation-Special menu.)

CITING AND LISTING SOURCES IN APA STYLE

In APA style (the format recommended by the American Psychological Association and often required in courses in the social sciences), your sources are identified twice: first, briefly noting the author and the date as you refer to the source and later identifying the source in full in an alphabetical list of references at the end of your paper. As you use this style, keep in mind these two key questions: Who wrote it? What type of source is it? For more detailed advice, turn to the *Publication Manual of the American Psychological Association* (6th ed.; Washington, DC: APA, 2010), usually available in your campus bookstore and library.

APA DIRECTORY

CITING SOURCES IN YOUR TEXT

LISTING SOURCES AT THE END

Citing Sources in Your Text

The core of an APA citation is the author of the source. That person's last name links your use of the source in your paper with its full description in your list of references. Next comes the date of the source, which often establishes its currency or its classic status for readers. A common addition is a specific location, such as a page number (using "p." for "page" or "pp." for "pages"), that locates the material in the original source. Unless the source lacks page numbers or other locators, this information is required for quotations and recommended for paraphrases and key concepts. When you supply these elements in parentheses, separate them with commas: (Westin, 2005, p. 48). This basic form applies whatever the source—book, article, or Web page. (See also p. 237.)

Who Wrote It?

Naming the author of a source is part of your ethical obligation as a researcher. As a writer, however, you can decide whether to tuck that name away in parentheses or to emphasize it in your discussion.

INDIVIDUAL AUTHOR NOT NAMED IN SENTENCE

Some experts feel that adolescent boys who bully are not merely aggressive but are depressed and acting out in an aggressive manner (Pollack, 2000).

INDIVIDUAL AUTHOR NAMED IN SENTENCE

Pollack (2000) contends that boys tend to contain their pain for fear of appearing vulnerable and inviting ridicule.

TWO AUTHORS

List the last names of coauthors in the order in which they appear in the source. Join the names with "and" if you mention them in your text and with an ampersand (&) if the citation is in parentheses.

Anderson and Ross (1998) maintain that the development of a group's culture provides both physical and psychological protection.

A group's cultural development enhances its chance for survival, providing both physical and psychological protection (Anderson & Ross, 1998).

THREE OR MORE AUTHORS

For three to five authors, include all the last names in your first reference. In any later references, identify only the first author and add "et al." (for "and others"), whether in the text or in parentheses. For six authors or more, simply use the name of the first author with "et al." for all citations.

> The discipline of conservation biology has developed in response to the accelerating rate at which species are being lost (Purves, Orians, & Heller, 1999). Purves et al. specifically explore the consequences of human activities in relation to this acceleration.

ORGANIZATION AUTHOR

> Important as nutrition is for healthy people, it is even more critical for cancer patients who may have specific dietary requirements such as the need for more protein (American Cancer Society, 2003, p. 7).

UNIDENTIFIED AUTHOR

When you don't know the author of a work, identify the source with a short title, beginning with the first few main words so that it can be located in your alphabetical list of references.

> Parents of middle school students are encouraged to monitor their online activities (*Safe Kids,* 2005).

SAME AUTHOR WITH MULTIPLE WORKS

> Five significant trends in parent-school relations have evolved (Grimley, 2005) since the original multistate study (Grimley, 1985).

DIFFERENT AUTHORS WITH MULTIPLE WORKS

Within a single citation, list the authors of multiple works in alphabetical order (as in your reference list). Separate the works with semicolons.

> Several studies have been designed to determine reasons for minority underperformance in educational attainment (Bowen & Bok, 1998; Charles, Dinwiddie, & Massey, 2004; Glazer, 1997).

What Type of Source Is It?

Naming the author and adding the date are the essentials of the APA citation, but a few types of sources may present complications.

INDIRECT SOURCE

If possible, locate and cite the original source. Otherwise, begin your citation with "as cited in," and then name your source.

> According to Claude Fischer, the belief in individualism favors "the individual over the group or institution" (as cited in Hansen, 2005, p. 5).

GOVERNMENT OR ORGANIZATION DOCUMENT

If no specific author is identified, treat the sponsoring agency as the author, and give its full name in the first citation in your text. If the name is complicated or commonly shortened, you may add an abbreviation in brackets. In later citations, use just the abbreviation and the date.

> The *2005 National Gang Threat Assessment* (National Alliance of Gang Investigators Associations [NAGIA], 2005, pp. vii–viii) identified regional trends that may help account for the city's recent gang violence.

Here is the next citation: (NAGIA, 2005)

PERSONAL COMMUNICATION

Personal communications—such as face-to-face interviews, letters, telephone conversations, memos, and e-mail—are not included in the reference list because your readers would not be able to find and use the originals. In the text of your paper, name your source, identify it as a personal communication, and supply the date of the communication.

> J. T. Moore (personal communication, November 10, 2005) has made specific suggestions for stimulating the local economy.

LONG QUOTATION

If you quote forty words or more, indent the quotation one-half inch and double-space it instead of using quotation marks. After it, add your citation with no additional period, including whatever information you have not already mentioned in your launch statement as student Ross Rocketto did in "Robin Hood: Prince of Thieves? An Analysis of Current School Finance Legislation in Texas."

This phenomenon is explained further by Hoxby (1998):

> First, districts that are good, efficient providers of schooling tend to be rewarded with larger budgets. This fiscal reward process works because a district's budget nearly always depends on property taxes, which in turn depend on home prices within the district, which in turn depend on how the marginal home buyers value the local schools. (p. 48)

APA CITATION CHECKLIST

☐ Have you double-checked to be sure that you have acknowledged all material from a source?

☐ Have you placed your citation right after your quotation or reference to the source?

☐ Have you identified the author of each source in your text or in parentheses?

☐ Have you used the first few main words of the title to cite a work without an identified author?

☐ Have you noted the date (or added "n.d." for "no date") for each source?

☐ Have you added a page number or other location wherever needed?

☐ Have you checked your final draft to be sure that every source cited in your text also appears in your list of references?

Listing Sources at the End

In APA style, your list of sources appears at the end of your paper. Begin a new page with the title References centered. Double-space your list, and organize it alphabetically by authors' last names (or by titles for works without an identified author). If you need to list several works by the same author, arrange these by date, moving from earliest to most recent. (See the checklist on p. 244.)

As you prepare your entries, begin with the last name and initials of the author. The various author formats apply whatever your source—article, book, Web page, or other material. Then find the type of source you have used in this section, and follow its pattern in your entry. Keep in mind these two key questions, which are used to organize the sample entries that follow: Who wrote it? What type of source is it?

Who Wrote It?

INDIVIDUAL AUTHOR

Pollack, W. (2000). *Real boys' voices.* New York, NY: Random House.

TWO AUTHORS

Anderson, R., & Ross, V. (1998). *Questions of communication.* New York, NY: St. Martin's Press.

THREE OR MORE AUTHORS

Provide names for three to seven authors; for eight or more, list the first six followed by three ellipsis dots and the last author's name.

Evans, B., Joas, M., Sundback, S., & Theobald, K. (2005). *Governing sustainable cities.* London, England: Earthscan.

SAME AUTHOR WITH MULTIPLE WORKS

Arrange the titles by date, the earliest first. If some share the same date, arrange them alphabetically and letter them after the date.

Gould, S. J. (1996). *Full house: The spread of excellence from Plato to Darwin.* New York, NY: Harmony.

Gould, S. J. (2003a). *The hedgehog, the fox, and the magister's pox: Mending the gap between science and the humanities.* New York, NY: Harmony.

Gould, S. J. (2003b). *Triumph and tragedy in Mudville: A lifelong passion for baseball.* New York, NY: Norton.

ORGANIZATION AUTHOR

American Red Cross. (2004). *CPR/AED for the professional rescuer.* Washington, DC: Author.

UNIDENTIFIED AUTHOR

Findings. (2005, April). *Harper's, 310,* 100.

What Type of Source Is It?

Once you have found the appropriate author format, look for the type of source and the specific entry that best matches yours. Mix and match the patterns shown here as needed.

Printed or Electronic Book

PRINTED BOOK

> Rosenthal, A. (2004). *Heavy lifting: The job of the American legislature.* Washington, DC: CQ Press.

ONLINE BOOK

> Oblinger, D. G., & Oblinger, J. L. (Eds.). (2005). *Educating the Net generation.* Retrieved from http://www.educause.edu/ educatingthenetgen/

MULTIVOLUME WORK

> Friedman, H. S. (Ed.). (1998). *Encyclopedia of mental health* (Vols. 1–3). San Diego, CA: Academic Press.

SELECTION FROM A PRINTED BOOK

> Martin, P. V., & Hummer, R. A. (2003). Fraternities and rape on campus. In M. Silberman (Ed.), *Violence and society: A reader* (pp. 215–222). Upper Saddle River, NJ: Prentice Hall.

SELECTION FROM AN ONLINE BOOK

> Brown, M. (2005). Learning spaces. In D. G. Oblinger & J. L. Oblinger (Eds.), *Educating the Net generation* (chap. 12). Retrieved from http://www.educause.edu/educatingthenetgen/

ARTICLE FROM A REFERENCE WORK

> Norman, C. E. (2003). Religion and food. In *Encyclopedia of food and culture* (Vol. 3, pp. 171–176). New York, NY: Charles Scribner's Sons.

Article in a Printed or Electronic Periodical

ARTICLE FROM A PRINTED JOURNAL PAGINATED BY VOLUME

If the pages in all the issues for the year's volume are numbered consecutively, no issue number is needed. Italicize the volume number as well as the title of the journal.

> Martin, J. (1997). Inventing sincerity, refashioning prudence: The discovery of the individual in Renaissance Europe. *American Historical Review, 102,* 1309–1342.

ARTICLE FROM A PRINTED JOURNAL PAGINATED BY ISSUE

If each issue begins with page 1, add the issue number in parentheses with no space after the volume number. Use italics for the journal title and the volume number but not for the issue number.

> Lipkin, S. N. (1999). Real emotional logic: Persuasive strategies in docudrama. *Cinema Journal, 38*(4), 68–85.

ARTICLE FROM AN ONLINE JOURNAL

Include the DOI (digital object identifier) if the article has one. If the article does not have a DOI, give the URL for the home page of the journal.

> Kingstone, A., Smilek, D., & Eastwood, J. D. (2008). Cognitive ethology: A new approach for studying human cognition. *British Journal of Psychology, 99*(3), 317–340. doi:10.1348/000712607X251243
>
> Rothfleisch, J. (2001). Mid-dermal elastolysis. *Dermatology Online Journal, 7.* Retrieved from http://dermatology.cdlib.org/

ARTICLE ACCESSED THROUGH A LIBRARY OR SUBSCRIPTION SERVICE

Include the DOI (digital object identifier) if the article has one and do not include the name of the database. If the article does not have a DOI, give the URL for the home page of the journal. If you access only an abstract, add "Abstract" in brackets after the title.

> Allison, S. (2004). On-screen smoking influences young viewers. *Youth Studies Australia 23*(3), 6. Retrieved from http://www.acys.info/journal

ARTICLE FROM A PRINTED MAGAZINE

> Lankford, K. (1998, April). The trouble with rules of thumb. *Kiplinger's Personal Finance Magazine, 52,* 102–104.

ARTICLE FROM AN ONLINE MAGAZINE

> Chandler, K. (2005, June 18). Anger management. *Salon.com.* Retrieved from http://www.salon.com

ARTICLE FROM A PRINTED NEWSPAPER

> Stein, R. (2004, March 11). Breast-cancer drug changes suggested. *The Boston Globe,* p. A4.

ARTICLE FROM AN ONLINE NEWSPAPER

> Grady, D. (2005, June 23). Studies lead to big changes in lung cancer treatments. *The New York Times.* Retrieved from http://nytimes.com

Printed or Electronic Report or Other Document

Start with the agency name if no specific author is identified. In parentheses, add any report number assigned by the agency right after the title, but add any number from a document service (such as ERIC, Educational Resources Information Center, or NTIS, National Technical Information Service) after the entire entry, without any period at the end.

PRINTED GOVERNMENT DOCUMENT

> U.S. Bureau of the Census. (2003). *Statistical abstract of the United States* (123rd ed.). Washington, DC: Government Printing Office.

PRINTED RESEARCH REPORT

> Liu, J., Allspach, J. R., Feigenbaum, M., Oh, H.-J., & Burton, N. (2004). *A study of fatigue effects from the new SAT* (RR-04-46). Princeton, NJ: Educational Testing Service.

ONLINE RESEARCH REPORT

National Institute on Drug Abuse. (2005). *Inhalant abuse* (NIH
Publication No. 00–3818). Retrieved from http://www.nida.nih
.gov/PDF/RRInhalants.pdf

ONLINE RESEARCH REPORT FROM A DOCUMENT SERVICE

Berger, S. (1995). Inclusion: A legal mandate, an educational dream.
Updating School Board Policies, 26(4), 1–4. Retrieved from ERIC
database. (ERIC Document Reproduction Service No. ED386789)

REPORT FROM AN ACADEMIC INSTITUTION

Bunn, M., Wier, A., & Holdren, J. P. (2003). *Controlling nuclear warheads
and materials: A report card and action plan.* Cambridge, MA: Harvard
University, Belfer Center for Science and International Affairs.

Internet or Electronic Source

See the directory on page 233 for entries for other electronic sources,
including books and articles.

SECTION OR PAGE FROM A WEB DOCUMENT

Instead of referring to an entire Web site, whenever possible identify the
specific material that you have used by supplying its section number or
its own URL.

Detweiler, L. (1993). What is the future of privacy on the Internet?
In *Identity, privacy, and anonymity on the Internet* (sec. 2.12).
Retrieved from http://eserver.org/internet/Identity-Privacy-
Anonymity.txt

DOCUMENT FROM A CAMPUS WEB SITE

Identify the university and sponsoring program or department (if applicable) before giving the URL for the specific page or document.

Allin, C. (2004). *Common sense for college students: How to do better than
you thought possible.* Retrieved from Cornell College, Department of
Politics website: http://www.cornellcollege.edu/politics/
common-sense_cwa.shtml

Visual or Audio Source

AUDIOTAPE OR RECORDING

> Ellis, A. (Writer/Producer). (1995). *Helping students develop their IEPs* [Audiotape]. Washington, DC: National Dissemination Center for Children with Disabilities.

PROGRAM ON TELEVISION OR RADIO

> Clark, L. (Writer/Director/Producer). (2004). Descent into the ice. [Television series episode]. In P. Aspell (Executive Producer), *Nova*. Boston, MA: WGBH.

FILM

> Lustig, B., Molen, G., & Spielberg, S. (Producers). (1993). *Schindler's list* [Motion picture]. United States: Universal.

APA REFERENCES CHECKLIST

☐ Have you started each entry with the appropriate pattern for the author's name? Have you left spaces between the initials for each author's name? Have you followed each initial with a period?

☐ Have you used "&," not "and," to add the last coauthor's name?

☐ Have you included the date in each entry?

☐ Have you followed the sample pattern for the type of source you have used?

☐ Have you used capitalization and italics correctly for the various titles in your entries?

☐ Have you included the conventional punctuation—periods, commas, colons, parentheses—in your entry?

☐ Have you accurately recorded the name of the author, title, publisher, and so on?

☐ Have you checked the accuracy of dates, pages, and other numbers?

☐ Have you correctly typed or pasted in the address of each electronic source? Have you split a long URL only before a

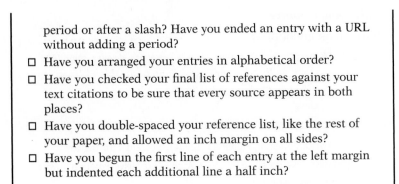

period or after a slash? Have you ended an entry with a URL without adding a period?

☐ Have you arranged your entries in alphabetical order?

☐ Have you checked your final list of references against your text citations to be sure that every source appears in both places?

☐ Have you double-spaced your reference list, like the rest of your paper, and allowed an inch margin on all sides?

☐ Have you begun the first line of each entry at the left margin but indented each additional line a half inch?

Checklists, Tables, Figures, and Other Visuals

ARGUING

INTEGRATING SOURCES

Acknowledgments (continued from page iv)

Benjamin S. Bloom, *Taxonomy of Educational Objectives, Handbook 1: Cognitive Domain*. Copyright © 1956 by David McKay, Inc. Reprinted with the permission of Random House, Inc.

Joe Brooks, excerpts from "How to Catch More Trout" from *Outdoor Life* (May 2006). Copyright © 2006 by Time4 Media, Inc. Reprinted with the permission of the publishers.

Ann Carr, excerpt from "Deporting Resident Aliens: No Compassion, No Sense" from *America* 180.6 (February 27, 1999). Copyright © 1999 by America Press, Inc. Reprinted with permission.

Jeff Chu, excerpt from "You Wanna Take This Online?" from *Time* (August 8, 2005). Copyright © 2005 by Time, Inc. Reprinted with permission.

David Edmonds and John Eidinow, excerpt from "Fear and Flight" from *Rousseau's Dog*. Copyright © 2006 by David Edmonds and John Eidinow. Reprinted with the permission of HarperCollins Publishers.

Guy Garcia, excerpt from "Influencing America" from *Time* (August 13, 2005). Copyright © 2005 by Time, Inc. Reprinted with permission.

Jon Gertner, excerpt from "The Futile Pursuit of Happiness" from the *New York Times Magazine* (September 7, 2003). Copyright © 2003 by The New York Times Company. Reprinted with permission.

Ellen Goodman, "Kids, Divorce and the Myth" from the *Boston Globe Online*, September 28, 2000. Copyright © 2000 by the Boston Globe Newspaper Co./Washington Post Writers Group. Reprinted with permission.

Naomi Klein, excerpt from "Purging the Poor" from *The Nation* (October 10, 2005). Copyright © 2005 by The Nation. Reprinted with permission.

Figure 7.1 from www.Howtostudy.org. Copyright © 1998–2006 by Lucy Tribble MacDonald. Reprinted with permission.

Jay Matthews, "Class Struggle: Is Homework Really So Terrible?" from the *Washington Post* (February 18, 2003). Copyright © 2003 by the Washington Post Writers Group. Reprinted with permission.

John McCain. Adapted from "The Virtues of a Quiet Hero." From *This I Believe*. Copyright © 2005 by John McCain. Copyright © 2006 by This I Believe, Inc. Reprinted by permission of Henry Holt and Company, LLC.

Index

A

Academic institution report, APA listing of, 242

Academic readers, targeting, 8–9

Adjectives, 171–72

Adverbs, 171–72

Advertisement, MLA listing of, 230

Allness, 198

Alternating pattern of comparing and contrasting, 128

American Psychological Association style. *See* APA style

Analogy, argument by, 199

Analysis
in critical thinking, 27–28, 29
reading levels and, 16, 18

Analytical reading skills, 16–18

Analyzing process, 122–24

Analyzing subject, 119–21

Annotated bibliography
summary with evaluation in, 213–14
summary with interpretation in, 214

Annotating text while reading, 14–15

Antecedent-pronoun agreement, 169–71

Anthology, MLA citation of, 222

APA style
for citing sources, 234–37
for listing sources, 237–44

Apostrophe, 176–77

Appeals, evidence for, 194–96

Application, reading levels and, 16, 17

Appositive, definition of, 175

Argument, 190–203
ad hominem, 199
by analogy, 199
developing, 190–200
from dubious authority, 199
from ignorance, 199
presenting, 200–03

Art, MLA listing of, 230

Articles. *See* Periodicals

Articles (*a, an, the*), definition of, 186

Assignments, generating ideas from, 41–44

Audience
revising for, 140–41
shaping topic for, 60–62
writing process and, 7–10

Audio sources
APA listing of, 243
MLA listing of, 230–31

Austin, James H., 92

Authors
APA citation of, 234–35
APA listing of, 238
MLA citation of, 220–21
MLA listing of, 224–25

B

Baker, Russell, 94

Bandwagon argument, 199

Bar graphs, 133, 134

Be
forms of, 166, 167
wordiness and, 148

Begging the question, 199

Berry, Cecelie S., 108

251

CORRECTION SYMBOLS

Many instructors use these abbreviations and symbols to mark errors in student papers. Refer to this chart to find out what they mean.

Boldface numbers refer to sections of the Quick Editing Guide (pp. 160–89)

abbr	faulty abbreviation		**,**	comma **C1**
ad	misuse of adverb or adjective **A7**		*no,*	no comma **C1**
agr	faulty agreement **A4, A6**		**;**	semicolon
appr	inappropriate language		**:**	colon
awk	awkward		**'**	apostrophe **C2**
cap	capital letter **D1**		**" "**	quotation marks **C3**
case	error in case **A5**		**. ? !**	period, question mark, exclamation point
coord	faulty coordination		**— ( ) [ ]**	dash, parentheses, brackets, ellipses
cs	comma splice **A2**		**...**	
dm	dangling modifier **B1**		*par,* ¶	new paragraph **D3**
exact	inexact language		*pass*	ineffective passive
frag	sentence fragment **A1**		*ref*	error in pronoun reference **A6**
fs	fused sentence **A2**		*rep*	careless repetition
gr	grammar **all of A**		*rev*	revise
hyph	error in use of hyphen		*run-on*	comma splice or fused sentence **A2**
inc	incomplete construction			
irreg	error in irregular verb **A3**		*sp*	misspelled word **D2**
ital	italics (underlining)		*sub*	faulty subordination
lc	use lowercase letter **D1**		*tense*	error in verb tense **A3**
mixed	mixed construction		*v*	voice
mm	misplaced modifier **B1**		*vb*	error in verb form **A3**
mood	error in mood		*w*	wordy
ms	manuscript form **D3**		*//*	faulty parallelism **B2**
nonst	nonstandard usage		*^*	insert **D3**
num	error in use of numbers		*x*	obvious error
om	omitted word		*#*	insert space
p	error in punctuation **C**		*‿*	close up space **D3**